Egypt and Its Betrayal

Also from Westphalia Press

westphaliapress.org

The Idea of the Digital University

Bulwarks Against Poverty in America

Treasures of London

Avate Garde Politician

L'Enfant and the Freemasons

Baronial Bedrooms

Making Trouble for Muslims

Philippine Masonic Directory ~ 1918

Paddle Your Own Canoe

Opportunity and Horatio Alger

Careers in the Face of Challenge

Bookplates of the Kings

Hymns to the Gods

Freemasonry in Old Buffalo

Original Cables from the Pearl Harbor Attack

Social Satire and the Modern Novel

The Essence of Harvard

The Genius of Freemasonry

A Definitive Commentary on Bookplates

James Martineau and Rebuilding Theology

Bohemian San Francisco

The Wizard

Crime 3.0

Anti-Masonry and the Murder of Morgan

Understanding Art

Spies I Knew

Lodge "Himalayan Brotherhood" No. 459 C.E.

Ancient Masonic Mysteries

Collecting Old Books

Masonic Secret Signs and Passwords

Death Valley in '49

Lariats and Lassos

Mr. Garfield of Ohio

The Wisdom of Thomas Starr King

The French Foreign Legion

War in Syria

Naturism Comes to the United States

New Sources on Women and Freemasonry

Designing, Adapting, Strategizing in Online Education

Gunboat and Gun-runner

Memoirs of a Poor Relation

Espionage!

Bohemian San Francisco

Tales of Old Japan

Egypt and Its Betrayal

Personal Recollections

by U.S. Consul General Elbert E. Farman

WESTPHALIA PRESS
An imprint of Policy Studies Organization

Westphalia Press
An imprint of Policy Studies Organization
1527 New Hampshire Ave., NW
Washington, D.C. 20036
info@ipsonet.org

ISBN-13: 978-1-63391-136-9
ISBN-10: 1633911365

Cover design by Taillefer Long at Illuminated Stories:
www.illuminatedstories.com

Daniel Gutierrez-Sandoval, Executive Director
PSO and Westphalia Press

Rahima Schwenkbeck, Director of Marketing and Media
PSO and Westphalia Press

Updated material and comments on this edition
can be found at the Westphalia Press website:
www.westphaliapress.org

EGYPT AND ITS BETRAYAL

PREFACE

EGYPT has been, through all historic periods, a fruitful subject for writers. Interest in this small country, from the time of the "father of history" to the present day, seems never to have waned. Recently, a large amount of very incorrect information has been given to the public concerning its people and Government. This has been to a large extent for political reasons; in the interest of and by the inspiration of a Government whose ideal policy is the extension of its sway over all countries from which substantial revenues can be derived.

With a powerful press and a great number of able writers at its command, constantly waging a campaign as studied and often as unjust as any of our Presidential contests, with no counter campaign working against it, only success could be expected. Articles thus inspired and published form the basis for others often written by conscientious but misled authors.

Having held a diplomatic position in Egypt during its modern crucial period, I was in a position to learn the real facts. It is thought necessary by those in power to excuse or in some manner justify the imposition upon this people of the grossly unjust burdens they are compelled by military force to sustain. The old story of carrying the Bible under the left arm and the sword in the right hand to Christianize heathen people would not fit the case. The impression of service rendered in some other manner must be given.

An illustration of this manner of justification appeared in a late number of a magazine issued by an honorable publish-

ing house of New York. The article is entitled, "The Story of
Lord Cromer in Egypt." Lord Cromer was educated for the
military service and reached the rank of major before going
to Egypt. He is a man of rare administrative ability, and his
work in Egypt from an English standpoint, that is, with a view
to "English interests," cannot be too highly praised, and from
this standpoint there is no need of misrepresentation, and certainly not of gross misrepresentation.

The article is not only extravagantly laudatory, but, to add
to its interest and increase the effect of its praises, is profusely
illustrated. Among these illustrations is one representing a
palanquin borne by two gaudily decorated camels. These are
standing, and two women are looking from the windows of the
palanquin waiting for the work of the photographer, a scene
not at all Egyptian. Respectable Egyptian women would not
thus publicly exhibit themselves. In the background appear
the tombs of the Khalifs. Under this illustration is printed,
"Egyptian Transportation as Lord Cromer found it."

On the same page is an illustration of a railroad, having beneath it the inscription: "Transportation in Egypt as Lord
Cromer left it."

The meaning intended to be conveyed by these illustrations
and the accompanying inscriptions, and the only one that
could be conveyed to those not acquainted with the facts, is
that the palanquin was, on the advent of Lord Cromer in Egypt
as its real ruler, an ordinary means of transportation, and that
the introduction of the railroads, that have taken the place of
this primitive mode of conveyance, is one of his Lordship's
"great works." This wonderful transformation, if true, of the
Christian, altruistic, English rule would naturally redound to
the glory of the governing power.

What are the facts?

I resided in Egypt for eight years preceding the arrival of

Lord Cromer as its real Governor; five years in its principal city, Cairo, and three years in its emporium, Alexandria. I visited all of its cities and places of commerce, most of them many times, traveled on all of its railroads and made a special study of the country and its people. Yet I never saw a palanquin, nor anything resembling one except the Mahmal. This is a litter carried on a camel in the caravan that leaves Cairo annually on the pilgrimage to Mecca, and described in this work on page forty-nine. No one, however, is ever carried in it. During my residence in Cairo, I was informed that the palanquin had formerly been used sometimes in the often fantastic ceremony of conveying the bride to the home of the bridegroom. I have seen many of these processions, but in none of them was there a palanquin. The bride on all of these occasions was carried in a closely covered carriage, or walked under a canopy carried by four men by means of poles under each corner, the canopy having curtains coming to the ground.

There is still the question of the railroads, that Lord Cromer is represented as having substituted for this alleged primitive mode of conveyance that had had no existence for many years before his arrival. There were in Egypt, on the accession of Ismaîl Pasha to its Government, over two hundred miles of railway. During the next twelve years Ismaîl added about nine hundred miles. There was thus in Egypt over a thousand miles of railroads, ten years previous to the advent of Lord Cromer's administration. If anyone had substituted the railway for the supposed primitive mode of conveyance, it was the much slandered Ismaîl Pasha. Years before the end of his reign Egypt was covered with a network of railroads connecting all its cities and places of commerce. Egypt then had all the railroads that it has to-day that are of any substantial value to its people. Besides the railroads in Lower Egypt, there was one extending up the Nile to Assiût, two hundred and forty miles above Cairo. Above Assiût the valley is very narrow, only from one to ten miles wide, on either side of which are high desert hills and mountains. For this narrow strip of land the great river is by far the least expensive highway for its commerce.

The extension of the railroad above this point was for military purposes, to enable the English to reconquer the Sudân that had been lost to Egypt through the interference of France and England in its affairs. The reconquest was made at the expense of Egypt, but the territory became an English province or, as they delight to call it, "The New British Empire of the Sudân." All the railroads built since the reign of Ismaîl Pasha have been constructed with Egypt's money for the advancement of "English interests."

The illustration of the palanquin was the work of an enterprising photographer. He had an old palanquin mounted and the camels gaudily decorated to make a salable photograph. This was innocent enough, but on its being purchased with others for the illustrations, the writer of the article or the illustrator added the inscriptions by which the reader is deceived.

Others of the illustrations taken, with their inscriptions, are equally deceptive. A picture of the Barrage near Cairo has printed under it, "One of the great irrigation works of Lord Cromer's administration." The Barrage was commenced in the reign of Mohammed Ali, in 1835, and has been one of the "sights" visited by travelers for the last fifty years. It is true that, owing to the treacherous nature of the soil, its foundations became in time insecure; and during the financial pressure in Egypt from 1867 they were neglected and the Barrage became of little or no value as an aid to irrigation. The original structure is a grand and imposing work, until recently the largest weir in the world. This structure has been strengthened by an Eng-

Barrage near Cairo.
From a Photograph Taken about 1875 during the Reign of
Ismaîl Pasha.

lish engineer, Colonel Sir Colin Scott-Moncrieff. He successfully accomplished a difficult task, but the Barrage can in no sense be called one of the works of Lord Cromer.

There is an illustration of an encampment of wandering Arabs, such as frequently pitch their tents on the deserts bordering on Egypt. Under it is printed, "Dirt, poverty and misery " . . . "Lord Cromer's Problem." It is well known that the people of Egypt have not lived in tents for centuries, though the rude dwellings of the laboring classes are not much better and they have not been improved during Lord Cromer's administration.

Under a view of Cairo taken from the Citadel we read: "The Egypt of Lord Cromer's administration." "The modern sanitary, orderly city of Cairo—Lord Cromer's solution." To my personal knowledge Cairo was a sanitary and orderly city under Ismaîl Pasha. One could then wander anywhere about the city, night or day, in perfect safety, which could not then and cannot now be done in any city of its size in Europe or the United States.

There is also an illustration of fellâhîn raising water by means of shadufs, entitled "Primitive irrigation as Lord Cromer found it." On the next page is the picture of the Assuân dam, with the inscription, "Irrigation in Egypt under Lord Cromer." It is thus intended to say that the dam has taken the place of the shaduf.

If the writer of the article will make the voyage of the Nile in the month of March of the present year, he will find in use as many shadufs as at any time in the past. He does not tell us that the great dam that is causing the destruction of all the grand and marvelous monuments of antiquity above the First Cataract, and has added $800,000 a year for thirty years to the burdens of the poor Egyptians, has proved a great disappointment to its sanguine promoters; and that now it is proposed to increase its height twenty-three feet, at what further cost to Egypt we are not informed.

The only illustrations of the article that are intended to represent improvement in Egypt under its present government, that are not misleading, are those of the marching and drilling of the Egyptian soldiers who have been or are being disciplined by their English officers, as are the soldiers in India, to keep their own people in servile subjection.

The article will not bear any closer examination of its statements relative to changed conditions of Egypt than the illustrations. The writer even has the temerity, in his attempted justification of a continuance under military force of the "spoiling of the Egyptians" commenced many years ago by the Jewish bankers of Paris and London, to compare the English occupation with that of Cuba by the United States. It will be news to many Americans that Lord Cromer, however meritorious his rule, left no native mourners in Egypt outside the official group and a small favored class. The English, however, well understand the facts. They accuse the natives of being ungrateful for all they have done for them, and even of hating their benefactors!

I am fully aware that the preparation and publication of any statements of the wrongs suffered by a people already "bound hand and foot," and under a close military surveillance from which they can never escape, is a thankless task. However, writings that are constantly appearing of the character of those I have mentioned have induced me to include in this work a number of chapters that would not otherwise have appeared. I have been urged to adopt this course not only by Americans, but by loyal Englishmen.

A large part of the work relates to personal experiences from which it is hoped the reader, who has not had better means of procuring information, may obtain a general knowledge of the country, its inhabitants, their occupations, modes of life, religion and character. This is followed by chapters descriptive of the manner and means by which the people have been and are being "spoiled" for the benefit of Europeans, a narration of the facts relative to the riots of Alexandria, the bombardment and burning of tha tcity, and the subjugation and military occupation of the country.

E. E. FARMAN.

NEW YORK, February, 1908.

CONTENTS

Contents

Contents   xvii

Contents · xix

LIST OF ILLUSTRATIONS

EGYPT AND ITS BETRAYAL

EGYPT *and its* BETRAYAL

CHAPTER I

FIRST IMPRESSIONS OF EGYPT

AFTER a passage of six days from Marseilles on one of the steamers of the Messageries Maritimes, I arrived, at early dawn of a May morning, off Alexandria. The noise of lifting trunks and boxes from their place of storage announced to the passengers that they were approaching their destination. All were quickly on deck to catch the first view of the land of the Nile.

The low coast is treeless and without any background of highlands. A light yellow line of sandy beach is first discerned through the morning haze. Beyond, farther to the east, soon appear the lighthouse, Pompey's Pillar, some fortified points, the masts of numerous ships in the harbor, and many windmills along the coast.

We passed Point Marabout and, a little further on, Bâb el-'Arab (Gate of the Bedouin), an ancient canal a mile in length which crosses the belt of land separating Lake Mareotis from the sea. Along this belt, from Marabout to the harbor, were fortifications, which gave no signs of hostility, but which, six years later, I was to behold enshrouded in the smoke of battle, amid the din of bursting shells and the roar of cannon.

Near Bâb el-'Arab is Mex and the ruins of the summer château of Saîd Pasha with its picturesque domes and towers. An Arab pilot having been taken on board, we continued our course eastward in a tortuous and difficult channel near a line of fortifications. Passing on our left the lighthouse, erected on what was once the eastern end of the historic Island of Pharos, we entered the capacious "Old Harbor of Alexandria" and dropped our anchor opposite Râs et-Tîn (Cape of Figs) the summer palace of the Khedive. Here was the first scene of that panorama of Oriental life which was to be constantly unrolled before me during a series of years, often grotesque but always charming.

At that time there were no docks for large steamers and we were a mile from the place of landing. As soon as we were at anchor, the water around us was covered with small boats manned with turbaned Arabs in flowing robes ready to serve the passengers. And such a bedlam! A hundred animated and apparently angry voices were shouting the jargon of an unknown language. Rival boats were pulling and pushing desperately for a position near the landing-stairway. Several Arabs pounced upon the hand baggage of the first passenger who descended, and a fierce struggle followed which was only settled by actual blows from some one in authority. Such was my introduction to the Arabs of Egypt, whom, in the end, I was to find a submissive and easily governed people.

The Governor of the city had sent for me his private boat manned with soldiers, to which all the other boats quickly yielded their places. I was thus saved the annoyance of this apparent mob of Arabs, who, from the first twilight of the morning, had awaited our coming. Eight well-trained oarsmen brought our light boat quickly to the landing at the arsenal instead of to the usual landing at the custom-house.

The arsenal is on the neck of land connecting the ancient Island of Pharos with the site of the original city. This island, previous to the time of the Ptolemies, was a mile from the mainland. It is said that Alexander the Great, floating out of the Canopic branch of the Nile, followed the coast and ran in behind the island. It was the only shelter for ships on the coast of Egypt. Seeing its natural advantages, he ordered a city to be laid out and built. There was then on the mainland a village of fishermen called Rhakotis.

Ptolemy Soter, or his son Philadelphus, connected the island with the mainland by an embankment called, from its length, the Heptastadium, seven stadia (about three-fourths of a mile). Through it were bridged passages for boats. These were long since filled by the débris of the city and the natural deposits of the sea, and the Heptastadium, now over half a mile in width, constitutes a considerable part of the Arab quarter of the city.

On my way to my hotel in the European quarter I caught glimpses of those fascinating Oriental street scenes which never fail to delight the traveler. Some time afterwards, an American lady on her first visit to Egypt, whom I was accompanying from a steamer to the same hotel, exclaimed, on beholding one of the scenes of an Arab market day, "This alone is worth a trip from America."

I found at Alexandria the U. S. Vice-Consul-General, who had come from Cairo to meet me, with Hassan, one of the consular guards or kavasses.

Hassan had already held his position eighteen years. He was an honest, faithful Arab, proud of his place, which was regarded as far above that of the common fellâhîn. He wore a showy, blue cloth costume trimmed with gold braid and carried a curved sword. On first seeing him with the Vice-Consul-General I was not aware of his precise position and duties.

Having occasion to remain some time in my room at the hotel, I found him, when at last I went out, seated in the hall at my door. I probably, by look or word, expressed surprise, for he said, "I am always with you." No words could better express the facts. At the office in the city, on my numerous excursions—up the Nile, to Palestine, to Mt. Sinai—everywhere, he was "always with me," my faithful and invaluable servant, guard, and, with the Arabs outside of Cairo, my interpreter. In my drives he acted as footman, sat on the box beside the driver and carried a staff or baton surmounted by an eagle.

His long experience, natural capacity, and absolute devotion to his duties, made him very useful. He had already gained a good name and had been frequently mentioned in the published writings of travelers. He had watched over two Consuls-General in their last hours and been faithful to all he had served. He had accompanied Consul-General Butler on his trip to Khartum with General Stanton, acting as generalissimo of a caravan of forty camels in a fourteen days' journey across the deserts, during which time water was found only once.[1]

After taking a drive through the city, visiting Cleopatra's Needle, which is now in New York, and Pompey's Pillar, which marks the site of the Serapeum, we left for Cairo on the afternoon train, reserving the further study of Alexandria for a future day.

The distance to Cairo is one hundred and thirty miles. It was a hot, dusty ride, since it was the time of the low Nile, the most uninteresting part of the year. In this latitude the days are never long, and, while we were in time to get a distant view of the Pyramids at the setting of the sun, it was dark on my arrival at the "Grand New Hotel."

Though I was weary with a journey of nearly a month, my first night in Egypt was sleepless. The sudden change from the cool air of the sea intensified the effect of the tropical heat. The music in the gardens across the street, first European, and then Arab (or rather those discordant, grating sounds, both instru-

[1] This was at a period when the Khedive frequently entertained visitors in royal splendor. The journey was made at the expense of his Highness, Ismaïl Pasha, in special steamers to the first and second cataracts of the Nile, thence by camels across the desert to Berber and again by steamer to Khartum. The distance traveled going and returning was nearly four thousand miles. The time then required for the journey was one month each way.

The Two Hassans.

mental and vocal, which the Arabs call music), did not cease until a late hour. Afterwards, the barking of dogs and the singing and screaming of youthful Arabs—the gamins of Cairo whose only homes are the streets—continued until dawn. It did not require many nights, however, to become accustomed to these strange noises. They were then no more the enemies of sleep than the winds and waves of the sea, or the ticking of the clock in the bedchamber.

Dogs in Cairo, as in Constantinople and other Oriental Moslem cities, have no owners. They are called "wild" simply because they are not domestic. They live in groups. Each group remains in its own well-defined quarter, and woe to the unfortunate cur who trespasses upon the grounds of another group than his own. The moment he crosses the line, he is unmercifully attacked by the united forces of the invaded territory. In these cities where the garbage is emptied into the streets or upon unoccupied grounds, the dogs become the city scavengers, like the turkey buzzards of Vera Cruz, and often dispute with the street beggars the choice morsels from improvident kitchens.

The morning gave me my first view of Cairo. The hotel, an immense building, was then the private property of the Khedive. It was constructed to give ample accommodations to the guests at the celebration of the opening of the Suez Canal. It had a marble-floored terrace upon which its guests, protected from the sun by a canopy, could sit and view, while breathing the salubrious air of a delightful climate, passing scenes of unspeakable charm. Indeed, a visitor with leisure might spend hours and days there intently watching a constantly unfolding, never ending picture.

The streets are thronged with passers-by. They resound with the continual and hurried tramp of a motley multitude. There are donkeys carrying travelers or the black-robed and closely veiled women of the lower middle class, which the hammars, or donkey-boys, follow on a full run, urging them with loud cries and frequent applications of the whip. There are groups of camels loaded with grain; others, more fleet, bearing Bedouins; carriages with the thinly veiled beauties of the Khedivial harem attended by their eunuchs; other turnouts, less pretentious, with more conservative women (the wives and daughters of Beys and Pashas), also accompanied by their eunuchs.

The sakka, or water-carrier, bearing his goatskin of water, is sprinkling the street, or giving drinks in brass cups to the passers-by, crying, "May God recompense me!" in the hope of receiving a pittance. Consuls-General and Pashas pass in showy equipages preceded by picturesque and fleet seis, and the Khedive, with his guard of outriders and his seis crying, "Clear the way!" There are soldiers escorted by bands of music, squalid beggars, jugglers, a continual tramp of Jew, Copt, Mohammedan and Christian, of Arab, Turk, Syrian, Armenian, Persian and European, each in his characteristic costume. Such are the daily views of the endless panorama of enchanting street scenes in Cairo.

On each side of the hotel terrace are gardens filled with tropical trees and plants. Across the street in the heart of the European quarter is the garden of Ezbekiyeh, with its lake, fountains, artificial mounds and grottoes, covering twenty or more acres. It has fine walks, and numerous rare shrubs and trees, many of which were brought from India. Among the trees are several banyans whose branches have dropped to the ground, and their shoots taken root and formed new stocks. Ducks chatter in the artificial streams, black and white swans sail gracefully on the lakes, and little pleasure boats ply the waters for the amusement of the children. In the afternoon and evening, the middle and lower class Cairenes swarm in this garden to enjoy music and jugglery, thereby giving the stranger an admirable opportunity to see at its best the medley of people of all shades

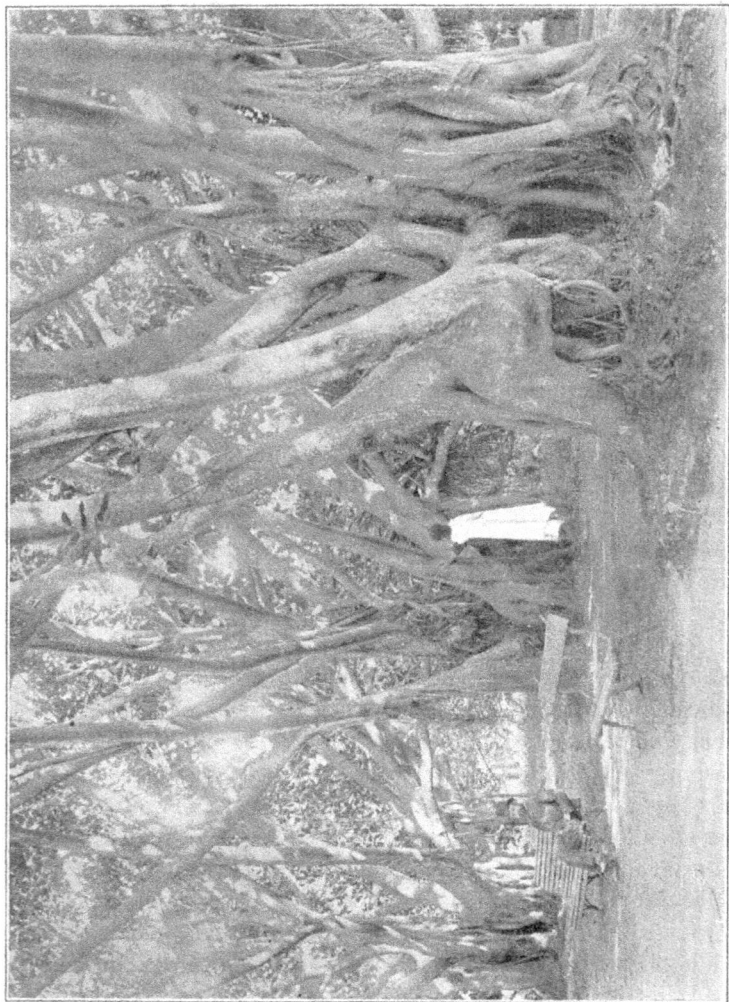

Banyan Trees in the Garden of Esbekiyeh, Cairo.

of color and of many religions and nationalities who make up the population of Cairo. Fine buildings, among them the Opera House and the large school of the American Mission, surround the garden on all sides.

A short morning walk gave me a pleasant impression of my temporary home and a promise, which was to be fully realized, of a pleasant sojourn in the capital city of the Khedive.

CHAPTER II

My first duty in Cairo was a visit to the Khedive, Ismaîl Pasha. This was made at the palace of Gezîreh, the "Palace of the Island," on the west side of the Nile opposite the city. His Highness had been notified of my arrival through Cherîf Pasha, his Minister of Foreign Affairs, and had fixed the time and place of my informal and unofficial reception.

I crossed the Nile, by the Great Bridge, to a long oval island and turned to the right into a broad avenue, between which and the river were many stately palms. On the other side, to the left, were botanical and zoological gardens, the latter then containing a variety of African and Asiatic animals, among them a small herd of elephants attended by their Indian keepers. These elephants were afterwards, on the advice of General Stone, sent to the upper Nile regions to perform carrier-service.

At the end of this avenue was Gezîreh, a comparatively small but magnificent palatial residence, which was commenced during our War of Secession, when Egypt was giddy with its suddenly acquired wealth, resulting from the high price of cotton. It was designed as a residence of pleasure only for a portion of the year. Adjoining it were large and beautiful gardens, in which was a kiosk decorated in Moorish style, and, at some distance from the palace, a building for the harem.

This palace was occupied at the time of the celebration of the opening of the Suez Canal in 1869, first, by the Empress Eugénie, and, later, by Francis Joseph, Emperor of Austria. It was subsequently occupied by other distinguished people, including the Prince of Wales. The property has been sold and transformed into a hotel largely patronized by English officers. The island is such only at the time of the high Nile, the western branch of the river being at other times dry.

I entered the palace and was escorted by the Master of Ceremonies up a grand stairway of Carrara marble, and received by the Khedive in a magnificent reception room. His Highness met me at the door with a cordial welcome. After the introductions and the usual salutations, I took a seat at one end of a divan and the Khedive at the other, his feet drawn under him in Turkish style. Our conversation was of a very general character. His Highness welcomed me to his country, asked me if I was pleased with it and inquired as to the health of the President and the prosperity of my country. He hoped I would enjoy my residence at his Court and expressed himself as desirous of doing anything in his power to make it agreeable. As he did not speak English, our conversation was in French, a language which he spoke fluently.

Physically, he was not prepossessing. He was then about forty-seven years old, short in stature, broad-shouldered, stocky and corpulent, his complexion slightly darker than that of Europeans. His eyelids drooped—the left more than the right. When his features were in repose, his dark eyes seemed half closed. His eyebrows were dark, coarse, thick and projecting, and his dark brown beard was cut short. His ears were large and ill-shaped. He wore a black European suit, except that his coat was a stamboul, that is, a single breasted coat with a low standing collar. He wore also the red tarboosh.

The Turks never appear with their heads uncovered. To do so would be a mark of the greatest disrespect. A young man, whose father had been one of the Sultan's Cabinet, and who was himself employed in one of the departments at Cairo, told me that he had never, not even in his early childhood, appeared before his father with his head uncovered, that he would not dare to do such a thing, since he could not offer his parent a greater indignity. Riaz Pasha, afterwards the Khedive's Prime Minister, speaking of his first visit to Europe, told me of his astonishment at being requested to take off his tarboosh by the sexton of a church in Germany, which he was visiting. If a Mussulman should enter a mosque with his head uncovered, he would be ejected forthwith, and, if not with such force as to cause him bodily harm, he would be very fortunate.

The fez, tarboosh, or turban is worn in the mosque, at public and private receptions, at meals, everywhere in fact that the Turk or Moslem goes. A woman who appears on the street must not only be veiled, but must have her entire head covered. It would be as unpardonable a breach of decorum to show the back of the head as the face. To do either would mean disgrace for life.

The Khedive had the habit of talking with one eye closed, while, with the penetrating gaze of the other, he scrutinized, in the minutest details, the movements, the manner and almost the thoughts of those with whom he conversed.

With all his peculiarities and physical disadvantages, he was a delightful conversationalist, frequently smiling, always affable and interesting. His voice was low and pleasant, his words, well chosen and expressive. He had remarkable intelligence and accurate knowledge, even of the details, of all that pertained to his Government and his very extensive private affairs. The keen and intelligent glances of his eyes (when once they were fairly opened by animated conversation), his quick and apt responses, and his information regarding subjects with which he would naturally be supposed to be unacquainted, showed him, to all who had the pleasure of conversing with him, to be a man of no ordinary ability.

Ismaîl Pasha.

According to the custom of the country no American could be presented to the Khedive except by his diplomatic representative. I had occasion during my five years' residence in Cairo to perform this duty frequently, and it often happened that the visitor was astonished at the Khedive's remarkable intelligence. On the occasion of the presentation of the commander of one of our war vessels, the Khedive, after having asked him a series of questions relative to his ship, some of which he could not answer, entered into a detailed account of the same particulars upon his own ships. The captain and other officers who accompanied him expressed their great astonishment, after leaving his Highness, at his knowledge of a man-of-war. It was the same in other matters. Soldier and civilian were equally surprised by his detailed information. He had, furthermore, the rare faculty of gaining the confidence of his visitor by relieving him of all embarrassment, and putting him completely at his ease.

My official reception was long delayed on account of the non-arrival of the necessary papers from Constantinople. Nominally, the Khedive is the subject of the Sultan and, therefore, before a representative of a foreign government can be officially recognized in Egypt, the consent or order of the Sultan must be obtained. This is done through the minister of the government to be represented. The Government of the Sultan communicates with the Government of the Khedive to ascertain whether the appointee is satisfactory, whether he is a "persona grata."

The work of the bureaucracy at Constantinople is notoriously slow, the slowest, perhaps, of that of any government in the world, and the murder of the Sultan, Abdul Aziz, which occurred two weeks after my arrival, added to the delay in the arrival of the required official documents. The death of Toussoum Pasha, Minister of the Marine and husband of the Princess Fatma Hanoum, the second and favorite daughter of the Khedive, also intervened and caused further delay.

The papers sent from Constantinople by Hon. Horace Maynard, then our Minister at the "Sublime Porte," consisted of a
firman, addressed to the Khedive, and a *berat*, addressed to me,
specifying my official prerogatives. They were in the Turkish
language, written in an ornamental style in large characters,
the alternate lines being in different colors. They are now among
my many souvenirs of Egypt. I insert a translation of the *firman*. It is a curious illustration of Orientalism.

"To my noble Minister and high Khedive, the model of the world, the wise
director of the affairs of State, the prudent provider of humanity, founder of
the edifice of happiness and glory; you who fortify the columns of happiness
and salvation, the favorite of the grace of God, Khedive of Egypt, decorated
with the orders of the Osmanieh and Medjidieh of the first class; my Vizier,
Ismaïl Pasha, glorious and mighty Emir, chosen by the grace of God.

"On the receipt of the present be it known to you, that the United States
Legation, residing at my gate of happiness, has made a 'takrir' informing me
of the death of Mr. Beardsley, who was Consul-General of the United States
in Egypt, and attended to the business of the merchants of the United States,
going and coming in that country, and also informing me of the appointment
of Mr. Elbert E. Farman, who has been supplied with my imperial berat, which
is given to this Consul-General to be kept by him. My imperial command is,
that he must be empowered to attend to the business of the citizens and merchants of the United States, who frequent that place, and that also, without
any hindrance from any outsider, he be treated and assisted according to the
terms of the existing treaties. A new firman has been given to him, and you
will also treat him personally in accordance with the treaties. You, who are
the aforesaid Khedive, will act according to the prescriptions of the said berat,
and allow him to collect the consular duties on the imports and exports by
American merchants, and you will see that no interference of any kind be
allowed in his consular prerogatives.

"This 2nd day of Djemaziul Ahir, 1293.

"Seal of the Sultan,
"by the Grand Vizier.

The Porte omitted any mention in the *berat* of the diplomatic
functions of a Consul-General to Egypt. The duties of the Agent
and Consul-General of the United States to Egypt are both diplomatic and consular, but principally the former. The Agents

and Consuls-General of the Great Powers of Europe, which have consuls to perform the consular duties, are wholly diplomatic. These exclusively diplomatic representatives are recognized by the Porte, however, only as Consuls-General, and their rank at the Court of the Khedive is the same as that of the other Agents and Consuls-General.

At the official reception, which took place at the palace of Abdîn, I presented personally to the Khedive, in accordance with my instructions, the letter of credence of the President, General Grant, a copy of which, furnished by the State Department at Washington for that purpose, had been previously delivered to Cherîf Pasha.

This letter was as follows:

"Ulysses S. Grant, President of the United States of America,
"To his Highness, the Khedive of Egypt.
"Great and Good Friend:

"I have made choice of Elbert E. Farman, a citizen of the United States, as Agent and Consul-General of the United States of America to Egypt, to reside at Cairo, to watch over our interests, and by all honorable means to cultivate and to maintain the harmony and good will between us.

"Therefore, I request your Highness to receive him in that character, to cause him to be duly respected, to give full credit to what he shall represent from his government, more especially when he shall assure your Highness of our cordial friendship.

"Written at Washington the 13th day of April in the year of our Lord, one thousand eight hundred and seventy-six.

"Your Good Friend,
"U. S. GRANT.

"By the President,
"J. L. Cadwalader,
"Acting Secretary of State."

Before the presentation of this letter, following the custom, I made a short address, in which I assured his Highness of the cordial friendship of the President and his desire to continue the relations of amity existing between the Government of Egypt and that of the United States.

The Khedive replied in French, affirming his appreciation of the "friendly words," as he termed them, that had been spoken in the name of our Government and country, and requesting me to convey his sentiments of friendship to his Excellency General Grant.

He also expressed a desire, not only to continue, but to strengthen the cordial relations which had always existed between the United States of America and Egypt, and assured me that, under all circumstances, he would be disposed to aid me in the mission which had been confided to me by my Government.

On this visit, I was accompanied, according to usage, by my Vice-Consul-General, my secretary and my four dragomans. The positions of the dragomans were simply honorary, as they only served on public, official occasions. They were persons of influence and, generally, of wealth, who rendered the occasional small services demanded of them in return for the protection given them. Being *attachés* of the Consulate-General, they were entitled to the rights and privileges of American citizens, and were thus frequently saved from the extortionate demands of the governors and other local officials of an autocratic government.

The Ottoman Government, in pursuance of an old custom, permits four dragomans to each Consul-General. Theoretically, they form a part of the Consul-General's suite and act as secretaries, interpreters and aids to him. There was also a regular employee of the office, who acted as Arab interpreter.

After the presentation of the letter of credence, those present, including some Egyptian officials among whom was Cherîf Pasha, were seated on Turkish divans. Pipes with long stems set with diamonds were presented, the bowls resting on silver plates placed on the floor. The stems were sufficiently long to permit of the convenient use of the pipes in this manner. A few whiffs were taken, Turkish coffee was served, and, after a short conversation between the Khedive and myself, his Highness arose and accompanied me to the door of the reception room. As I was about taking final leave, he expressed his regret that circumstances had prevented him from receiving me in the customary manner, adding that he would have the pleasure of so doing at a future time.

I had supposed that this reception was to take the place of the more ceremonious one which I knew was customary in Egypt. The usual forty days of mourning had not elapsed since the death of Toussoum Pasha, and, in the letter fixing the place and date of the reception, we had been notified that the reception would be "without ceremony."

At the time appointed for the final reception, Zecchi Pasha, then Master of Ceremonies, came to my residence, as the representative of the Khedive, with two coaches. One of these, intended solely for the Pasha and myself, was the royal gala coach, gilded as gaudily as a Barnum band-wagon, drawn by richly caparisoned white horses and accompanied by footmen and outriders. The other was for the consular suite. The Pasha was also attended by a body of cavalry mounted on white and gray horses, which escorted us to the palace. There a regiment of infantry was drawn up on either side of a large square in front of the main entrance. As we approached, firing of cannon from the Citadel commenced, and the soldiers saluted as we passed.

At the palace entrance, we were met by Tonino Bey, the Assistant Master of Ceremonies, and others of the Khedive's attendants. Ascending the grand stairway, we were received at its head by the Khedive and conducted into the reception room. After a few complimentary words between his Highness and myself, we were all seated, and pipes and coffee were served as on the previous occasion. When I took my leave, the Khedive presented to me, as an emblem of my authority in his country, a curved sword with a Damascus blade and a scabbard with gold mountings.   On quitting the palace we passed between the lines of soldiers, who again saluted us, and were conducted to our residence in the same manner, and with the same escort that had accompanied us to the palace.   Official visits were then exchanged, according to usage, with Cherîf Pasha, with the sons of the Khedive and with certain other leading personages.

The next morning, as a sequel to the reception, the coachmen, footmen and other servants of the Khedive, the Master of Ceremonies and the Minister of Foreign Affairs, who had had the good fortune to be present at the ceremonies, came for the bakshîsh (gifts) to which, according to the usage of such occasions, they were entitled.   Custom had regulated the amounts to be given, which were as follows: Khedivial coachman, six pounds sterling;   second coachman, four pounds;   footmen, four pounds; guards of Master of Ceremonies, five pounds; guards of Minister of Foreign Affairs, ten pounds; coachman of Minister, footmen and servants, five pounds; consular guards, one pound twelve shillings—a total of thirty-five pounds, twelve shillings sterling, or one hundred and seventy-three dollars.

The Khedive gave our kavass, Hassan, sixteen napoleons (a little over sixty dollars) to be used in buying the new uniform which he was supposed to need on entering the employ of a new Agent and Consul-General.   It was then the custom for the Khedive, on the occasion of the official reception of a newly arrived Consul-General, to present to him a fine horse, saddled and bridled in the most costly Oriental style—the large saddle cloth wrought with gold and all the other trappings ornamented with corresponding richness.

This present had been accepted by the Consuls-General of all the Powers, including those of the United States, with the exception of my immediate predecessor who had been instructed not to receive it. This prohibition was repeated in my instructions. As it was known that the horse could not be accepted, it was not offered to me. Cherîf Pasha had previously asked me, however, in a conversation on the subject, what right the United States had to interfere with their ancient customs and had intimated that he should offer the horse, leaving it to me to refuse the gift.

The Khedive's groom, who would have followed me from the palace leading the horse had it been given and accepted, did not fail to come for his share of the bakshîsh. Why should he? It was not his fault that the Government of the United States, after permitting the acceptance of the horse for a long period, had come to the conclusion that it was unconstitutional.

The custom of giving the horse was an old one which originated when there were no carriage-roads in Egypt, not even in the large cities of Alexandria and Cairo, and when a riding horse was a necessity for a person of position. At the time of my arrival, there were no carriage-roads outside of these two cities and their immediate vicinities, and there are very few now. The longest one of which I have any knowledge is that from Cairo to the Pyramids, a distance of about nine miles.

Previous to my final official reception, I had frequently visited the Khedive and, thanks to his amiable, sociable character, I already felt quite well acquainted with his Highness. I frequently had to perform the unpleasant duty of requesting unofficially, but with polite persistence, the payment of American claims against the Egyptian Government. While this was generally done before the Minister of Foreign Affairs, or the Minister of Finance, it was sometimes necessary to press the matter personally before the Khedive. The Egyptian Government was then in great financial embarrassment, and the mere mention of a pecuniary claim must have been annoying. With this exception, however, I had nothing to ask, while the European representatives had not only to make constant pecuniary demands, but to further political projects, which were of vital importance to the Khedive and, in the end, lost him his throne.   When my arrival at the palace was announced, he had no fear of an unjust demand or of a political intrigue on the part of my Government, and could receive me with sincere cordiality without fear of jeopardizing his interests.   In fact, at that time the United States and Russia were the only Great Powers that did not have some political ambition, direct or indirect, relative to Egypt.   This state of affairs was of much aid in securing the payment of American claims, which were finally all satisfactorily adjusted, being paid in full.   For this result I was greatly indebted to the friendliness of the Khedive.

CHAPTER III

MYSTERIES OF THE NILE AND IRRIGATION

EGYPT is a land of surprises and Cairo is one of the most fascinating cities in the world. No other city is so picturesque. No other country is so marvelously novel in its scenes; no other has so much which interests both the seeker after pleasure and the seeker after knowledge. At every turn in both city and country there is a fresh surprise, a new pleasure. The mosques, the tomb-mosques of the Mameluke Khalifs, the tombs of the present dynasty, the Arab cemetery, the old palaces, the narrow streets with their surging masses and overhanging Arabian architecture, the wonderful bazaars, filled with gorgeous, Oriental trappings, the collection of Pharaonic antiquities, the Citadel with its palaces, the alabaster Mosque of Mohammed Ali, the glorious views, the deserts, the petrified forests, the white fossiliferous rocks of the Mokattam Hills, the Pyramids, the Sphinx and the marvelous ancient tombs, the Nile and the fields of its valley, the varied costumes and habits of the people,—all these combine to produce an effect not equaled anywhere else upon the planet.

These scenes are so indelibly engraved upon the memory, that after many years of the prosaic, commonplace scenes of life, one, "who has once drunk of the waters of the Nile," longs again to bask in Egypt's genial atmosphere and re-enjoy the delights that in the retrospect seem only the dream of a mysterious land, lighted by the transforming rays of Aladdin's lamp.

Twenty-three hundred and fifty years ago, Herodotus, "the

father of history," in speaking of Egypt said, "It possessed more wonders than any other country and exhibited works greater than could be described, in comparison with all other regions." [1] Since that date, it has never ceased to excite the admiration of the traveler, the historian, the lover of the marvelous, the beautiful, the grand. Geographically, it is simply an oasis surrounded, except on the north, by vast deserts. By the ancients it was called the "Black Land" from its dark alluvial deposits, "the gift of the Nile," [2] which produce a marked contrast with the yellow sands of the desert.

From the earliest times, it has been the garden and the grain field of that section of the Orient, its one reliable source of food. It supplies its own people (formerly more numerous than at present) and the nomadic tribes of the adjoining deserts, and furnishes large amounts of grain, sugar and cotton for exportation. Thirty-six centuries ago, Jacob said unto his sons, "I have heard that there is corn in Egypt, get ye down thither and buy for us from thence, that we may live and not die." Since that day, with few exceptions, Egypt has not failed to bring forth abundant annual and semi-annual harvests.

In 1880 it contained only about five million acres of productive land, an area less than one-sixth of that of the state of New York. Small as it is, it has never ceased (either in ancient or modern times) to attract the cupidity of foreigners. It has suffered many conquests, and to-day the very riches of its soil subject its people to burdens and sufferings from which those dwelling in mountainous and sterile regions happily escape. The mysterious Nile, the "issue of Osiris," is the source of its fertility and wealth.

In the small oases, water is taken from the wells and springs, and a small amount of land is thus irrigated and cultivated. In the valley and delta of the Nile, water is taken from the river for the same purpose. There are no rains of any practical im-

1 Her. II, 35.   2 Her. II, 5.

portance. The Nile sustains all vegetation, and the inhabitants of Egypt and their herds drink only of its waters. It is to this country the source of life, animal and vegetable. Its waters, if too abundant, produce great destruction, if too scanty, famine. Should it cease to flow, every plant, shrub and tree would wither and die. In less than three months, the whole country would be as arid, as desolate and uninhabitable as the Great Sahara. The millions of native inhabitants, who have never drunk any other water, await its accustomed annual rise with more solicitude than a northern farmer awaits the return of spring.

To the ancient Egyptians the Nile was a deity, whose mysteries were the most sacred secrets. Its sources, the cause of its annual overflow in the heat and dryness of summer, its decline in winter, and its life-giving properties were, to them, like the attributes of other deities, phenomena beyond the ken of mortals and too sacred for their investigation.

Many wise men of other nations speculated and wrote upon these subjects and generally advanced the most absurd theories. Herodotus relates that, of all the Egyptians, Lybians or Grecians with whom he conversed, the only man who pretended to know anything about the sources of the Nile was the registrar of the treasury of Minerva at Sais in Egypt. His account was as follows:

"There are two mountains rising in a sharp peak, situated between the city of Syene in Thebias and Elephantine. . . . The sources of the Nile, which is bottomless, flow from between the mountains; the half of the water flows over Egypt to the north, the other half over Ethiopa to the south." [1]

This account fixes the sources of the Nile at the First Cataract, a point which Herodotus afterwards visited, learning the in-

[1] Her. II, 28.

correctness of his information, but without obtaining any knowledge of the real facts.

The Greek philosopher and mathematician Thales, one of the "seven wise men," who went to Egypt about 600 B. C., gave his opinion of the cause of the rise of the Nile as follows :

"The Etesian winds that beat fiercely upon the mouth of the river, give a check and stop to the current, and so hinder it from flowing into the sea, from which cause, the river swelling and its channel filled with water, at length overflows the country which is low."

The philosopher Anaxagoras "ascribed the rise to the melting of snow in Ethiopia."

His pupil Euripides, has left us these lines :

"The river Nile . . . . which, flowing from the Negro's parched land, swells big when the melting snow to the river takes."

Ephorus says :

"The whole land of Egypt is cast up from the river, and the soil is of a loose and spongy nature, and has in it many large cliffs and hollow places, wherein are abundance of water, which in the winter time is frozen up, and in the summer issues out on every side, like sweat from the pores, which occasions the rise of the Nile."

There are other equally absurd and, to us, amusing theories, brought forth with much labor by ancient Greek sages. When we read of the winds stopping the flow of a mighty river, causing it for months to inundate the country, or of waters frozen up in a country of perpetual summer and coming forth in abundance in the excessive heat, we wonder if two thousand years hence much of the wisdom of the sages of the nineteenth century will appear equally absurd and childish.

Homer, though he knew nothing of the facts, was correct in calling the Nile "heaven descended" in the line "Back to Egypt's heaven descended stream." [1]

Simple as they now appear, it required more than two thousand years to solve the mysteries of the sources and the annual overflow of the Nile. It was only in the present generation that the facts were fully known and the phenomena satisfactorily explained, though the problem had long ceased to be other than a geographical one.

With a full knowledge of the wonderful provisions of nature for the supply of the waters, and the regulation of their flow, admiration took the place of idolatry. The Arab of to-day, without the blindness begotten by superstition, can spread his carpet and, turning toward Mecca, bow in silent prayer to Allah, offering devout thanks for the rise of the waters that are to give him green fields and an abundant harvest.

There are two seasons in Egypt, a long, hot summer and a short winter. In the latter, the temperature descends to the freezing point only once in a score of years, producing a little white frost. In the month of June, the heat becomes excessively oppressive, the soil, dried and parched, opening in great seams. The plants are withered, the foliage drooping, and the whole face of the country scorched and seared. Then the Nile, which has sunk deep in its bed, having reached its lowest point, suddenly begins to rise. Without a cloud in the heavens, and in spite of the augmenting heat, it continues to increase in volume until September, sometimes until October, when it overflows all the lands not protected by dikes.

The regions whence came the great river were, so far as they were known to the ancient Egyptians, like their own country, without rain. It is not surprising that they should have regarded phenomena which they were unable to explain with

[1] Od. IV, 581.

superstitious awe, and ascribed to the river the attributes of Deity.

The Nile has its sources in the Albert and Victoria Nyanzas, great lakes of Central Africa, the latter eight hundred miles in circumference. These lakes are the recipients of the rainfall of a large surrounding country. They are in great basins of mountainous regions where it rains almost continually for more than six months of the year, during which the Victoria Nyanza is said to rise more than three feet. This lake is the unfailing source—nature's vast reservoir—which, with great regularity, supplies the Nile.

The waters of the Victoria Nyanza flow into the Albert Nyanza, and the outlet of Albert Nyanza is, strictly speaking, the commencement of the Nile. There are large tracts of low country below this outlet which are overflowed during the rainy season, adding largely to the amount of storage.

The annual rise of the river and the consequent inundations are the result of the rains in the mountainous districts of Occidental Abyssinia, which form the Blue Nile and the Atbara. The former makes its junction with the White Nile at Khartum, and the latter empties into the Nile two hundred miles below. These two tributaries supply the sand and soil which make the Nile a muddy stream, as the Yellowstone does the Missouri. In the dry season they are small rivers, especially the Atbara, which nearly ceases its flow. In many places it then presents only a dry bed of rocks and sand with an occasional deep pool—the home of the crocodile and the hippopotamus. To these pools, the rhinoceros, the elephant, the tiger, the lion and the wild boar come to slake their thirst. In the rainy season it becomes a raging river, deep, broad and rapid, bringing down immense quantities of earth, sand and trees.

Below the Atbara, the Nile has no tributary, not even a rivulet, in its course of sixteen hundred miles to the sea. Consequently it does not, like other rivers, constantly increase in volume in its onward flow. On the contrary, as it passes through the desert regions of Sudan, its waters are continually diminished by absorption and evaporation, and, in Egypt, by their abundant use for irrigation. Yet they reach the sea through two great branches, each large enough to constitute a magnificent river, carrying with them immense alluvial deposits.

From a very early period man has employed his skill in utilizing the waters thus munificently and providentially furnished.

Strabo says :

"The attention and care bestowed upon the Nile is so great as to cause industry to triumph over nature. The ground by nature, and still more by being supplied with water, produces a great abundance of fruits. By nature also a greater rise of the river irrigates a larger tract of land; but industry has completely succeeded in rectifying the deficiency of nature, so that, in seasons when the rise of the river has been less than usual, as large a portion of the country is irrigated by means of canals and embankments, as in seasons when the rise of the river has been greater." [1]

This gives us the conditions at the beginning of the Christian era; but Egypt's system of irrigation did not originate with the Romans, nor with their immediate predecessors, the Greeks. It dates far back, to a time earlier, perhaps, than the dawn of Pharaonic history.

The luxuriance of the agricultural products of Egypt is not surpassed by that of any country. The labor required is proportionately great. No one, who has not made a special study of the subject, has more than the vaguest conception of the amount of labor necessary to raise, conduct and distribute the waters

[1] Strabo, XVII, 3.

of the great river, at precisely the right time, and in the required quantities, upon every acre of cultivated land.

The processes of flooding, plowing, sowing and harvesting are often carried on simultaneously in adjoining fields. It is necessary to irrigate the lands several times before the maturity of the crop, the quantity of water depending upon the kind of produce. Rice and sugar-cane require large amounts of water; wheat, oats and rye, much less.

There are in Egypt eight thousand five hundred miles of large irrigating canals, of which two thousand miles are navigable. These form the great system of arteries for the conveying of water to all parts of the country, while forty-five thousand miles of small canals, or ditches, serve to distribute the water upon the lands and to facilitate the drainage.

There are also great dikes, twenty and thirty feet high, and two to three times as many feet in breadth, on either side of the river and its branches in the Delta—to keep the waters in their beds during the high Nile.

In Upper Egypt there are hundreds of miles of collateral embankments of the same character as the Delta dikes, and others of serpentine form running across the valley. There are also numerous small dikes throughout the country. All of these serve some important purpose in this great system of irrigation. Whether we look upon that part which nature has done, or that which has been the work of man, it is a system of water supply that in its perfection and magnitude has no equal. It furnishes all the water, and that of the best quality, used by eight millions of people and their animals. It irrigates and fertilizes all the land. Without it, not a cask of sugar, a bushel of wheat, nor a pound of cotton could be produced.

Earth is a good disinfectant and the waters of the Nile below the Blue Nile and the Atbara are filled with soil. When this is removed by filtration, or even by allowing the waters to settle, they are both palatable and wholesome. No water is more healthy or more agreeable to the taste. The same is true of the waters of the Missouri, and for the same reasons. In both cases, a current of three miles or upward per hour causes the water to float constantly a large quantity of earth, thus continuing and perfecting the process of disinfection.

The deposits, which are distributed upon the land by repeated irrigations, contain a large percentage of carbonate of lime, oxide of iron, and carbonate of magnesia. They are generally sufficient to maintain its fertility, though land that is also otherwise fertilized produces much more luxuriantly. The amount of deposits is large, rendering the frequent cleaning of the canals necessary. This requires, for the large canals, the labor of at least two hundred thousand people six months in each year.

The high waters injure the dikes, carrying away large amounts of earth and thus necessitating frequent repairs. When the waters are the lowest, in April, May and June, the people are seen in throngs repairing the damaged embankments, and cleaning the canals. This work was done until recently by a system of enforced labor, known as the *corvée*,[1] which had existed in Egypt since the days of the Pharaohs. It was a "*levée en masse.*" All the people (men, women and children) were taken from the rural villages, often to a considerable distance, and kept without pay, twenty, thirty, or more days, according to the requirements of the service. Within a space of three or four miles as many thousand people could be seen working on the embankments or cleaning the canals. These works literally swarmed with human beings. Under their overseers, who stood by, whip in hand, they were as busy as ants. The adult men dug up the earth with rude

[1] In 1890, the *corvée* was nominally abolished, and the fellâhîn now receive compensation for their labor, which is paid from the tax receipts; but they must continue to perform the required service as formerly, if reasonable contracts for the work cannot be made.

mattocks and filled baskets, which were carried by the women and children, on their heads, up the steep embankments of the dikes and canals.

At the time of the digging of the Suez Canal, these *corvée* slaves did not always have the luxury of baskets. They improvised baskets by clasping their arms over their backs. They climbed the high embankments with bended forms and straightened themselves at the top, permitting their loads to fall. Many thousands died while engaged in this great work.

When the *corvée* system was in force, the overseer was not only always ready, but quick, to chastise the laggard, old or young, male or female; and, if the work did not progress with sufficient rapidity to satisfy the governor of the province or his agents, the overseer himself was whipped in his turn, as in the days of Moses. "And the officers of the children of Israel, which Pharaoh's taskmasters had set over them, were beaten." [1]

The overseers were generally the sheiks (chiefs) of the villages in which these people resided, and were held responsible both for their taxes and for the performance of their allotted share of public work.

The traveler who remains in Egypt till May and June can witness the novel scenes presented by these dense masses of laborers, of both sexes and all ages, with their peculiar dress (or, frequently, lack of dress) and their mode of work.

They sleep upon the ground at the place of their labors, literally covering it with a mass of humanity. If there is a dry sand bank in the vicinity, it is a great luxury. It is soft, fits the tired, aching body that has borne the toil and heat of the day and, in the warm nights of summer, makes a most enjoyable bed. Besides, the atmosphere is dry and invigorating. With the always clear, deep, blue vault of heaven lit by myriads of celestial lamps for their canopy, they rest from their toils, sleep-

[1] Ex. V, 14.

ing as soundly as the more favored sons of man. For covering, they have whatever they have worn during the day, and, sometimes, a blanket. They are awakened at the early dawn. No time is required for the making of toilets. A piece of coarse bread and a draught of Nile water suffice for the breakfast. After these summary preliminaries, they are hurried to their tasks.

The canals that are thus cleaned by public service are the main arteries conducting the waters from the river to the vicinity of the lands to be irrigated, and it is at this point that the great work of the proprietors of the land begins.

During the continuance of the high waters irrigation is not difficult, though the constructing of sluices and dikes, the digging of ditches, the cleaning and repairing, and the distributing of the waters requires a very large amount of labor.

At the time of the high Nile, the whole country would be flooded were it not for the dikes. In a considerable part of Upper Egypt and a portion of the Delta, this is still permitted. The country then assumes in many places the appearance of a great lake dotted with numerous islands, the latter being formed by the fellah-villages with their ever-accompanying groups of palm-trees. These village-islands are often connected with each other by the dikes or by high embankments along the canals formed by the earth accumulated from the cleanings of long periods.

The waters slowly recede, the lands are prepared, often with much labor, and are sowed or planted. The grain quickly sprouts in the warm, moist soil and sends forth its young blades. The fields are clothed in the rich, dark green of spring, though it is really late fall or the beginning of winter. Soon, more water is needed. If the river or canals are still full, it is let upon the lands, as in the first irrigation. If they are too low, it must be raised by pumping or in some other manner.

In much of the Delta the water is kept, by means of the canals,

on a higher level than the lands for the larger part of the year.
But the raising of the water by pumping, or otherwise, commences in some parts of the country within one or two months
after the high waters and continues till the rise of the river the
following summer. For the second crop, which is quite generally
produced, the larger part of the water must be thus raised.

The fall of the river from its highest rise is, at Cairo, twenty-
five feet, at Thebes, thirty-eight feet, at Assuan, forty-seven
feet. At the time of the lowest waters, the river is in some
places thirty or forty feet below the top of the bank, and the
water, when it has not been brought by canals from points higher
up the river, must be raised this distance for purposes of irrigation.

Dipping, drawing and pumping are continued in some sections
the greater part of the year and more than half of the lands are
irrigated a portion of the time by some of these means. If the
water is required to be raised twenty feet up the banks of the
river, as in Upper Egypt during the winter months, it is generally
done by the shaduf. This is a rude appliance resembling the old
well-sweep, with a basket-shaped bucket attached to one end
by palmsticks, and a mud-weight, to act as a balance, at the
other. The bucket is made of matting, leather or woolen stuff,
fastened to a hoop, which forms the rim. The sweep is short and
rests upon a horizontal bar supported by two posts set in the
ground. By this means water can be raised about eight feet
with great rapidity.

When the Nile is very low, it sometimes requires four or five
shadufs, one above the other, to raise the water to the level of
the lands to be irrigated. The mean height during the season,
in Upper Egypt, would be about twenty-five feet. The water
is ordinarily raised this distance by the use of five shadufs, one
worked singly and the others in pairs. By the first shaduf, a
man near the river raises the water four or five feet, emptying

Raising Water with Shadufs for Irrigating Rice Fields.

it into a basin made in the side of the bank. From this point, two men, each with a shaduf, lift it to a second basin, then two more to a third basin and so on till the required height is attained. It is then conducted onto the land, sometimes a mile or more distant, by earth-sluices constructed on the top of low embankments.

If the water is to be raised twenty-five feet, the constant working of five shadufs for forty-eight hours would be required to irrigate one feddan (acre). In other words, by changing once in six hours, ten men would work twenty-four hours each to water one acre. The process must be repeated at least three times for each crop. Thus the labor required for the irrigation of one acre would be seventy-two days of ten hours each.

Crops requiring a large amount of water, such as cotton, rice and sugar-cane, are generally produced where the labor of irrigation is less. On some of the larger estates steam pumps are used, but the fuel (coal) is brought from England, and is too expensive for general use, where labor is so cheap. There were in 1880 about four hundred steam pumps employed.

When water is raised by the shaduf, or other hand process, the minimum labor per acre is fifteen days, and the maximum not less than one hundred; yet, so cheap is labor, large areas of land are thus irrigated.

In 1873, according to official records, there were in four provinces of Egypt eighty thousand five hundred and thirty-six common field-laborers, whose average pay was five and three-eighths to seven and a half cents a day. In only two provinces did it exceed ten cents a day, and the average price of all the labor of this class was seven and a half cents a day. It must not be understood that the laborer was furnished with food, as is generally the case on farms in the United States. This he furnished himself. Hence, the prices above named were the full cost of the labor.

Even at these low prices the laborer did not find constant
employment. He was only hired by the day at such times as
his services were required. He was also subject to a personal
tax, which, though small, represented from ten to twenty-five
days' labor a year. The present average price of labor is ten to
fifteen cents a day, but the price of food has been proportionately
increased.

Of the means of irrigation other than those above mentioned,
the Sâkîyeh is the most employed. The Sâkîyeh is in common
use in the Delta where there are said to be over fifty thousand
of them. It is a rude machine on the principle of the endless
chain. It is propelled by oxen, cows and horses, sometimes,
by camels and donkeys, and raises the water by means of earthen
jars attached to an endless rope-chain passing over a vertical
wheel. This machine is generally used in raising water from
large wells having openings into canals. Throughout the Delta
the water generally stands in the soil on a level with the waters
of the river in the same locality. A large well, having no direct
connection with a canal or the river, will generally yield a goodly
amount of water, but only sufficient to irrigate a small parcel of
land.

CHAPTER IV

MYSTERIES OF THE NILE

At the time of my residence in Cairo, there were many festivities and ceremonies connected with the rise of the Nile, which had their origin in periods when the river was still a solemn mystery and an object of awe and veneration. On the night of the 17th of June, according to the belief of the ancient Egyptians, a tear of Isis dropped from the heavens into the river, causing the rise, which was supposed to commence at that date. It is, as a matter of fact, at about this date that the annual rise commences. This night, though less observed than formerly, was still celebrated in the seventies by those living on the banks of the river and such friends as chose to join them, with various superstitious ceremonies.

Soon after this date, the rise of the waters becomes perceptible to the anxious watchers along the river, and, each morning, criers in different parts of the city pass along the narrow, crowded streets, announcing in a loud voice the amount of rise, or the point to which the waters have attained according to the official statement of the sheik in charge of the Nilometer.

One of the most interesting ceremonies I witnessed was the cutting of the dam, built each year at the time of the low water, across the canal El-Khalîg, which, previous to the construction during the reign of Ismaîl Pasha of an admirable system of water works, furnished the water for the city of Cairo. Until a very recent date it supplied a large number of native inhabitants, who preferred the old system, erroneously believing it more conducive to health.

The canal was deep and ran from a point in Old Cairo, opposite the Island of Rôda, to and through the native or old part of the present city. It is said to have been made by Amru, Khalîf Omar's General, after his conquest of Egypt in A. D. 641, for the purpose of connecting the Nile with the Red Sea. He continued it to a point near Bubastis, where it joined with an old canal running to the Bitter Lakes and probably thence to the Red Sea. It has long been filled up, except that part running through Cairo, which emptied, immediately after leaving the city, into the great canal constructed to convey fresh water to the Suez Canal at Ismaîlîya and thence to Suez.

This short canal, supplying the city of Cairo, was kept open by frequent cleanings. It was dry for several months each year. At the time of the high water, large cisterns along its line were filled and from these the water was taken throughout the year and carried in skins to the consumers.

Water-carriers are constantly seen in the streets selling water, and also furnishing it to the thirsty passers-by gratuitously, or for such pittance as they may choose to give. It is usually sold from skins, but sometimes from earthen vessels. In either case, the water is served in small brass cups, which the carrier constantly strikes one against another, calling attention to his vocation by their sharp ring.

Previous to my departure for Europe, during my first summer in Cairo, I was invited by the Governor of the city to be present at the ceremonies of the cutting of the dam. This took place near the middle of August, when the Nile had reached a height which gave promise of sufficient water to insure a plentiful harvest. It was an event which was then celebrated with real joy and, as might be expected from the nature and habits of the Arabs of the lower classes, with noisy festivities.

The principal ceremony took place in the early morning at the head of the canal in Old Cairo. All Cairo was alive soon after dawn. Boys carrying flags attended the criers, who announced with unusual emphasis the glad tidings of an abundant flow of the Nile. A ride of about three miles over a road of deep, fine sand, through a then sparsely built quarter, brought me to the dam, at the entrance of Old Cairo.

What is now known as Old Cairo is a small town built on and around the site of the "Babylon in Egypt" of the Romans. This was an immense fortress, in which were stationed the Roman soldiers who aided in holding Egypt in subjection first to Rome and then to the Byzantine emperors, until it was taken by Amru after a long siege. The place was known in the early Mohammedan period as Fostât. The ruined walls of the fortress still exist and within them is the principal part of the present town, including a number of old, interesting, Coptic convents and churches.

On my arrival at the dam, I found a throng of many thousands of people, mostly of the lower classes, many of whom had been there throughout the night. There were tents along the banks of the Nile and the canal and boats loaded with people on the small branch of the river separating the Island of Rôda from the mainland. The tent of the Governor, to which I was invited, was on the bank of the canal directly above the dam, and in its front was a platform built out even with the edge of the water.

The tent was guarded by soldiers, who had accompanied the Governor, and was occupied by his Excellency, his assistants and a number of Europeans. From the platform was a view on the west of the river, of the Island of Rôda with its high surrounding walls, its beautiful gardens, palm trees and Nilometer. Beyond, a few miles distant on the other side of the valley, were the Pyramids. In front was the high wall of the ruined aqueduct of Saladin, rebuilt in 1518, obstructing the view of the domes and minarets of the mosques, the towers of the Coptic churches, and the prison-like walls of the convents of Old Cairo.

The booths of the sellers of bonbons, fruits, bread and other edibles, who are always in evidence on festive occasions, were surrounded by crowds. The clinking of the cups of the ever-present water-carriers, the discordant sounds of native music, the cries of the Cairene gamins and the general noise of the multitude were, I doubt not, manifestations of sufficient joyousness to satisfy even an Arab's love of the tumultuous, though scarcely surpassing in this respect an American Fourth of July.

The dam was a thick, high bank of earth and the waters on its upper side reached nearly to its top. A large number of men had been at work during the night digging down this bank, on the lower side, and carrying the earth out in baskets.

The men were still at work, but cautiously and ready to move at a moment's warning. We had not long to wait. The waters burst through, quickly sweeping away the balance of the embankment and, moving with great force down the canal, soon filled it nearly to the level of the river.

The Governor then appeared at the front of the platform and commenced sowing newly coined piastres broadcast on the waters. These are of the value of five cents, nominally of silver, but much alloyed. At the same moment many Arabs, each slipping off his single garment, plunged into the waters in search of the treasures. Some were unable to stem the current, and others with the agility of fish dove and scoured the bottom bringing up the shining pieces. In a few moments the canal was filled with men swimming, grappling and struggling with each other for a place in this amphibious throng.

At the cutting of the dam, Arabs were sometimes carried away by the current and drowned, although many of them are expert swimmers. The throwing of the silver into the waters was an old custom which had probably succeeded other customs.

The Great Pyramid of Khufu or Cheops.

It was continued to satisfy the superstition of the people who had come to believe that it had some influence in producing the rise of the river.

In a conversation with the Governor, on a subsequent similar occasion, he told me that the question of discontinuing the throwing of silver into the waters had been considered, but that no Governor had been willing to assume the responsibility of the omission, knowing that, should it be followed by a low Nile, he would be looked upon by many as the cause and suffer in reputation and influence among a large class. The canal El-Khalîg has recently been filled and the ceremonies of cutting the dam will henceforth exist only in history.

According to Moslem tradition, the Coptic Christians, previous to the conquest of Omar, sacrificed at this place every year to the God of the Nile a beautiful virgin, whom they dressed in bridal robes and cast into the river. This tradition has not been authenticated. According to some writers, an image, instead of the virgin, has in recent times, even within a few years, been thrown into the waters, but nothing of the kind took place on the occasions when I was present at these ceremonies.

As soon as the canal was sufficiently filled, boats, gorgeously pavilioned, sailed in from the river, the Governor and his escort retired and the people commenced dispersing.

I have already mentioned the Island of Rôda as lying near the canal just described. It is now principally visited on account of its famous Nilometer. An Arab tradition that it was among the flags on its shore that Moses was found by the daughter of Pharaoh lends it an additional attraction. It also possesses the "tree of Moses" and the "tree of Saint Mandûra," a venerable millenarian planted by Fatima, the daughter of Mohammed. This tree has survived many generations, is still vigorous, and is believed to have the miraculous power of healing the sick, making the lame walk, and the blind see.

It is true that not all of the devout pilgrims who spread their garments on its branches are relieved of their infirmities, but this fact does not injure the reputation of the "Great Physician." Only one in many thousands of the devout Catholics who visit the shrines of Lourdes claims to be benefited. This does not prevent an annual pilgrimage of several hundred thousand believers to this sacred place, where, as they believe, the Holy Virgin appeared in 1858 to the shepherd girl, Bernadette Soubirous. If the most enlightened people of this enlightened age have such faith in holy places, who can deny to the poor Arab the solace of a like superstition?

The Island of Rôda is in the form of an elongated ellipse, two miles long by nearly a half mile broad in its centre. It is surrounded by a high wall and was once fortified. It was here that the Copts took refuge on losing the fortress of Babylon with which it was connected by a bridge of boats. After this retreat they opened negotiations with the victorious Amru and finally capitulated. They were humanely treated and were allowed to retain their property. In fact, many of them welcomed the followers of the Prophet as a means of relief from their Byzantine oppressors.

The island was formerly a summer resort, on account of its cool breezes, for the families of a few Cairene Pashas who owned the property. It is covered with beautiful gardens replete with tropical trees and plants, among which are the orange, the lemon, the banana, the henna, and, towering high above them, the date-palm. Henna is a shrub, from the leaves of which is made a paste long used by the Egyptians in dyeing their nails and the palms of their hands.

The Nilometer is at the upper end of the island. Crossing from the mainland in a small boat, I mounted a long flight of stone steps to the top of the wall and entered a garden whose walks were paved with small stones in ornamental designs. After a short stroll among the shrubs and flowers, I was conducted by the custodian to the mysterious measurer of the rise and fall of the Nile. But what can there be of mystery in a simple device for determining the depth of water? It is only a large rectangular well with cut-stone walls, each of its sides measuring about five yards. In the centre is an octagonal column on which are Kufic inscriptions. A passage leads from its bottom to the river. It is true that very few, even among the most learned Arabic scholars, can read the Kufic. The only person I found in Egypt who could read the inscriptions on my Kufic coins was an Englishman, who had devoted many years to the study of early Mohammedan coinage. But the mystery is not in the inscriptions on the column and the sides of the well, many of which are only quotations from the Koran. Strange as it may seem there are few people in Cairo who know or can ascertain the exact rise of the river.

The unprecedented low Nile of 1877 gave just grounds for fears of the most serious consequences, the highest point attained being only seventeen pics and three karets. According to the official statements for the fifty-two preceding years, which was as far back as they could be obtained, this was three feet and three inches less than that of the lowest rise during that period, and nearly ten feet lower than the medium rise.

It was estimated by competent judges that five hundred and fifty thousand acres of land, one-fourth of all Upper Egypt, could not be irrigated, and, consequently, must remain uncultivated. I had been informed that the official statements did not give correct measurements. Wishing to make a correct report to Mr. Evarts, then Secretary of State, of so important an event, I undertook to ascertain the exact facts.

I first applied to General Stone, who, as chief of the staff of the Khedive, was at the head of the military department at Cairo and had kept a record of the rise and fall of the Nile for

a number of years, taking his figures from the statements which
were published in the daily official paper. He had had prepared
for reference in military affairs altitudinal charts, based on the
data thus obtained, which showed the heights of the water during
each month for a number of years. I found that he knew nothing of the measurement, except that the Nile-pic was about
twenty-one inches, and he supposed that all the statements
given were based upon these figures.

I next applied officially to the Governor of Cairo to whose jurisdiction the Nilometer belonged. He replied that, personally,
he had no knowledge of the manner of taking the measurements
of the rise of the river, nor of the exact length of the Nile-pic;
that these were secrets known only to the family having charge
of the Nilometer. In a conversation with Cherîf Pasha, then
Minister of Foreign Affairs, I found that he was equally ignorant
upon the subject.

The Nilometer of the Island of Rôda was first constructed,
according to some writers, A. D. 716, according to others, nearly
a century later. The present system of measurement may be
of a much earlier period. It has been long transmitted from
father to son or to the lawful successor in the family which, by
hereditary right, is charged with the duty of measuring the rise
and fall of the river. Each sheik on assuming these duties is
sworn to secrecy.

After much inquiry and search, my interpreter found an old
Arabic book, containing a statement of the facts, which I afterwards verified. The book was published a hundred years ago,
soon after the French scientific expedition to Egypt which first
discovered the fraud that was being practiced upon the people.

Theoretically, land which cannot be irrigated by the natural
overflow of the Nile, or by means of the canals at the time of the
highest waters, is not taxed. But the decision as to what land
is taxable is not left to the taxpayer nor to the lower local au-

thorities. The question is determined by the official statements of the rise of the river. In cases of partial or insufficient overflow, the proportionate amount of the tax is fixed in the same manner.

During the reign of the Pharaohs, there was a Nilometer at Memphis, and others at different points on the river. The registers kept of the rise of the Nile were always factors in determining the amount of taxes at that period, as in modern times. The priests then formed the educated class, were supposed to be the depositaries of all knowledge, and were often more powerful than the king. They kept the Nile-records and decreed the amount of taxes to which the king was entitled. That he and the priests counselled together and took into consideration the necessities of the exchequer is highly probable, but the motives for secrecy can easily be seen. If an Arab should be admitted to a view of the Nilometer, he would be no wiser for what he saw. If anyone capable of reading the record, except an authorized custodian, is allowed to do so, even now, it is an innovation of recent date.

The facts, as I ascertained them, are, that a Nile-pic is a measure of twenty-one and one-fourth inches; that the zero of the Nilometer is seven pics below the mean low-water mark; that in giving the height of the waters from zero to and including the sixteenth pic, the measure of the pic is twenty-one and one-fourth inches; that from this point to the twenty-second pic, inclusive, the measure of the pic is just half of this amount, ten and five-eighths inches, and, above this point, again twenty-one and one-fourth inches. A karet is the twenty-fourth part of a pic, whether the pic be short or long. After having deducted from the published statements of the height of the Nile the seven pics that are below mean low-water mark, and reduced the balance to inches according to the foregoing rule, it is still necessary to deduct seven inches to obtain the real rise of the river.

One explanation, or defense, of this system is, that when the Nile has risen at Cairo to sixteen pics, which is nine pics above the mean low-water mark, the people become anxious concerning the necessary additional rise. To quiet their fears, a half pic is counted as a whole, thus giving an apparent rapid increase. When the point of twenty-three pics is reached, there is the amount of water necessary for an abundant harvest. If the river continues to rise, there is fear of too much water, of the breaking of the dikes and the consequent damage, and, therefore, the full pic of twenty-one and a fourth inches is again used. This is in accordance with the common habit of the people of saying to you whatever they believe will best suit your wishes.

The real original reason for the practice of varying the pic was that relating to taxes, and the secret continuance of this practice and the mystery with which the whole subject was surrounded, so far as the mass of the taxpayers was concerned, could have had no other object. To understand how such a state of ignorance can exist, on a subject so vital to the interest of everyone, it is necessary to remember that very few of the people can read or write; that in an autocratic government, those who can read and write seldom take any interest in, or in any way meddle with matters that are supposed to be the special prerogatives of the sovereign, or of those he places in authority.

The Nile-pic is an obsolete measure and should you ask every educated man in Egypt what measure it represented, not one in two thousand could tell you, though they are constantly talking about the number of pics of the rise and fall of the river. They only know that what is published as twenty-three pics is necessary for abundant crops, and the rise most to be desired.

The rise in 1877 was, in reality, only about five feet below the mean rise, and twenty inches below the lowest rise for the fifty-two preceding years. The year of the next lowest rise during

Valley of the Upper Nile at Time of Low Water, Showing a
Traveler's Dhahabîyeh and the Shadufs along the Banks.

that time was 1833. The disastrous results of the low rise of 1877 show the inestimable importance of a normal rise of the river.

Herodotus, in speaking of the Nile, says: "Unless the river rises sixteen cubits or fifteen, at least, it does not overflow the country." [1] He has reference to the measurements made at Memphis, ten miles above the Island of Rôda.

Five and six hundred years later, in the time of the Roman reign in Egypt, the same height was required. Among numerous other designs on Egyptian coins of that period, that of Nilus, the God of the Nile, is very frequent. He is represented as lying on the ground and holding a cornucopia, or a branch of a vine. Near by there is generally a crocodile or a hippopotamus. These coins, when struck in a year in which the Nile reached sixteen cubits, had, in addition to their other usual characters, the Greek letters IS, representing sixteen, showing that it was a year of abundance. It is probable that the measurement then commenced at mean low-water mark, and that the ell was an equivalent of the present Nile-pic. If so, the height of water required to flood the Delta is about the same as formerly.

[1] Her. II, 13.

CHAPTER V

FASTS AND THE MECCA PILGRIMAGE

No scenes in Cairo are more interesting to the stranger than those connected with the annual pilgrimage to Mecca and Medina —the departure of the caravan, its return and the subsequent festivities, formerly ending with the Dosseh. The holy month of Ramadân immediately precedes that in which the departure of the pilgrims takes place and is most opportune for their preparation for this sacred duty. Ramadân is the ninth month of the Moslem year, always has thirty days and is devoted by Mohammedans to fasting.

However lax the Moslem may be in obeying the other cardinal precepts of his religion, he is very rigid in the observance of the prescribed fasts. He may cease to give alms, neglect to make his pilgrimage or to wage war against unbelievers, and not always remember to repeat in their fixed time his five daily prayers; but he will strictly observe the fasts of Ramadân. He believes that on the night of the 27th of this month the Koran was sent down to Mohammed. The gates of heaven are that day opened. God especially devotes Himself during this month to listening to the prayers of the penitent and granting them pardon for their sins. This is the month in which God made His "revelation to Abraham," delivered the "laws to Moses" and revealed the "Gospel of Christ."

The Moslem year consists of twelve lunar months of three hundred and fifty-four days, with three leap years in thirty, each adding one day. Consequently, any fixed Moslem date will occur, according to our calendar, ten to twelve, generally eleven, days earlier each year than the next preceding year, the date making the circuit of the year three times in a century.

The Coptic year is different from the Moslem. The Julian year, still used by the Greeks, commences on our 12th day of January. As if this did not already complicate sufficiently the question of dates in Egypt, the Government, at the time of the institution of the Mixed Tribunals (1875), adopted the Gregorian calendar. This is used only by the Department of Finance, the Mixed Tribunals and the Europeans. All of these systems are used by different individuals, according to their nationality or religion.

The Moslem day begins at sunset, and the month with the new moon. To fix the date of the commencement of Ramadân, the moon must actually have been seen, and the fact of its appearance a little after sunset must have been judicially determined by the Kadi. This is not difficult in the ever clear atmosphere of Cairo. Men are sent out upon the high hills just beyond the Citadel. Having obtained a view of the expected crescent above the Lybian mountains, they return. Their evidence is reduced to writing and a decision is made and announced to the numerous dignitaries who assemble on this occasion at the house of the Kadi. Cannon are immediately fired from the Citadel and processions are formed which, escorted by bands of music, march through the city proclaiming that the month of fasting has commenced. At the dawn of the next day, the district "messenger of the morning" announces the fast, and, just as the sun begins to appear, the cry is heard from the minarets of all the mosques of Cairo, "Hearken, the fast has begun!"

Mohammedan fasting consists in abstaining from food, drink and tobacco, between sunrise and sunset, during the period of the fast. No one is exempt from its strict observance except soldiers in battle and the sick. By reason of the short Egyptian winters, Ramadân falls for many years in succession in the warm season. The abstinence from food and drink during the long, hot, dry and dusty days of summer for an entire month is no inconsiderable sacrifice. It often produces upon the physical condition of the people an effect, which is marked by an indisposition to labor, peevishness and ill-humor, frequently resulting in misdemeanors.

The fasting of the day is, in a measure, compensated by the feasting of the night. It is sometimes painful to see the people toward the close of a long, hot day watching the slowly descending sun. As the weary hours are about to end they listen in breathless silence for the report of the cannon fired from the Citadel, announcing that the day's fast has ended. Then cigarettes are quickly lighted, dates and other fruits are ready, and the water-bearer is in great demand. Thirst is the first appetite to be appeased. The laborer drops his rude tools, the coachman jumps from his carriage and the cameleer from his camel, and each waits with nervous impatience his turn to seize a cup of the sacred water of the Nile. Then comes the feasting in which each person indulges according to his means.

Other branches of business are dull or suspended during Ramadân, but that of the cafés and restaurants is then at its height. There are bright illuminations, native or European music, song and story-telling until an hour before dawn, when the cry from the minarets, "Arise and prepare for the fast!" is heard. Then comes the early morning meal, the principal one during Ramadân, wholly contrary to the habits of the Orient, where usually but little and very light food is taken in the morning.

It is a long thirty days, but the cannon at the Citadel finally announce the end. On the morrow (the first day of Shawwâl, the tenth month), the three days' festival known as the Little

Beirâm commences. It is a general time of visits, receptions, rejoicing, making presents to servants and children and putting on new clothes.

The Khedive gives a reception, beginning at six o'clock in the morning, when the officers of the army are received. Afterwards come the various classes in a prearranged order, heads of departments, high officials, sheiks of religious orders, judges of native courts, representative merchants, notable civilians and dignitaries of all classes, judges of the Mixed Tribunals, and lastly, at eleven o'clock, the diplomatic representatives. The last-named are the only visitors honored by being seated. They are served with coffee, smoke the shibûk, and have a short conversation with his Highness in which they present and receive congratulations.

Immediately after this festival, in which religious rites have not been neglected, preparations commence for the departure of the pilgrim-caravan, which takes place on the twenty-third of the month. Each year, the caravan carries a new Kisweh, usually called "the carpet," a rich covering for the outer wall of the Kaaba. The Kaaba is a small building situate in the interior of the temple, or mosque, at Mecca, containing the sacred black stone. The Kisweh is of black brocade, wrought with gold, and covered with inscriptions from the Koran. It is made at Cairo, and some idea of its magnificence may be formed from the fact that its cost to the Egyptian Government is $23,000. The annual expense of the pilgrimage to the Government is over $330,000, a sum nearly double that appropriated for schools under European control.

The Kisweh is first made in small pieces, which, soon after the Little Beirâm, are taken to the mosque of Hasanên and there sewn together. When the body of the Kisweh has been completed, a broad, rich border and a veil or portière for the door of the Kaaba are attached. The caravan also takes another orna-

mented cloth to serve as a covering for the tomb of Abraham,
and still another of green material wrought with gold and various
colored silks for the inside of the Kaaba.

A covering for the tomb of Mohammed, at Medina, is brought
by the caravan that is organized at Damascus. A third caravan
comes from Bagdad. The three leave their respective cities at
about the same time, enter the great Arabian desert, after a few
days' travel, and, continuing southward, arrive at Mecca in
about forty days.

There is little difference in the general character of the scenes
and ceremonies each year on the departure of the pilgrim-caravan
from Cairo. The foreign representatives receive official invi-
tations to be present. I will write only of what I saw on one
occasion.

The invited guests arrived early in the morning at the Place
Mohammed Ali near the Citadel, whence the caravan takes its
departure. Bodies of different classes of troops were already
assembled there and, in the vicinity, various religious organizations were being formed into a procession. A gorgeous tent of
red velvet and gold had been erected for the Khedive or his
representative, and for the ministers, kadi, mufti and other
military, civil and religious dignitaries. His Highness, Tewfik
Pasha, then Crown Prince, represented the Khedive.

The Khedive, Ismaîl Pasha, did not attend public religious
ceremonies, but was represented by his son Tewfik, who was
regarded by the faithful as the more devout Moslem. Tewfik,
after he became Khedive, continued to be present on all occasions of this character. When his Highness arrived, he was
seated in the center of the tent, surrounded by the officials and
invited guests. Soon afterwards, that section of the procession
in which the Mahmal was carried advanced, and the camel carrying it was halted in front of the Khedivial tent. His Highness
stepped forth, took the camel by the halter and handed the halter

to the sheik who was to be the leader of the pilgrims. By this act, he entrusted him with the caravan and gave him authority over all who accompanied it.

The Mahmal is a magnificent litter with a highly ornamental pyramidal top. It is covered with cloth wrought in gold and two copies of the Koran are suspended from it, one on either side. This litter is now carried only as an emblem of royalty, but it, or the litter it represents, was formerly designed for the wives of the Khalîfs, who made the pilgrimage. It is said that the Mahmal had its origin in the time of the beautiful and wise Sultana, Shegeret ed-Durr, who made the pilgrimage (A. D. 1250) in a magnificent litter carried between two camels. It has accompanied the pilgrims annually to Mecca for centuries and is regarded as sacred by the simple devotees of Islam, who eagerly force their way through the throng to touch it and thereby be blessed. The camel that bears it is richly decorated, leads the caravan when on the desert, and becomes to such an extent holy that it is not customary to use him afterwards for any other purpose, though he continues to carry the Mahmal on the pilgrimages as long as he is able.

Near the Mahmal followed the grotesque sheik of the camels, who every year accompanies the pilgrims. He was a burly, almost herculean Arab, with long, matted hair and naked down to the loins. Mounted on his camel, he swayed backwards and forwards, his eyes closed, as if in religious ecstasy. Then followed pilgrims mounted on camels (in some instances whole families), with their baggage, tents, and other articles necessary for the desert journey. The camels were dressed in gaudy trappings and decorated with palm-branches, and, if their long, coarse hair had become too much whitened by the sun, its natural tawny color was restored by a free use of henna.

The main part of the procession, which was to honor the pilgrims by escorting them out of the city, had been the first formed, and was well in advance, pushing its way through the narrow streets of the native part of the town toward Bâb en-Nasr,[1] the gate of exit, two miles distant.   I did not wait to see the sheik of the cats, who is generally near the rear.   He goes half naked like the sheik of the camels, and is quite as rough and grotesque in appearance.   Mounted on his high, humpbacked animal, he is surrounded with baskets filled with tribes of cats, which thus make the sacred pilgrimage.   They look out upon the multitude, receiving its applause, fully realizing and enjoying, apparently, the distinction which places them above the rest of the feline race.

All business had been suspended for the day.   Shops, stalls and stores remained closed and the many thousands who had been on the streets in their best attire, since early morning, were now massed along the line of the route of the pilgrims, even the women mingling in the crowds.   Our seis, preceding us, cleared the way for our carriage and we entered and continued for some distance in the current of this stream of humanity.

This native part of Cairo, with its narrow streets and quaint arabesque architecture, was always attractive, but at no other time was it so interesting and picturesque as when it donned its holiday dress for the pilgrim procession.   Its buildings were gorgeously decorated.   Besides the traditional palm-branches, there were flags, streamers and banners of various colors and devices in superabundance.   The roofs and windows were filled with throngs of both sexes and of all classes and ages eager to obtain a view of the passing pageant.   The scene on either side, to us, as we passed, was a panorama of a mass of joyous, festive, enraptured human faces, surrounded with and embedded in the deep, rich colors of Oriental costumes, drapery and bunting.

Leaving the route of the pilgrims, we passed to a side street and hurried on to the outer gate in order to obtain a view of that

[1] Gate of Victory.

part of the procession which had preceded us. Companies of soldiers, infantry and cavalry had already passed, and were moving toward a desert camping ground near by. Each section of the procession was preceded by a native band of music, some of the bands being mounted on camels. There were court officials, military, civil and religious, other high dignitaries, with rich uniforms, decorations and abundance of gold lace. Many of them were accompanied by their guards or kavasses in equally showy dress. There were companies of dervishes, each order with a different colored turban (blue, green, white and red) and with flags and banners to be equalled in richness of decoration only in the Orient. Some, engaged in their peculiar form of worship, were saying their prayers and whirling and throwing themselves into a religious frenzy. Others were eating serpents, swallowing pieces of broken glass and walking on the sharp edges of swords. Still others had spikes passing through their cheeks from one side of the face to the other. And all these things, it should be remembered, were done under the guise of religion and with a pretense of being miraculously preserved from harm.

There were half-naked swordsmen, civic orders or guilds with various devices, people on horses and donkeys, desert Arabs on camels with spears, shields and all their wild fanciful costumes and trappings, interspersed with bodies of regular troops. Such were some of the features of the long train of believers in the Prophet which required more than two hours for its passage through Bâb en-Nasr.

Those who were to make the pilgrimage and various orders of dervishes went into camp in the desert just outside of the city. Here, two or three days were spent in further preparations and religious festivities. The Whirling, Dancing and Howling dervishes continued nightly their peculiar devotions. They thus aroused a religious frenzy which stimulated and encouraged those who were about to undertake, in fulfilment of a pious duty

for which no sacrifice is too great for the true Moslem, the long
and perilous journey to the Holy City. And this pilgrimage is a
real sacrifice. Exposed to the contagious diseases that frequently prevail at Mecca and to the privations of ninety days on
the deserts, many of the pilgrims fail to return. Mecca and the
sands of the deserts along the routes thereto are strewed with
the bones and ashes of generations of the faithful.

The first day's journey is to the Birket el-Hagg—Lake of the
Pilgrims—about ten miles distant. The dervishes accompany
the caravan to this place, where there is one more night of devotion. Then come the farewells to families and friends and the
departure.

On leaving Cairo, going east, one immediately enters and
continues in the desert. The Derb el-Hagg—Route of the Pilgrims—crosses the Suez Canal near the ruins of the "ancient
Arsinoe," ten miles north of Suez, and thence continues a little
south of east across the Sinai peninsula to the head of the Gulf
of Akabah. It then runs near the coast of the gulf and of the
Red Sea, until it reaches Mecca. The whole distance traveled
is a continuous waste of rocky, sandy deserts, with only rare,
small, verdant spots. At Mecca, the three caravans meet the
great mass of the pilgrims who have journeyed, by way of the
Red Sea, from Persia, India, Turkey, and the northern states
of Africa, including Egypt, and have landed at Jeddah, two
short days' journey from the Holy City. The whole number
assembled is often a hundred thousand.

After the performance at Mecca of the customary religious
rites, the splendor of which is said to be unsurpassed, the pilgrimage is continued eastward, six hours, to Mount Arafat.
Here, according to Mohammedan tradition, Abraham prepared
for the sacrifice of his son, not Isaac, but Ishmael, whom they
regard as the father of the Arabic race. The pilgrims ascend
the mountain, or hill, as it really is, and remain there during

the night. The next day, the tenth of the twelfth month, they sacrifice a lamb in commemoration of the sacrifice made by the prophet, Ibrâhîm,[1] as they term him, in obedience to the command of God. That night, at the foot of Arafat there is a great slaughter of lambs, and feasting is universal throughout the Moslem world. Those who are unable to procure a lamb or the meat of some pure animal are supplied by their more fortunate neighbors.[2] It is the Id el-Kebîr, the Kûrbân Beirâm, the time of giving alms to the poor and gratuities to servants, of providing new garments for children, of official and private receptions, of congratulations and general feasting and rejoicing—in a word, for festive observances similar to those at the close of Ramadân.

The caravan occupies sixty days in returning. It travels slowly, going by Medina to visit the tomb of Mohammed, and passes a considerable time in quarantine near Suez. It arrives in the vicinity of Cairo, the last of Safar, the second month of the new year.

The pilgrims are met at some distance from the city by relatives, friends and dervishes with music and loud demonstrations of joy. But, mingled with the din of kettle-drums and other harsh native instruments of music, and the firing of guns, are to be heard the agonizing cries and lamentations of wives and children, who, coming out to welcome husband and father, find only his vacant place in the procession. After remaining encamped outside the city until the arrival of the date for the closing ceremonies, the caravan enters the town with the same pomp and display with which it departed.

The Kisweh and the other coverings which have been replaced by new ones are brought back, cut into the original pieces of

---

[1] It was this prophet who, according to Moslem belief, first established the true religion.

[2] More than fifty thousand sheep are slaughtered at Mecca for this festival, which continues three days.

which they were formed and given to the mosques and religious sheiks as holy relics. The entrance into the city is made at the beginning of the religious festivities that are held in honor of the birth of Mohammed, the second day of Rabî el-Awwel, the third month of the Moslem year. There is, on this occasion, a great assemblage of different religious organizations, mostly dervishes, from various parts of Egypt. Cairo again puts on its festive, picturesque garb. The celebration continues until the eleventh of the month, ending, at the time of which I am writing, with the Dosseh.

The streets were filled with natives in their gayest costumes, with a sparse sprinkling of European residents and travelers. There were long lines of booths with candy-toys, bread, cakes, coffee, stalks of sugar-cane, gourds, melons and other fruits and edibles of the country. Native amusements abounded; music and the story-teller (at the coffee-booth), the swing, the see-saw, the Egyptian Punch and Judy, the merry-go-round. Companies of soldiers and frequent processions of dervishes with their music, gay flags and banners were passing.

After the heat of the day came the soft, dry, agreeable atmosphere of the evening. Apparently everyone was on the streets, and the festive scenes were at the height of their gayety. The booths were brilliantly, often fantastically, illuminated. Minstrels and bands of music were heard at every turn. The dervish processions carried colored lamps. Harem carriages passed rapidly, preceded by flashing torches borne by torch-bearers, their outrunners loudly crying, "Clear the way!"

A spacious field had been appropriated for an encampment in which each religious order had its large and gorgeous tent. Throughout the day and night, dense masses of people were wandering over the grounds. The Dancing or Whirling dervishes and those popularly known as the "Howlers" continued incessantly their accustomed devotions, edifying the Mussulman and amusing the Christian or arousing in him feelings of pity.

During the last three nights, there were extensive fireworks, an artifice in which the Arabs excel. The animation of the moving masses, the brightly lighted tents with their canvas lifted on one side, exposing the dervishes in all their rhythmic movements, the festoons of light made by lamps suspended to ropes of various lengths and heights, each order having its own color, combined with the display of Roman candles, rockets and other beautiful or fantastic fireworks to produce a magnificent spectacle. All classes were present. The Crown Prince was in his tent, surrounded with high officials and male members of his family. Numerous carriages passed containing richly dressed, thinly veiled inmates of the harems of the Khedive and pashas or European residents. Peasants mingled with the laborers and artisans of the town, the rich with the poor. The ubiquitous traveler appeared on his donkey, afoot, or in his carriage, according to his tastes or the size of his purse.

From the beginning to the end of this long celebration of the birthday of the Prophet, there seemed to be no decrease of enthusiasm. There was to be a final act, however, changing the long and pleasing drama into a disgraceful, sickening tragedy, and leaving a lasting impression both upon the Moslem and the Christian, but for very different reasons.

CHAPTER VI

THE DOSSEH AND DERVISHES

THE word Dosseh, literally translated, means "a stepping," or "treading upon," and conveys, in its original language, the idea of crushing under the feet. The ceremony consists of a sheik of the Saadîyeh dervishes riding, on horseback, over a large number of devotees. These prostrate themselves upon the ground, lying upon their faces, packed closely together.

In the forenoon of the eleventh of the month, the Rifâ'i dervishes, of which the Saadîyeh is one of the orders, assembled near the mosque of Hasanên. Others of the more fanatical dervishes joined them, and a procession of several thousand was formed. The Sheik of the Saadîyeh, having passed the night in fasting and religious ceremonies in preparation for the miracle of the day, came to this mosque for his midday prayer. When it was finished, he mounted a medium-sized stallion, joined the procession in the rear and rode with it to the encampment, where, since ten o'clock, an immense mass of people, fifty thousand or more, had been anxiously awaiting their coming.

On one side of the field, to the left of the entrance, was a long row of tents. The most distant tent was that of the Sheik of the religious orders taking part in the Dosseh, the next, that of the Khedive, was occupied by his Highness Tewfik Pasha and his friends; the third, by prominent Europeans; and the others, by dervishes. A space about thirty feet wide in front of these tents was kept open for the entrance of the procession. Soldiers were stationed in front of the tents to keep back the pressing crowds.

Those who had been selected or had volunteered as martyrs for the occasion marched down the open space in front of the tents accompanied by an equal number of dervishes, so that each man had his attendant. When the head of the column had arrived in front of the tent of the Sheik of the dervishes, it halted, and the men along the line, about four hundred in all, prostrated themselves upon the ground at a right angle to their line of march with their heads toward the tents. They were packed as closely together as possible.

They were dressed in the ordinary manner of the poorest classes and were undoubtedly from the lowest and most fanatical elements of the people. They wore only loose garments, fastened at the waist with a sash or cord, their feet and limbs being bare. The attendant remained sitting at the head of each man during the passage of the horse.

The placing of the men and the other preliminary arrangements occupied from half to three-quarters of an hour after the arrival of the procession. During this time the men were lying on their faces and the pressing masses of people, each eager for a place in the front rank, were kept back by the soldiers. I was in the tent next to that occupied by the Crown Prince and had a good opportunity to observe what took place. Opposite, across the line, were a large number of carriages, those of the harems in the front rank, and, back of them, those of strangers and foreign residents who were obliged to stand on the carriage seats to see what was happening. Among and beyond the latter was a seething mass of people who could not approach, and could only obtain a view of the Sheik, above the heads of those in front, as he rode down the line.

The bodies of the deluded devotees, when arranged and packed, formed a kind of corduroy road for the triumphal march of the holy Sheik, so holy that the Prophet miraculously protected from harm those who prostrated themselves to be trampled upon by his horse. If perchance it became known that some one had been harmed, it was attributed to want of faith.

At a certain signal, the attendants along the line and the thousands of faithful among the people commenced crying, "Allah" (God), "Allah-la-la-la-la-lah-lah," emphasizing and prolonging the last syllable of the word so that nothing else could be heard. At the other end of the line, two men side by side were seen walking on the bodies, carrying green [1] flags, the staffs of which were surmounted by spear heads.

Close behind followed the Sheik, mounted on a horse led by two men. They came hurriedly down the line, amid the cries of "Allah-la-la-la," "Allah-la-la-la," which gradually deepened and, mingling with the excited clamor of the great multitude, became a continuous, deafening roar unlike any sounds to be heard except among the dervishes. The Sheik was apparently a large man. He wore a green turban and a brownish-yellow burnoose fastened at the waist by a sash. His eyes were closed and he swayed one way and another, yielding to the motion of the horse, according to the usual manner of those in a state of religious ecstasy. Two men walked near him, one on either side, with their hands upon his robes to prevent him from falling.

The men on the ground made no movement. Their faith was strengthened by the continued invocation of Allah, whose Prophet was to protect them and thus show His power to all unbelievers. As the horse moved along the line, there was a general rush and the crowd quickly closed in behind him the moment he had passed. Whether this was prearranged by the managers, or whether it was because the people could no longer be restrained, I do not know. The result was to prevent the obtaining of much information as to what had taken place.

[1] Green is the color of the order of the Saadîyeh.

The Dosseh. Showing the Devotees Arranged To Be Ridden Over by the Sheik of the Dervishes Who Has Started on His Horse at the Further End of the Line.

The space in front of our tent had been kept clear of people. As the horse approached, I obtained a position next to the attendants seated at the heads of the men. Horses in the East are used mostly under the saddle and this one, according to custom, had been taught to amble. He was shod in the Oriental style, with a flat circular shoe covering the whole lower surface of the hoof. He passed quickly with a shuffling, nervous, unsteady gait, between a walk and a pace, his feet sometimes sliding down between the prostrate men, sometimes striking with much force directly upon their bodies and at other times upon their limbs. As the people closed in behind him, the men were hurriedly assisted to their feet by their attendants or carried away by them to the dervish tents near by. In less than a minute, not a person was to be seen lying on the ground, and the facts as to injuries were as far as possible concealed.

On two occasions I forced myself quickly, but with much difficulty, into the crowd immediately after the passage of the horse. On the first occasion I saw a young man arise apparently uninjured and laughing as if it had been a play. Another man, however, was carried away in a seemingly helpless state with blood running from his nose and mouth. In the crowding and scrambling, this was all the information I could obtain. On the second occasion I saw some getting up unhurt; but one man was unable to conceal his agony, caused by some wound, and another was carried away without the power of moving his limbs, apparently almost lifeless. I thought at the time that his spinal column had been dislocated or otherwise injured, but the rapidity with which all these people were moved away left little opportunity for observation.

By some, it was boldly maintained that no one was injured, that they were all miraculously protected by the Prophet. This was undoubtedly the belief of the greater part of the Moslem population. By others, it was affirmed that there was a large number wounded each year, and among them some whose injuries were fatal. A local paper, published by Europeans, claimed that in 1879, when the number of believers who prostrated themselves was greater than usual, there were three hundred and forty wounded. This was undoubtedly a random and much exaggerated statement. Even an approximate number of those injured could not have been obtained.

The bodies were packed so closely together that a single body occupied but a small space and the steps of the horse, in the manner he moved, were very long. I estimated, at the time, that he did not touch more than one in every three or four persons. In any event, the results were sufficiently horrible and sickening to condemn the Dosseh and to class it among the most barbarous relics of religious superstition that have been bequeathed to this generation. That it should have survived until the last quarter of the nineteenth century is a remarkable commentary upon human nature, as well as upon the fanaticism still existing in the human family.

Soon after one of these scenes, wishing to ascertain the real belief of the Moslems, I questioned Hassan, than whom there was no truer believer in the Prophet. He frankly informed me that no one was injured on these occasions, that it was a miracle, that he would have no fear of throwing himself before the horse, since he would not be injured. I told him he was mistaken, and related to him what I had seen. He was somewhat startled, having great confidence in what I said, but I could see that his faith, though a little weakened, was still strong.

The next day Hassan asked to speak with me. He said that he had come to tell me that he had been to see a high sheik of his religion, in whom he had great confidence. The sheik had informed him that there were people injured at the Dosseh and sometimes killed, but that the Dosseh was no part of the Mohammedan religion. He had explained that the Dosseh was an old practice of certain fanatical dervishes which disgraced their religion and had affirmed that he would be glad to have it, as well as many other practices of certain orders of the dervishes, discontinued. This was the opinion entertained by all the better classes, including the professors of el-Azhar, the great university of Cairo. This institution is the central point of Moslem education, and the fountain head whence flow the true doctrines of El-Islam to all parts of the Mohammedan world. This religion embraces more devotees than any other and its numbers are constantly increasing.

Happily, the Dosseh now exists, at least in Cairo, only in history. This marvelous city will henceforth have one less memorable entertainment for the traveler. The lover of barbarous public spectacles must content himself with the bull fights of Spain.

In February, 1880, I witnessed the last exhibition of the Dosseh. At the urgent request of the Khedive, the sheiks having control of these ceremonies discontinued them along with certain other practices, such as the public eating of snakes and glass, marching with needles and spikes apparently piercing the cheeks, the nose, the arms, and the flesh of various parts of the body and walking on the edges of sharp swords. These were mostly acts of jugglery, sometimes indecent, which had been up to this time common scenes in religious processions and had been considered by fanatical devotees as miracles.

His Highness, Tewfik Pasha, then Khedive, and the members of his Ministry were certainly entitled to much credit for the suppression of these practices. The fact that the change was made without serious opposition was an indication of an advancing moral sentiment. The Khedive had wished to abolish the Dosseh. His Ministers, the Ulema and the Sheik of Islam, however, while all agreeing with him that it was no part of their religion and was, in principle, contrary to the doctrines of the Koran, did not dare to take the responsibility of so radical a measure.

In the year 1880 several incidents occurred to aid the Khedive. During this year, Allah kindly removed to the Moslems' Paradise the fanatical Sheik el-Bekri, who was at the head of the dervishes, and the sheik who rode the horse, both of whom were bitterly opposed to any interference with the old religious customs. The old horse, also, which had long served to trample upon the devotees, became very sick a little before the time to celebrate the Prophet's birthday. The superstitious leaders interpreted these incidents as an augury in favor of the proposition of the Khedive and, without further opposition, consented to the discontinuance of the ceremony.

Nothing definite is known as to the origin of the Dosseh. While in Cairo, I heard an oral tradition to the effect that about the tenth century a religious sheik, on returning to Cairo from his Mecca pilgrimage, was kept outside the walls of the city for the alleged reason that he had not given any proofs of such piety, holiness and divine favor as to entitle him to the position he occupied. It was said: "If he is worthy of being such a religious sheik, let him give evidence of it." Irritated by these imputations, he caused a large number of glass bottles to be placed close together on the ground, mounted his horse and rode over them without breaking one.

Among the people present to witness this trial of the sheik's power were many women, who, in the enthusiasm inspired by the miracle they had witnessed, threw their children before him. He rode over these also without injuring them. The gates of the city were then opened, and, as he entered, the people threw themselves down before him and he rode over them. No one was harmed, and the same miracle was afterwards repeated each year, until the Dosseh became a recognized part of the religious ceremonies immediately following the return of the pilgrims from Mecca.

It is believed by many, however, that the Dosseh was a continuation or an imitation of some usage of a far earlier period, perhaps of Indian origin. Mohammedanism is a strange mixture of all religions known to Mohammed. In it, Judaism, Christianity and paganism are skilfully blended together, forming a system well adapted to the people among whom it was to be propagated, and the miraculous was one of its most essential elements. Pagan customs that were not forbidden by the Koran were continued.

No religious leader could obtain great renown without the aid of a popular belief in his power to work miracles. Any ceremony of the character of the Dosseh, that was grounded in the religious habits of a people who became Mohammedans, would have been readily accepted and adopted by the fanatical devotees of the Prophet.

Mohammedanism is better than the paganism it supplanted, and is still supplanting, and its adherents are no more superstitious than large numbers of certain branches of the Christian church; but even in its greatest purity it has many elements of barbarism, and its manifestations of superstition are of a grosser character than those of the Christian religion. Its wonderful hold upon the people of the Orient is shown by the number and the unwavering faithfulness of its adherents.

There is a fanatical element in all religions, and this is represented among the Mohammedans by the dervishes, who number many thousands. They are the monks of the Orient, but only a small part of their numerous orders make religion their sole business. They are mostly married men, artisans, tradesmen and fellâhîn, who take part in religious ceremonies at stated times, generally on Friday, the Moslem Sunday, and during the great festivals. Some, however, are mendicants and make it their business to attend religious ceremonies and funerals. These are the performers and miracle workers in the processions.

The religious exercises of the dervishes are called zikrs. They are a continued rhythmic invocation of Allah, accompanied by some motion, the whole company present joining in both the invocation and motion. This is sometimes kept up for hours without change or rest, but generally not more than twenty-five or thirty minutes. The motion of some orders is whirling, and these are consequently called Whirling or Dancing dervishes. They become very proficient in this exercise. They turn on the left foot and propel themselves by touching the floor with the right, making from fifty to sixty rotations in a minute with a graceful pose of the body, arms and hands, scarcely excelled by the best dancers.

The motion of some orders is a movement of the head from right to left or up and down, in the form of a nod or bow. Sometimes, there is a movement of the upper part of the body backwards and forwards, to the full extent of its bending capacity. The head is brought forward and down to the knees, and thrown back until it nearly touches the lower part of the body. The whole company keep time in this motion, and shout in concert their prayers, in which the principal sounds are those of "Allah-la-la-la." These dervishes and others whose zikrs are of a similar character are called by strangers the Howling dervishes.

Some make their invocations sitting, and some reclining or lying on their breasts; but all continue their prayers in concert, in a fixed measure of time and with frequent cadences, and prolongations of the "la." Their eyes are closed, and they often reach such a state of religious ecstasy that they fall into convulsions. It must not be inferred that the dervishes are not sincere in their devotions. They are faithful believers in the Koran, genuine and devout disciples of the Prophet.

CHAPTER VII

A JOURNEY TO MOUNT SINAI

THE peninsula of Sinai is a part of the territory of Egypt. Only an occasional traveler visits the sacred mountains. The trip is ordinarily made on camels starting from Suez. For those who have no special official aid, this is the only practical route. The journey requires three weeks, sixteen days of the time being occupied in traversing the deserts. If the dragomen and camels are hired by the day, without limit as to time, several days more will probably be needed.

Food must be taken for the whole trip—except bread, a poor quality of which can be procured at the Sinai-convent. In case of necessity, rice, lentils and dates are sometimes furnished by the monks, but at the time of our visit nothing could be obtained but coarse bread. In the dry season, palatable water will be found only in two or three places on the route, and supplies must be taken from these points. To insure admission to the convent, letters from the monastery of the Sinaites at Cairo are required.

Instead of taking the ordinary route, our party went by sea from Suez to Tor, one hundred and sixty miles, thence to Sinai by camels; an arrangement by which our desert travel was reduced to eight days—going from and returning to the sea. We had letters from Cherîf Pasha to the Governor of Suez, asking him to aid us in securing passages, and to the Governor of Tor, to procure camels for our party. Without these letters, it would have been difficult to procure either on reasonable terms, especially the camels. The company consisted of General Loring, an ex-Confederate officer; the consular clerk, Mr. Edward A. VanDyke; the consular kavass, Hassan; a cook and a colored servant. We took two tents, beds, blankets, canned meats, fruits and necessary arms and personal effects with us by railway to Suez.

When we left Cairo, we expected that passage to Tor would be obtained on a steamer that had been fitted out by the Government to transport Captain Burton and a company of laborers and soldiers to the "land of Midian," on the east coast of the Gulf of Akabah, in search of gold. The Captain had represented to the Khedive, that he had found gold in that country, on the route to Mecca, and had claimed that it was the real Ophir of the Bible. He had thus induced the Khedive to fit out for him an Argonautic expedition. This was one of the many cases in which his Highness, Ismaîl Pasha, was imposed upon by Europeans. Specimens of iron pyrites and a little copper were the only results of this expensive expedition.

There was a delay in the starting of the steamer, which made it necessary for us to obtain a boat for our excursion. After the usual long negotiations, inevitable in dealing with Arabs, an arrangement was made for an open twenty-five ton sailing vessel. Two days would be required, it was claimed, to prepare for the voyage. We utilized a part of this time in making a visit to the Springs of Moses, Ain Mûsa, which are on the regular camel route to Sinai, not far from the sea, and about three hours distant from Suez.

We were taken across the shallow waters and the Suez Canal in a small native boat, and thence by donkeys. After crossing the Canal, we were in Asia and on the border of a vast desert. East and south, there was an extended view of plains, hills and mountains of sand, gravel, earth and rock, without vegetation, and of a dull, monotonous yellow tint. It was the last of November. The long, dry, hot summer had parched and burned up all vegetation, and a brisk north wind enveloped us in a continuous cloud of dust.

On our right was the Red Sea, or more correctly speaking that arm of it which is known as the Gulf of Suez. It is only a few miles in width at this point, but deep, and as blue as the sky it reflects. Beyond it, rising from near the water line, are the mountains of Atâka, nearly three thousand feet in height, and wholly destitute of vegetation. On our left was only the desert, bordered by the mountains in the distance.

The Springs of Moses consist of a number of small basins of brackish water, some on the surface of the ground, and others on the tops of mounds in the form of truncated cones. The largest of the springs forms a pool about fifteen feet across, and was surrounded, at the time of our visit, by a garden with a few palm- and acacia-trees, thus making a little oasis. These are the springs, according to tradition, the waters of which were made sweet by casting into them the branch of a tree shown to Moses by the Lord.

There were several mud huts occupied by Arabs who irrigated and cultivated a small plot of ground. Most of the mounds with their basins of water were but little above the desert. One of them was remarkable for its size and altitude, rising, according to our estimate, to a height of thirty feet. It was very regular in form and had on its top a basin of shallow water, five or six feet in diameter, whence a very little water ran over the rim and down the sides. Standing on the top, I looked about the country to discover a higher point that might be the source of the water that fed the spring, but I could see nothing nearer than the Raha mountains, ten to twenty miles to the east. The desert gradually descended westward to the sea, distant one or two miles.

The mound was a solid mass of rock—a coarse sandstone. The water contained lime or some other element which cemented together the drifting sands. The mound being thus commenced, the water that ran over its sides united the particles of sand blown into it, thus continuing its growth.

A geologist, who has lately examined the mound, asserts that the cementing element is the calcareous integuments of a small transparent insect, the water flea, of which he found myriads in the water of the basin. Whatever it may be that unites the sand and solidifies it into solid rock, it is evident that the mound was formed and is still forming in the manner stated.

According to tradition, this is the point of the assembling of the Israelites after their passage "through the sea," the place where "Moses and the children of Israel sang their songs of triumph, and Miriam the prophetess, the sister of Aaron, took a timbrel in her hand; and all the women went out after her with timbrels and with dances."

We were to have sailed from Suez on the morning of the third day after the making of our contract. As usual with the Arabs, there was delay and, before all was ready, the last rays of the evening twilight had disappeared. There was a strong north wind, which is the prevailing wind on the Red Sea at that season of the year. Our tent and our provisions for two weeks, including casks of Nile water, the only good water in Egypt, were on board, and the last tardy sailor had made his appearance. Our Consular Agent at Suez, with some friends, had come to see us off; but, when we were seemingly ready to sail, the captain came to me to say that we would do better to wait till morning, that he thought the wind would increase and that we should have a disagreeable night.

This was what I had expected. In Egypt it is always "tomorrow," "bookra." After much talk, we moved out of the harbor. There was a splendid sailing wind and the stars shone brightly, but there was no moon and it was damp and chilly. The tall Atâkas soon shut off half the western sky and increased

Springs of Moses, near Suez.

the darkness. The wind, hugging the sea between the mountain ranges, gathered strength. We were making good time, but the boat pitched and rolled badly. Exposed to the wind and spray in an open boat, the prospects for the night were not very promising either for comfort or sleep.

At that season, bad storms were unusual, but the Red Sea, on account of the numerous coral reefs along its shores, is regarded as so dangerous for large sailing vessels, that those bound for India and other Oriental countries go around the Cape of Good Hope. This part of the sea is narrow, and, as we were on the direct track of the great number of ocean steamers that pass through the Suez Canal, a good lookout was kept. Thanks to the wind and the movement of the boat, there was little danger of the men sleeping on their watch.

The Arabs are cautious and timid sailors and take as little risk as possible. With their small vessels, they generally follow the coasts and, when a safe landing-place can be found, pass the night on the shore. This sea has been the highway of Oriental commerce through all historic periods, its vessels competing, up to the present age of steam, with the camels, "the ships of the deserts," on the overland routes. The boat we were in was probably no better than the boats sent out by Solomon with the servants of Huram in the expeditions to Tarshish for gold, silver, ivory, incense and precious stones; [1] nor than those sent by Queen Hatshepsu in her famous expedition to the land of Punt; nor than those afterwards used by the later Pharaohs, the Ptolemies, the Romans and the Arabs, whose craft have successively plowed these waters.

We had a disagreeable night, but the next morning found us well on our voyage. Our boat was light, the lateen sails large, and the north wind still strong. Not a cloud was to be seen and the sun rose over the Wuta mountains, bright and warm, and

[1] II Chronicles, IX, 21.

gave us the first day-view of the crew. The captain and sailors were barefooted and barelegged, with long blue cotton shirts fastened tightly with a girdle about the waist, as outside garments. They wore the ordinary skullcap and turban.

The warm sun soon took the moisture out of our blankets and garments, and a cup of coffee, made on a camp stove we had brought, relieved our fatigue and restored our natural amiability. During the day, mountain ranges were seen on either side, steamers were occasionally met or passed us. A little before sunset, the village of Tor, with its groves of palms, appeared and we were soon at anchor in its harbor.

From Suez to Tor, on either side of the sea, are only waterless deserts without vegetation, except the few winter-plants. There are no habitations nor inhabitants. One shipwrecked on these shores would not find a morsel of food nor a drink of fresh water in the whole distance.

While our tents were being pitched and dinner prepared, I called on the Governor, presented our letter from Cherîf Pasha and informed him of our wishes. He said that there were two encampments of Arabs then not far from the town and that he would send a messenger asking them to bring in the requisite number of camels.

Tor is a natural harbor, well protected by coral reefs, and furnishes the only safe anchorage for ships in this gulf, except the port of Suez. It is a small village of mud huts used chiefly as a quarantine station for pilgrims on their return from Jeddah, the seaport of Mecca. Every good Moslem is bound to undertake, once in his life, a pilgrimage to this holy city. The great mass of the population on the southern and eastern coasts of the Mediterranean, from Morocco to Turkey inclusive, are of the Mohammedan faith and the annual number of pilgrims is very large. Most of these pilgrims, to avoid the long desert trip, make the journey by water.

It has many times happened, that the pilgrims from India and Persia have brought with them to Mecca cholera and other dangerous, contagious diseases, which have thus been introduced into Egypt and Europe with fearful results. For this reason, the pilgrims have, in recent years, been stopped in Tor for examination and retained in quarantine there as long as the health officers have thought necessary.

Except when used for this purpose, Tor is only a very small, dead village. On the return of the pilgrims from Mecca, vessels are anchored in the harbor, and large numbers of tents are seen on the deserts near the sea. These are occupied by thousands of Moors, Arabs and Turks, from Morocco, Algiers, Tunis, Tripoli, Egypt, Syria and Turkey, and are guarded by Egyptian soldiers. These different nationalities and various tribes wear the burnoose—a flowing robe—and the turban; but, in the color and other characteristics of their dress, there are often striking differences which add to the picturesqueness of the scene.

The Sinai monks have a small convent at this place, occupied by several of their members, who receive and forward supplies of provisions to Sinai and have charge of some small palm-groves near the village, which belong to the order. Here also are large springs of good water from which the gardens are irrigated, but the supply is not sufficient for the pilgrims. The deficiency was formerly made up by water brought from Suez. It is now provided for by distillation.

The next morning, on coming from my tent, I found a group of Bedouins with their camels awaiting us. Nearly the whole day was spent in examining and trying the animals, choosing such as we thought the best, in bargaining and in various preparations. The camels of the desert are of a different race from those usually employed in Egypt. They are lighter, fleeter, and have an easier pace; but they must be carefully selected, since the comfort of a desert trip depends very much on having an easy riding camel.

During the day, we found time for a stroll along the shore, where we gathered a quantity of shells and coral which we placed on board our boat. The Red Sea furnishes many species of beautiful shells and some that are very large. At about four o'clock, we moved out of town. We had nine camels and one donkey, each camel being accompanied by a cameleer, on foot, and the donkey by a donkey-boy, who, in this case, was a full-grown man. The tents with their poles, pegs and other appurtenances, our folding iron beds, our bedding, camp chairs, cooking utensils, personal effects and provisions (including crates of live chickens and other fowls) were all loaded upon the camels. Four of them carried only baggage; the others, both passengers and baggage.

On account of the prevailing north wind and the consequent difficulty of returning by sea, directions had been given to have the boat taken back as far as Râs Abu Zenîmeh, about half way to Suez, there to await us. Râs means cape, or headland, and Râs Abu Zenîmeh is a point south of which vessels can lie, protected from the north winds. The boat would have about twelve days to reach this place, but, if we failed to find it on our arrival, we were to continue by camels to Suez. It was consequently necessary to provide provisions sufficient for over two weeks.

Our camels advanced in Indian file with such distances between them as to give our party the appearance, on the desert, of a fair sized caravan. We only rode out to Umm Saad, a little over an hour in a northeast direction, and encamped for the night. There are here a spring of fresh water, a few palm-trees, and a small piece of cultivated land irrigated by the water of the spring. It was the last green spot we were to see before arriving at the gardens of Sinai.

We were under way at an early hour the next morning, with the addition to our effects of goatskins of water attached to and swung under the camels' necks so as to rest against their breasts. We had also small sacks of drinking water which we had brought from the boat. Desert springs rarely furnish palatable water. It is generally charged with salts which give it a saline and disagreeable flavor.

We now commenced a long, weary, monotonous ride diagonally across the slightly ascending desert of el-Kâ'a. This desert plain, which runs in behind the coast mountains of el-Araba, extends northward from Tor, forty miles, and southward, along the coast, forty-five miles to the southern point of the Sinai peninsula. Opposite Tor it is twenty miles wide. On the east, it is bounded by the Sinai mountains. After a short distance of sand, we found the desert covered with small stones which gradually increased in size, becoming very large at the foot of the mountain range.

In 1863, Abbas Pasha, then Viceroy of Egypt, visited Sinai and conceived the intention of constructing a road from Tor to the holy mountain. He was assassinated the following year and little was accomplished, except the clearing of the stone from the route we were traveling across the desert of el-Kâ'a. This was an important improvement, as the stone so covered the ground in many places, that passage even with camels was difficult. Geologically speaking, this desert is of the cretaceous, tertiary formation.

After leaving the immediate vicinity of the coast, we saw neither animal nor vegetable life. It had not rained in eight months and the very few plants which grow on the desert had either disappeared or were dried and withered. Not an animal, not a bird, not an insect, not a leaf relieved the absolute desolation. The north wind was not strong enough to raise the sand; but the heat of the sun, its glare reflected from the desert, the continuous plain covered with stone which had been reddened and blackened by the heat of centuries, the seeming remoteness of the yellow-tinted mountain range, the foot of which was the goal of our day's journey, all contributed to make the day tiresome and long. Pack-camels travel only two to two and a half miles an hour.

I had been instructed how to avoid the excessive fatigue caused by the irregular motion of the slow-walking camel, which throws the body of the rider incessantly backwards and forwards with a jerking movement both disagreeable and tiresome. Light packages were placed upon each side of the saddle and covered with blankets and wraps, making a broad, flat seat. This enabled the rider to sit in any position and change as often as desired. If I felt fatigued, I urged the camel into a trot, and, when at a sufficient distance in advance of the caravan, dismounted and rested till the others arrived. In contradiction to what is said by some writers, I found the trotting of the camel easy and its walking unpleasant.

We reached the base of the mountains some time before night and continued our journey for about two hours up a deep, narrow, rocky ravine, Wâdi Hebrân, finding a camping place by a spring, which ordinarily had an abundance of water. It was then well-nigh dry. It contained the only water found on our route to Sinai. Near it were a few stunted palms. The gorge was narrow, only wide enough for a passage, and the granite rocks on either side rose precipitously to a great height.

The journey was resumed at a rather late hour the next morning and continued in this defile until some time in the afternoon. It was a constant and in some places a very steep climb. The path led over large masses of granite, in which places had been cut for the camels' broad feet. Over these rough, steep passes, the trusty animals moved as quietly and securely as a cat. At some points, the height of the rider on their backs increased the real or apparent danger, but there was no mishap. A little after noon, we espied a small bird, the only living creature seen on the whole route. There are several species of animals in these mountains. The hare, the jackal, the wild goat, the hyena and the leopard are said to live here, but they are rare and are seldom seen.

Some time in the afternoon we passed into the Wâdi, or valley el-Ejjawi, whence, soon afterwards, we entered the Wâdi Solâf on one of the ordinary camel routes from Suez. Near the junction of these two routes were a number of very ancient, beehive-shaped stone huts, of an unknown origin. They are called na-wâmîs, "mosquito houses," by the Bedouins and it was in them, according to tradition, that the rebellious Israelites took refuge from the plague of mosquitoes sent, as a punishment, by the Lord. The nawâmîs were in the form of an irregular circle and from twelve to fifteen feet in diameter. They were constructed in the following manner: a thick wall was built up perpendicularly about three feet and then gradually drawn in until a circular roof was formed, with a hole in the center which was covered with a flat stone.

At this point we were over three thousand feet above the desert of el-Kâ'a. Cliffs and mountain peaks were seen on every side. To the west, directly in our rear, towered Mt. Serbâl, high above all the others, nearly seven thousand feet above the sea. Serbâl was originally identified by the early Christians as the Sinai of the Bible. Many learned men are still of the opinion, that its claim to be considered the "Holy Mountain" is sustained by the stronger proofs.

We found an ideal camping ground for the night on a sandy plateau where there were a number of small thorn trees and many dried desert plants. The camels were relieved of their burdens and allowed to browse. Our tents were hastily pitched and dinner prepared. Dried plants, dead trees and roots, sufficient for a fire during the night, were collected and branches of thorn trees were brought in and cut up finely, with large knives resembling butchers' cleavers, for the camels on their return to camp. Our table was spread in the larger tent. There was served a dinner, as sumptuous as could be desired, which we ate with unsurpassed relish, thanks to the wearisome day's journey and the clear, cool, mountain air.

A large camp-fire was built and the camels were brought in and made to crouch in a circle around the fire, with their heads inward, and their legs folded under them after the manner of their race. Each was given a handful of beans brought from Suez and, afterwards, some of the chopped thorn tree branches. The Arabs had partaken of their scanty meal of coarse bread, a few cooked lentils, and the fragments from our table. Their day's work being ended and all preparations made for the night, these simple sons of the desert were seated, Turkish style, on the sand in an inner circle next to the fire.

Some of the more gifted of their number commenced the narration of wild tales resembling those Arabian stories which ever delight childhood. The auditors were certainly interested, for, till late into the night, I heard their warm applause, the prolonged "Aah! Aah! Aah! Allah! Allah! Allah!" The fire was well kept, but weariness finally came and one after another fell asleep. Only toward the morning hours did the hum of voices cease and leave the travelers in their tents, just outside this charmed circle, to the solitude, the fearful stillness of a night on the desert.

These solitudes produce peculiar emotions. They remind one of the old patriarchs, who, in their desert homes, far removed from the scenes of busy multitudes, surrounded only by their families and their flocks, seem, by reason of this isolation from the world, to have held a closer communion with nature and with God.

There are about five thousand Bedouins inhabiting the Sinai peninsula, and they are known under the name of Tawârah (people of Tor). The ancient name of the peninsula was Tute, whence the name Tur or Tor, as it is more generally written. These Arabs live upon the scanty products of their oases, the milk of their camels, goats and sheep, and upon what they receive for furnishing travelers with camels, transporting supplies from Suez and Tor to the convent at Sinai, and conveying millstone and other articles to Egypt. They are sometimes employed with their camels on the borders of the Delta and occasionally sell one of these animals. They have a very few sheep and goats, neither of which are often sold. They live in tents, except that there are a few huts near Tor and on the oasis of Fêrân through which we shall pass on our return to the sea. In these places, there are small parcels of cultivated land and a few date-palms, the ownership of the latter being divided between many persons not habitually dwelling there. A Bedouin often owns but a single tree. These people have the reputation of being very honest. It is said that no one ever partakes of the dates of an absent owner.

The different tribes of the Tawârah have for centuries served or protected the Sinai monks. The monks, in turn, are very kind to these children of the desert, feeding each day, just outside their gates, those who from age, decrepitude, or sickness are unable to sustain themselves.

On our arrival at the camping place I have just mentioned, Hassan was very ill with a high fever. I gave him aconite for a few hours, and the next morning he had so nearly recovered that we continued our journey. He ever afterwards had the strongest faith in my medical abilities.

The camp-breakfast was ready as soon as we were prepared for it. It was hastily eaten, the tents were taken down and the beds were carefully sacked to keep them free from the insects that are always found in an Arab camp. Then there was the bustle of packing, the kneeling of the camels, the loading and mounting, and the caravan was again under way. These are some of the usual incidents of the nightly camp on the desert.

Our route led, for some time, along the base of the mountains. During the forenoon, we left the Wâdi Solâf, and, taking our last distant view on this route of Mt. Serbâl, we entered the defile of Nugb el Hawa (Pass of the Wind). We then had a rise of about two thousand feet in a distance of five miles. The scene in this winding gorge was indescribably wild and desolate. The granite mountains rose, on either side, in precipitous shattered cliffs eight hundred to two thousand feet. The narrow and difficult pass, the bed of a deep, swift, winter torrent, was lined by massive pieces of rock, which had been detached from the towering cliffs. These rocks nearly blocked the way, leaving in many places but a scanty space for the loaded camel. There was an occasional stunted tree and a very little vegetation, but these in no way relieved the desolate grandeur of this high, rugged mountain pass.

The difficult work of clearing the camel path among these great blocks of stone was done by the early Christians. Some of the rocks were moved, the path was made to wind in and out among others and, in some cases, a way was made over immovable masses by laying other rocks beside them. This was the shorter of the only two passes through the mountain barrier, which rose in some places nearly seven thousand feet above the sea and was only a few miles distant, on the northwest of Sinai.

For two and a half hours the camels, carefully placing their feet, slowly mounted with their burdens. On reaching the summit, we were a mile above the sea, and at the entrance of the plain of Er-Râhâ (Rest).

CHAPTER VIII

MOUNT SINAI

SUDDENLY and unexpectedly we had before us a scene of imposing grandeur. In front was a plain, from one-fourth to a half mile in width and nearly two miles in length. It descended gently to the base of Râs Sufsâfeh (Mount of the Willow), a wall of naked rock which rose abruptly directly before us, nearly two thousand feet. Behind it, nearly a thousand feet higher, was Jebel Mûsa, the "Mount of Moses." These two mountains constitute the principal part of the Sinai group, their summits being nearly two miles apart.

On the left of this group, is the Wâdi ed-Dêr, at the base of which is the convent of St. Catherine with its high walls, trees and gardens. Opposite the convent, on the other side of the narrow valley, is another mountain group of about the same extent and nearly as high as that of Sinai. To the left of the plain of Er Râhâ, is Mount el-Eskûf, and to the right, Mount el-Ghabsheh. All these mountains are mere masses of angular, naked, igneous rock, composed mostly of granites and syenites.

The high, desolate, sandy plateau lying at our feet, amid the surrounding mountain walls, was the supposed place of the encampment of the Israelites before the "Holy Mountain." That mountain, rising before us, was the scene of the glory and power of God, of the delivery of the tablets of the law, of thunders and lightnings, of the "strong wind that rent the mountains and broke in pieces the rocks, before the Lord." It was the spot where came to Elijah, after the wind, the earthquake, and the fire, the "still small voice." [1]

On our arrival at the convent, we presented our letters, were kindly received and, by invitation, pitched our tents in the gardens, which were surrounded by high walls. The camels and Arabs remained outside, camping in the desert until the time of our departure. The gardens contain but a few acres and are irrigated during the long rainless summer by waters from a reservoir which is filled in the winter. They are at the base of the mountain slope, and a high retaining wall has been built on the upper side to protect them from the torrents caused by the winter rains. They form a small oasis, the fragrance of which is refreshing and delightful to one who has been traveling for days on the desert. They produce a variety of vegetables and among their fruits are the orange, quince, almond, peach, olive, fig and pomegranate. Vines climb the walls and a number of tall cypress trees lend, during the hot summer, their grateful shade.

It had been hazy during the latter part of the day and, after the setting of the sun, the heavens were completely obscured. In the evening, a monk came to our tent to say that the Prior sent us an invitation to come into the convent for the night, adding that he thought it would rain before morning. This change would require the removal of all our beds and effects, as only empty uninviting rooms could be furnished or rooms with beds we did not care to occupy. So, after consultation, we concluded to remain in our tents and sent our thanks to the prelate for his thoughtful kindness.

At about two o'clock, we were awakened by a sharp report of thunder. This was soon succeeded by another and then peal on peal quickly followed and reverberated from mountain to mountain, the sound being heightened, sharpened and quickened by its confinement between the lofty surrounding cliffs. Our tent

[1] I Kings, XIX, 12.

was intermittently as light as day. On going outside, we witnessed one of the grandest displays of nature. The heavens were ablaze. Piercing, dazzling lines of fire darted in every direction among the overhanging rocks, lighting up mountains and valleys. These were followed by sharp, deafening peals, that made the mountains tremble, as if they were rent asunder. The reverberation, at first sharp, quick and loud, slowly died away in the distance, like a roar of falling fragments crashing down the mountain sides.

Fierce thunder-storms are always impressive, and especially in childhood. The lightning, the thunder, the wind, the rain of such wild scenes remain vivid in the memory. But I have never witnessed anything approaching in its fierceness, its power, its awful grandeur, the thunders of Sinai. Their sharp crashing peals echoed from mountain to mountain, as if tearing away the summits and scattering the fragments in the surrounding valleys. I was reminded of the graphic Biblical account of the scene in the same place, thirty-two hundred years before, when "there were thunders and lightnings and a thick cloud upon the mount, and the Lord descended upon it in fire, and the smoke thereof ascended as the smoke of a furnace, and the whole mountain quaked greatly."

Wind and rain immediately followed and soon we heard the roar of the torrents coming down the mountain side. The ground, covered with water, was softening and our tent though doubly secured began yielding to the force of the storm. Hassan and the gardener were on the outside with mallets vainly trying to fasten the stakes and hold the tent in place. It was three o'clock and the convent bells were calling the monks to the chapel for prayers.

We were already well drenched, and the little protection we had seemed about to be removed. We began to consider whether we would not have done better to accept the invitation to enter the convent. General Loring with a soldier's tenacity still strongly insisted upon remaining outside. The prelate had not forgotten us. He sent a monk to renew the invitation, and to say that there was danger of the falling of the high retaining wall under which we were encamped. This settled the question, and we removed, as best we could, through a driving storm into the convent.

In the morning, all the mountains were white with a thin layer of snow. Thus suddenly had the long, dry summer changed to winter. We remained at the convent during our first day at Sinai, resting and viewing the objects of interest.

The mountains of the Sinai peninsula were regarded as sacred long before the time of Moses and have continued to be so regarded until the present time by a large number of people.

Early in the Christian period, perhaps in the first century, anchorites commenced locating in the mountains and glens of this remote desert region. They erected small stone structures, cut rooms in the rocks, or sought out natural caves in which to lead hermit lives. Their numbers increased and, at one time in the Middle Ages, it is said that there were no less than six thousand of these religious people among the mountains, either as hermits (anchorites), or in congregations (cenobites). They were frequently robbed and murdered and were sometimes massacred in large numbers by the Arabs.

Their sufferings and persecutions did not diminish their religious fervor, nor prevent their places from being filled by new converts. In many cases, they fled from persecution in their own country; but more often they were actuated by the religious idea, still very prevalent in various European countries, of leading a holy life in solitude. These wild mountain deserts, with their sacred historical associations, were naturally a favorite resort for persons disposed to indulge in this peculiar religious manifestation. Their number has been for a long time diminishing, and to-day there are no hermits and probably not more than forty monks dwelling on the peninsula.

There are chapels and convents in ruins and many grottoes, once inhabited, in various places among the mountains. These are generally in high valleys, but sometimes in almost inaccessible cliffs. At a very early period many anchorites settled in the vicinity of Mount Sinai and claimed it as the real "Horeb," the "Mount of the Law." In A. D. 530, the Emperor Justinian built at Sinai a church surrounded by a fortress for the protection of the monks who had previously lived isolated in natural or artificial caves and rude stone huts. The Empress Helena constructed about 326, on the site of the "Burning Bush," a tower and a chapel, which were included within the walls of the fortress. The true site of the "Burning Bush" was a long time in doubt, but the exact place was finally revealed by a pious monk to whom the Angel of the Lord had appeared in a dream.

The fortress of Justinian is said to be the present convent. It encloses a little over an acre of land, which is now covered with the convent buildings and their courts. On its high, thick, granite walls, are picturesque towers and covered promenades which provide the monks with a cool summer resort. Ancient loop-holes are still seen and, on the battlements, are a few old, useless cannon. Arabs have never been allowed within the walls and, until a recent date, visitors were admitted only by a door about thirty feet from the ground to which they were drawn by a windlass. There was at the time of our visit a very narrow side door opening from the gardens, through which entrance was made by a narrow stairway leading up to the level of the buildings. There was also, formerly, a well protected underground passage from the convent to the gardens.

Some of the convent buildings have been several times destroyed by fire and all of them have been restored or rebuilt with changes and additions to meet the necessities of the times or the caprices of the prelates. The whole interior is now a confused mass of buildings, connected by a labyrinth of small passages, through which the traveler is conducted. The buildings and their contents are interesting, but not very remarkable in comparison with those of other similar institutions.

The church, which was built at the same epoch as the fortress in the form of the Roman basilica, is massive and grand and has rows of granite columns between its aisles. It has chapels, altars, numerous paintings, mosaics of the seventh or eighth century, swinging candelabra, a hundred lamps, and many rich presents, including those of the Empress Catherine of Russia, and Alexander II. It has also many holy relics, among them, the skull and hand of St. Catherine, the philosopher, who was executed at Alexandria A. D. 312, and whose body was carried by angels, three hundred years after her martyrdom, from that city to the top of Mount Katarîna. As a proof of the fact, the monks point to a depression in the floor of an old chapel on the summit of that mountain, which they affirm was miraculously made by the body at the place in which it was found.   An account of the miracles performed in the holy mountains would fill volumes.

In the chapel of the "Burning Bush," a silver plate indicates the place where the bush stood, as shown by the angel to the monk. Over it is an altar with suspended lamps, which are kept constantly burning. On entering this chapel from the church, a descent of several steps is made, indicating that the chapel has been maintained in its original place and that the church and other buildings are higher than the earliest constructions. It is claimed that the chapel is the oldest building in the convent, some being of the opinion that it dates from the time of the Empress Helena.

Before entering, you are required, as Moses was, to take off

your shoes,[1] but the monks have thoughtfully covered the floor
with rich carpets. The silver plate was removed for us, as a
special favor, leaving an opening in the floor, that we might see
the exact place where the bush stood. "And the angel of the
Lord appeared unto him in a flame of fire, out of the midst of
the bush; and he looked, and behold, the bush burned with fire,
and the bush was not consumed." [2]

There is a small mosque near the church, said to have been
built by the monks to prevent the destruction of the convent,
at the time of the conquest of Egypt by Selîm, the Ottoman
Emperor. It has one minaret but contains nothing of interest.

The convent library is a valuable collection. It contains many
hundreds of ancient manuscripts, in Greek, Arabic, Persian,
Syrian and other languages, some of them beautifully illuminated. It is particularly celebrated for having contained the
famous Codex Sinaiticus, a nearly complete fourth century copy
of the Bible, second in age and importance only to the Codex
Vaticanus. This manuscript is now in St. Petersburg, having
been purchased by the Emperor of Russia, Alexander II.

Near the middle of the gardens, and connected with the convent by dark underground passages, are the vaults in which rest
the remains of the monks and priests who have died at Sinai.
There are two vaults and a small chapel. One vault contains
the remains of the lay brothers, the ordinary monks—a mass of
bones, the skulls in one heap, and the other bones in another.
The other vault contains the remains of the priests, bishops and
saints, in rude coffins. A few ghastly skeletons are placed against
the walls, and that of St. Stephen, the porter, who died in 580,
is sitting by the door of the priests' vault, with a violet velvet
skull-cap on his head and his mantle wrapped around him.

The convent had at the time of our visit about thirty inmates,
monks and priests. The former did the work of the establish-

[1] Ex. III, 5.   [2] Id. 2.

ment—the cooking, cleaning, washing, etc.—made the clothing and kept the buildings in repair. They also served as guides to the occasional travelers who visit this remote region. Their lives are those of ascetics. Their principal food is coarse bread, vegetables and fruits. They partake of neither meat nor wine, and, during their long fasts, use neither milk nor oils. They belong to the Greek church and have services, mass or long rituals, eight times during each twenty-four hours. Every monk is required to be present at two, at least, of these services during the day, and at the same number during the night.

It is difficult to comprehend the religious enthusiasm or devotion that causes strong men to leave their homes and kindred in order to spend their lives in this remote and desolate place. They submit here to a discipline and confinement nearly as strict as that of a prison. They have no luxuries, no comforts even, and, from a secular point of view, no prospects. They can hope for nothing more than passing a monotonous physical existence and adding their bones to the heaps already accumulated in the ghastly charnel-house of Sinai.

Their hardships, to-day, are slight in comparison with those of the periods when these mountain sides were covered with hermit dwellings. Then, as now, sufferings and loss of life, instead of deterring others, only acted as a stimulant, inciting them to take the places of the fallen and to assume, as a self-imposed duty, the same burdens and endure the same privations as their predecessors.

CHAPTER IX

ASCENT OF MOUNT SINAI

THE next day, we made the ascent of Jebel Mûsa, designated by the monks the "Mount of the Law." In the rear of the convent, there is a path up the mountain known as the "Pilgrims' Steps." Rough, irregular blocks of granite, of various sizes, are arranged to make a stairway. In the steeper parts of the ascent, they are sometimes two feet in height, making it necessary to climb or scramble over them. This is as fatiguing as the ascent of the Great Pyramid, and the rise is four times as great. Three hours of severe labor, by a good mountain traveler, is required to reach the summit. This route is said to have been constructed in the sixth or seventh century and, though in a bad condition, is still used. It leads diagonally up the mountain side and, in half an hour, we reach a cool, never failing spring, issuing from under a large granite bowlder.

According to the Arabs, this is where Moses watered the flocks of Jethro, and they have given it the name of the "Fountain of Moses." The monks, however, claim that the waters came forth in answer to the prayers of a holy abbot, at a time when the springs at the convent had failed, and that the real "Spring of Moses," where Jethro's flocks were watered, is at the convent. As there have been no revelations made to any pious monk, nor any edict of the church settling this important question, the traveler is allowed to choose between the Moslem and the Christian claims. The spring furnishes excellent water and has a right to be proud of the distinction of having supplied, in this desert region, either Moses, Jethro's cattle, or the holy monks.

Having rested a few minutes and partaken of the waters of this venerable spring, we continued our slow march, or rather climb, up the path that had been traveled by pilgrims for many centuries. There was no lack of convenient resting places. In a very short time, we were at a chapel dedicated to the Virgin Mary, a small building of rough stone. There is no dispute regarding the miracle, the memory of which is here perpetuated. All the books and traditions agree and we have no alternative but to accept the version given. At a time in the dim, distant past, the plague of fleas became so intolerable at the convent, that the good monks formed the hardy and solemn resolution to leave their cells and flee to the mountains. At this precise spot, the mournful procession was met by the Holy Virgin, who ordered them to return and promised relief. They obeyed like good Christians and, on their return, they found that their tormentors had disappeared. Whether the fleas remained away I am unable to give evidence, as we slept in our own beds and took ample precaution against annoying intruders.

Continuing our ascent, we soon came to a narrow pass, over which there was a rude arch forming a gateway and, a little further on, a second. Here, in the days of numerous pilgrims, priests were stationed to receive confessions and administer the sacrament. We next reached a small level place, green in its season, having a single gigantic cypress and near by a spring. It was surrounded with reddish granite rock, rising in masses and pinnacles. After climbing over a few more large blocks we reached a small stone building, in which are the two chapels of Elijah and Elisha, and the grotto where the former dwelt when he fled from Jezebel. "And he rose and did eat and drink, and went in the strength of that meat forty days and forty nights unto Horeb, the Mount of God. And he came thither unto a cave, and lodged there." [1]

We had been climbing the mountain side over two hours. General Loring had the aid of his colored servant, but was nearly exhausted and some distance in the rear. With his one arm and his years, this climbing and scrambling over the granite blocks were too much, both for his limbs and temper. I fear that the spirits of the departed monks, still lingering in these holy places, were much disturbed. Hassan, corpulent, unaccustomed in his hot climate to much exercise, and handicapped by his cumbersome Oriental dress, came struggling up, puffing and wheezing, vexed and disgusted, on account of the lassitude he was unable to conceal.

We had now reached a height which enabled us to obtain fine views of the surrounding mountains. We were at the base of the peak, Jebel Mûsa, which for the first time had come into full view. Its summit was yet an hour distant, directly south of us. A little to its right, several miles away, on the other side of Wâdi el-Lejâ, was St. Katarîna, the highest point on the Sinai peninsula, eight thousand five hundred feet above the sea. Near by to the west was a long ridge connecting Jebel Mûsa with Râs Sufsâfeh. Continuing our ascent of the "Mount of Moses," we were shown near its summit a small depression in the granite rock, which, according to Moslem tradition, was the track of the camel Mohammed rode on the occasion of his miraculous visit to Sinai. On the summit was another small chapel and a mosque built on the ruins of an ancient convent.

A cave beneath the mosque is the traditional place of Moses' sojourn on the Mount. "And Moses went into the midst of a cloud, and got him up into the mount, and Moses was in the mount forty days and forty nights." [2] A cleft in the rock near the chapel was shown as the place where the great lawgiver

[1] I Kings, XIX, 8.   [2] Ex. XXIV, 18.

stood when the Lord passed by. "And it shall come to pass while my glory passeth by, that I will put thee in a cleft of the rocks, and will cover thee with mine hand, while I pass by." [1]

The day was clear, but cold for that latitude. The mountains were still white with snow, except the steep cliffs where there was no place for it to lodge. The whole scene was wild and desolate, bleak mountain ranges rising one above another at nearly every point of the compass. In the immediate vicinity there was no visible valley, the valley views all being shut off by the lower projections of the mountain group.

On the east side of Jebel Mûsa there was a precipitate descent of one thousand feet, but no place where an assembled host, like the great body of the Israelites, could have encamped, and from or near their camp have witnessed the scenes described in the Biblical narrative. Our descent was made leisurely, in order to enjoy the fine mountain views on the north and west.

The next morning, General Loring concluded that he had had enough of mountain climbing, and decided to remain at the convent. Mr. VanDyke wished to visit Mt. Katarîna, and asked that Hassan might accompany him. They were fitted out and left at an early hour.

Mounted on a camel with a monk for a guide, I set out for Râs Sufsâfeh. The monk was a Greek, about thirty years old, over six feet in height and, in form and strength, a real Hercules. We went southeasterly up Wâdi Shu'aib, which is a continuation from the convent of Wâdi ed-Dêr and, turning gradually first toward the southwest and then west, crossed our track of the previous day at the small plain of the cypress.

Here, the camel was sent back to the convent with the cameleer. We continued on foot, following a difficult path on the northern slope of the rocky ridge that connects the two mountain peaks. We passed the remains of the ancient chapel of St. John

[1] Ex. XXXIII, 22.

the Baptist, several grottoes once occupied by hermits, and an old cistern. Descending slightly, we came to the chapel of the "Sacred Girdle of the Virgin." There were here a few trees, among which was the willow that has given its name to the mountain (Sufsâfeh).

There is a tradition that it was from this venerable willow that Moses cut his miraculous rod. Neither the age of the tree, nor the fact that the tradition does not accord with the Biblical narrative seem to weaken in the least the blind faith of the simple believer. Through some mishap, the rod, which might have been used as confirmatory evidence, has not been preserved. We shall, however, see later the rock it smote and this may cure us of our infidelity.

We had been over three hours in coming from the convent and had before us only a short, but difficult, ascent to the summit of Sufsâfeh. At first, we found steps, but afterwards we were obliged to scramble up the steep side of the mountain. On reaching the summit, we obtained our views, standing in a broad cleft of a rock closed above by a well-formed, natural arch. Nearly two thousand feet below us was the plain of Er-Râha, through which we had passed on the day of our arrival. We had then looked up to this towering mountain with its almost perpendicular face. Now the plain was in full view far below us, with lofty mountains on either side.

Every historical question or association apart, the scene was one of the grandest and most imposing. The historical questions are: Was this the real "Mount of the Law"? Were the valley and plains lying before us once covered with the encampments of the Israelites, who, looking up to the place where we were standing, saw the "glory of the Lord like a devouring fire on the top of the mount"? Many learned theologians believe this to be, contrary to monkish tradition, the "Mount of the Law."

It is not my intention to discuss or give an opinion upon any of the theories or beliefs regarding Mt. Sinai that have from time to time occupied the attention of Christian people. I will simply insert the words of one, who, like many others, believed this place to have been the theater of the scenes described in the book of Exodus.

"Here is a plain sufficient for the encampment of the whole people; there is the mountain rising up from it, which the careless, or the daring might approach and touch; and here, too, is the commanding peak, where dark clouds and lightning flashes would be visible to all. . . . All around are nature's own unchanging features. There are the mountains, and there the vales, that the Israelites gazed upon; there are the very peaks that were once shadowed by the clouds, that hid the Almighty from the view of His astonished people; that were once lit up by the lurid glare of the lightnings; and that once gave back in their echoes the awful voice of heaven's trumpet when it proclaimed the advent of heaven's King."

A little to the south of the place where we were standing was a circular elevation, a knoll of reddish gray granite, rising two hundred feet above us. On its summit was a small conical pile of loose stone, showing that some one had visited the place. I saw no way of approach, but was prompted to attempt the ascent by the very natural desire of reaching the highest point.

My Greek guide spoke no language that I understood, except that he knew a very few words of French. I succeeded in learning from him that the pile of stone had been placed there by an Englishman, Captain Palmer. As to whether we could make the ascent, he answered by a nod of the head. He also used the words "*dame Américaine,*" and, by gesture, gave me to understand that he had made the ascent with her. Thus encouraged, notwithstanding the cold, strong wind and the snow still lying in many places on the mountain, I also undertook to reach this summit, not apprehending any danger nor serious difficulty.

We scrambled for some time on the side of a dividing ridge to near its top. Here the monk sat down, took off his shoes, and indicated by a motion that I should also take off mine. Leaving our shoes we continued our ascent, he barefooted, and I in my stockings.

The monks are accustomed, like the natives, to going bare-footed. They sometimes wear sandals and, for mountain travel, shoes, but they are much more at ease without any pedal en-cumbrances. In this condition, they are certainly very sure-footed and able to climb among the cliffs with perfect safety. The change in my case was of doubtful utility. The monk led the way and I followed as best I could over the rough, sharp, angular granite, limping and trying to maintain my equilibrium, but without cognizance of what was around me or where I was going.

On passing over the ridge we were on the outer and western side of the mountain. We soon came to a kind of shelf or pro-jection, not more than twelve or fourteen inches wide, that ran along the side of the cliff. My guide took my hand and, without stopping, or giving me a moment to view the awful chasm below, led me about thirty feet along this projection to its end, where there was an elevation of about four feet. With the agility and sure-footedness of a chamois, he mounted and drew me after him and we were upon the granite knoll I had seen from below, but some hundreds of feet from its summit. The way was still steep, but presented no serious difficulty.

It was at this moment that I first fully realized my position. Below the narrow shelf along which we had passed, there was a descent, almost perpendicular in reality and quite so in appear-ance, of fifteen hundred feet. The wind was blowing with such force that, on further ascending towards the summit, we were obliged to stand still or sit down during the stronger gusts. The least misstep or loss of balance, while threading our narrow path along the side of the cliff, would have thrown us from these lofty heights into the abyss below. The rock above the shelf was also nearly perpendicular, and the only path by which it was possible to pass to the elevation above was the one by which we had mounted.

We proceeded to the summit, the place of the pile of stone. The views were no better than those I had already passed, and, had they been, I should not have fully enjoyed them. I was seriously considering how I should descend the steep decline to the edge of the precipice, and there, on the very face of the cliff, slip down to the narrow shelf. I knew by experience that climbing the sides of steep rocks was much easier and less dangerous than descending. In descending, you must go down backwards, without being able to see where to place your feet, and, in this case, there was nothing by which to hold with the hands.

I again resorted to pantomime to ascertain whether there was any other way of descent and received, in answer, a shake of the head. As we re-approached the edge of the cliff, the slant of the rock became so much steeper that I commenced slipping and was obliged to sit down and, in this position, approach the dreaded place. The monk had preceded me and had slipped down with the confidence and ease of a cat upon the narrow rock projection, where he stood ready to aid me. As I approached him I commenced sliding and was only held back by his taking hold of me. But get down I could not.

The valley of El-Lejâ and the plain of Er-Râha were lying stretched out before us, nearly two thousand feet below, and I was sitting on the edge of the cliff, as helpless as an infant, held in my position by a Greek monk. I need not say that I was frightened, that shudders ran over me and that lumps filled my throat. Many years have now passed, but my situation at that moment on the edge of the precipitous cliff, with the deep, broad valley below, and the surrounding mountains, still remains a vivid picture in my memory. I never think of it without a shudder, and even while I now write a strange feeling passes over me.

The monk tried to reassure me and to aid me to descend to the narrow shelf on the side of the rocks, but I could do nothing. Finally, he drew me towards him, took me in his arms, walked steadily along the shelf to the other end, carrying me as he would a child, and the peril was over.

Under all the circumstances, it was an athletic feat of no ordinary character, although my weight was not more than one hundred and fifty-five pounds. If he had conducted me into this place with any waggish mischievousness, he certainly took me out with a coolness and heroism deserving much praise.

Satisfied with the day's climbing and adventure, we sought our shoes and descended the mountain directly to Wâdi ed-Dêr. It was a rough and difficult path, but one giving us many interesting views of wild, fantastic rock formations. Mr. Van Dyke and Hassan returned late from the difficult ascent of Mt. Katarîna.

CHAPTER X

OASIS OF FÊRÂN AND RETURN TO THE SEA

THE weather continued unsettled and threatening and, as the season was far advanced (the commencement of December), we concluded to prepare for our return. Unexpected difficulties arose. Some Arabs had arrived who claimed the exclusive right of taking us back to the sea by the northern route. It appeared that the territory had been divided and that certain Arabs had the monopoly of the carrying trade in the northern, and others in the southern, part of the peninsula. After much loud talk and quarreling among the Arabs, in which General Loring took a vigorous part with his cane, a compromise was effected by which we retained our best riding camels, while the other camels were exchanged. Having made the usual donation to the convent, we bade adieu to the pious monks, not without regretting that we could not remain longer and make a more thorough study of the places which have been, according to the belief of many millions, the scenes of some of the most important events in the history of the Christian religion.

Retaining for the forenoon our faithful monk-guide, we sent our pack-camels on into the Wâdi esh-Shêkh, which unites with the valley by which we had come about a mile west of the convent. From the point of this junction we went in an opposite direction to the base of the Râs Sufsâfeh, the traditional place of the assembling of the Israelites. Here, they could touch the mountain and see what took place on its summit. Here it was that Moses descended and found the golden calf, which the people had set up as their God. Here, in his anger, he cast the tables of the law "out of his hands and brake them beneath the mount." Various places, which tradition connects with Biblical history, were pointed out to us by the monk, among them, the hole in the rock which served as a mould for the casting of the "molten image."

As we approached this point, I could see by looking up the face of the rocks almost directly over us, in the dizzy heights of the cliff, the place of my adventure of the previous day and the cleft in the rock, covered by the natural arch. Following the valley for some distance around the base of the mountain, we came to the rock of the "Miraculous Spring," the "Rock of Horeb." It is a reddish granite block, about ten feet in height, that has been detached and has fallen from the overhanging cliffs. Running through it diagonally is a vein of feldspar, in which are the horizontal crevices made by the rod when Moses smote it, and from which the water issued. Our knowledge of this miracle comes, as is said, through a Jewish tradition. The monks affirm that the rock accompanied the Israelites in their wanderings and afterwards returned to its place at the foot of the "Holy Mountain." "For they drank of that spiritual rock that followed them: and that rock was Christ." [1]

In this vicinity, as in several other places through which we had passed, there were many old Sinaitic inscriptions on the rocks. Retracing our steps and discharging our guide, we followed on the track of the pack-camels, overtaking them in the afternoon. We first traveled northeast and north ten miles, and then, turning to the west through the narrow pass of El Watîyeh, continued in that direction.

We followed the same valley for nearly two days, constantly, but slowly, descending. There were generally mountains on

[1] I Cor. X, 4.

either side, some of them rising in precipitous, wild cliffs. Sacred places were pointed out, and occasionally there was a scanty vegetation. A considerable stream had been formed on the night of the storm, and the subsiding waters had left many slippery places.

Camels are sure-footed and very rarely fall, either among the rocks or on the sandy desert; but where there is slipperiness, especially that slipperiness arising from the sediment of muddy waters, the feet of the camel often slide from under him, and he falls with startling quickness and great force. During the first two days of our return journey, we had some experiences of this kind, in which riders and packs were left in a ludicrous position in the mud. Poor corpulent Hassan, on one of these occasions, became very much mixed up in his roll, with camel, boxes and tent poles.

We found a dry, sandy place for our camp and the next day at noon were approaching the oasis of Fêrân, situated in a deep valley with high mountains on either side. Here we passed through a section covered with the Tarfah (tamarisk), the manna-producing shrub, a few of the specimens of which were the size of small trees. They are found in no other place. Very small holes are bored by an insect in the bark of the twigs, whence issue, from March to June, drops of sap, which fall and harden in the sand, forming a gum. The monks at Sinai keep this gum for sale put up in small tin boxes. It is claimed that it has certain medicinal qualities.

It was not much after midday when we arrived at Fêrân. I had heard and read much concerning the fertility of this oasis and anticipated finding a real Eden, but was much disappointed. Though our visit was at the end of a long, dry season and not at a time to see it in its verdure, I was inclined to believe that its reputation arose chiefly from its contrast with the surrounding deserts.

An oasis, however small the green spot, even a single palm or a tuft of grasses, is ever welcome to the thirsty traveler. By this he knows he is in the vicinity of water, and even the odor of vegetation is to him a real joy.

Travelers in Palestine have often wondered that such a dry, rough, rugged, rocky and what to us would be a barren land, should ever have been called a "land of milk and honey." Some writers have ventured the opinion that the country was formerly more fertile than at present. It was undoubtedly better culti-vated at some periods than at others, but, from its physical condition, it could not have been naturally more productive in the olden time than to-day. Whatever was obtained from the soil, except scanty pasturage, was then, as now, the result of much labor and, in many places, of artificial irrigation. All things are relative; and, to the thirsty wanderers of the deserts, to a whole generation who had never breathed other than the desert air, whose eyes had never rested upon fertile, green fields, it was in reality "a land flowing with milk and honey."

When in Palestine, I visited the Jordan, and stood upon its banks at the point where the Israelites are supposed to have entered the country. The river, as I saw it in the month of April, the "harvest time" of the Bible, was a swollen, angry stream and could not have been forded, or otherwise easily crossed. Recalling the Biblical narrative, I could readily under-stand how this people, as they appeared on the high eastern bank of the river, and looked across the broad valley upon the walls of Jericho, at the foot of the bluff lands on the other side, and, beyond, upon the green hills of Judea, must have felt that they were about to enter upon the fulfilment of the long deferred promise of Jehovah.

To them, the land when possessed was a real fulfilment of this promise, both figuratively and literally. Figuratively, it was all that their imaginations could have pictured. Literally, it was a "land of milk and honey." The hills and valleys furnished pasturage for their flocks and herds, and thus gave them milk, of which they could have had very little on the desert. In the rocky ledges of the country were many wild bees to furnish them with honey. With their habits and their ideas of luxurious living, what more could they have asked? It was to them a very paradise.

One has only to pass a few days upon the desert to understand the real joy with which they entered upon their promised inheritance. It will be remembered that the manna ceased the day after they crossed the Jordan and, perhaps, this people, a whole generation of which had been born and reared on the desert, ate then for the first time of grown products, the "old corn" of the land.

Fêrân is considered a large oasis, but there are not over two hundred acres of land that can be cultivated. It is a deep, narrow valley, three hundred yards wide, with high mountains on either side and a perennial brook running through it and then disappearing among the rocks. This brook, at the time of the very rare, heavy winter rains, has its source at the base of Mt. Sinai, and follows the route by which we had come, sometimes flooding the valley for a few hours. At other times, whatever water there is rises about five miles from the place at which it disappears. The rain is not sufficiently frequent to be of any importance in the cultivation of the land, which is irrigated by water dipped or drawn by shadufs from the stream. There are in the valley a large number of palm-trees, which produce an excellent quality of dates, many of them being owned, as I have stated, by wandering Arabs, who only occasionally come to Fêrân.

We saw at this place an Arab, assisted by his wife, weaving tent cloth in the most primitive manner. The piece when finished would not be more than ten or twelve feet in length. The warp was fastened, at each end, to small stakes or pins driven into the ground. The filling was wound on a stick and passed between the threads of the warp, which were separated by a rude harness moved by the hand, after the putting in of each thread of the filling. The filling was drawn together with a hook made of bone.

There were at Fêrân a few hovels and a number of Bedouin tents. We tried to buy a lamb, or some chickens, but were unable to obtain anything in the way of food. One Arab woman said she had a chicken she would sell, but on searching she was unable to find it.

The surrounding scenery is indescribably grand. The barren, naked mountains with their never ending variety of rock formations, the lofty pinnacles of the elongated summit of Mt. Serbâl apparently almost overhanging the narrow valley, though several miles distant, present a scene, the picturesqueness and grandeur of which are not surpassed at Mt. Sinai. The rocks were mostly composed of beautiful red granite and gray gneiss, with numerous veins of porphyry of nearly every color (green, black, flesh tint, blood-red) glistening with crystals of quartz, abbite and other minerals.

There are in this vicinity many ruins of ancient convents and numerous inscriptions on the rocks. This arises from the fact that Mt. Serbâl was originally believed to be the Sinai of the Bible. Until the fifth century, the oasis of Fêrân was the central place of influence in the Christian Church on the Sinai peninsula and the seat of an Episcopal see. Hermit cells were nowhere more numerous than about these mountains.

Fêrân was the city of the Amalekites, and it is claimed that it was in this valley that they fought the people of Moses. They came out to meet the hordes of Israel in defense of this little spot of tillable land and its never failing water, in the midst of their mountain deserts.

Oases are often called islands of the desert. They do not resemble islands in the sense of rising above the surrounding deserts, as islands rise above the waters. They are always in a valley, or in a deep depression in the desert, where there is sufficient moisture to sustain the date-palm, which, when the soil permits, sends its roots down twenty and thirty feet in search of aliment; and where water can be obtained sufficient to water flocks and irrigate a small piece of land. Sometimes, the water is taken from wells, often very deep, sometimes from springs, and occasionally from streams running a short distance and then disappearing as at Fêrân.

Neither are deserts what might be inferred from the definition, "vast sandy plains," that has often been given of the word. They generally consist of hills and valleys, high rolling table-lands, deep gorges, and lofty mountain ranges. They are deserts simply because in these regions there is no rain, or not sufficient to sustain vegetation.

To plainly understand what they are, it is only necessary to consider what the condition of our own country would be without rain. Should there be no rain for a number of years, all vegetation would cease. The springs and the streams, even the great rivers, would be dried up. All vegetable matter would disappear. The mountain tops would become denuded. The naked rock of the mountains, the bowlders and pebbles of the valley and plain would be blackened, or assume a dark brown color, from the effect of the constantly burning rays of the sun. Only in sandy regions would there be drifting sands, but everywhere there would be treeless, barren, desert wastes.

Dr. Schweinfurth, a great traveler, who has spent years on the deserts of northeastern and Central Africa in his favorite study of the botany of desert plants, informed me that he had never seen a "vast sandy plain." There are such plains, however, south of Algiers.

Having passed a few hours at Fêrân, we continued our journey a short distance and camped near El-Hesweh, the name given to the first cultivated spot met in approaching Fêrân from the west. The next afternoon we reached the ancient turquoise mines of Maghârah, in the Wâdi Maghârah, the Valley of the Cave. We had traveled during the day in deep, wild, desolate valleys, with numerous interesting rock formations, of various colors, and often of fantastic forms. In some places, the precipitate sides of the mountains were seamed in such a manner as to present the appearance of dilapidated walls, ready to fall.

Our only relief, during the day's journey, from the wild solitude of these desolate mountains and valleys was two Arab tents. Here, we tried again without success to buy a lamb. The Arabs claimed to have been visited the night before by a leopard, which had carried off a small goat.

The mines of Maghârah are not now worked. We did not find a hovel, a tent, or a living being in this once busy place. From hieroglyphic inscriptions on the rocks, it appears that the mines were worked by the Pharaohs six thousand years ago. The oldest inscriptions are those of Snofru, who was the first great king of the Fourth Dynasty, and of Cheops, the builder of the Great Pyramid. Subsequent Pharaohs continued or, from time to time, renewed the work for twenty-five hundred years. The extensive heaps of rubble and the shafts indicate a large amount of mining.

Condemned criminals, slaves and prisoners of war were compelled to work here and the treasures were taken to Memphis and Thebes to enrich or adorn the Pharaohs and their favorites.

The rock is partly granite and partly brick-red sandstone. In the red sandstone are many small turquoises, mostly soft and of little value, but occasionally small hard crystals are found which prove, when the crust is scaled off, to be beautiful bright blue turquoises of fine quality. They are easily detached from the rock with a knife. I saw many blue spots, but all the turquoises I examined were soft and worthless, except for cabinet purposes.

That night, we camped not far from the mines. Some Arabs, old men, came to our tents with turquoises, and I bought what they had that appeared to be of any value. Among them were several pieces which I afterwards had cut and which proved to be fine specimens. They were set and worn as ornaments, and are highly prized in the family as souvenirs. There has been no change in their beautiful, deep-blue color. The others I placed in my cabinet of minerals. Copper and malachite were also successfully mined in this place and carried to Egypt during the time of the Pharaohs. There are on the rocks here, besides the Egyptian inscriptions, many Sinaitic inscriptions, similar to those found elsewhere on the peninsula. There are also, in the vicinity, ruins of ancient origin in which tools made of flint have been found.

The next morning, we continued our journey to the sea in a slightly ascending valley enclosed by rocks of red granite. There had been no rain since the terrible storm on the mountain, the night of our arrival at Sinai. We were about twelve hundred feet above the sea, the weather was pleasant, warm during the day, and not disagreeable in the camp at night. It was about ten in the forenoon, when we arrived at a commanding summit and suddenly had before us the wild pass of Nugb et-Buderah (Pass of the Sword's Point), through which we were to descend to the sea and, beyond, in the far distance to the north, Râs Abu Zenîmeh, where we expected to find our boat. We tried to extend our vision so as to see it, but could only perceive the low sandy point stretching far into the sea. Two hours of descent would bring us to a sandy and stony plain near the sea. Two hours on this plain, and two hours more along the sandy beach of the coast and we should be at our objective point.

On our descent toward the sea we witnessed a new series of

geological formations of the most interesting character. We had left the granite region, and the pass we were in was of variegated sandstone. The descent was rapid and, as we passed from valley to valley, we had a series of views of rocks of fantastic forms and colors.

At some period, probably when the granite mountains of the Sinai group were thrown up from the furnaces of the earth, broad fissures, ten, fifteen, twenty and more feet wide, were opened in the primitive rock of this region. These were filled with melted lava, which, when it cooled, formed various kinds of igneous rock. Much of it, blackened by the sun, resembles volcanic slag. These formations generally run north and south and are harder than the sandstone. In the course of time the latter has been worn away, leaving the more enduring rock standing in relief. These projecting veins are sometimes twenty and thirty feet high. They run for miles, as far as the vision can reach, into and across the valleys and over low rounded mountains, appearing precisely like massive walls. There were not only two or three, but a great number of these formations. In places, they took the form of castles and battlements, and it was difficult not to believe we had in view some gigantic works of man.

There were also cliffs and pinnacles of grotesque form, and rocks of a great variety of colors. These colors, which are often brilliant and beautiful, have been produced by the mineral substances contained in the sandstone and by the different degrees of heat to which it has been subjected. The fact that rocks of such varied characteristics, composition, form and color, and of such vast extent, are all naked, makes this region a field of rare interest to the practical geologist and of enchantment to the traveler. The same facilities for observation and study exist in nearly all the mountainous districts of this peninsula.

Our file of camels, ten in number, accompanied by the same

number of cameleers on foot, moved slowly down the mountain passes, across the sandy and rocky plain, along the coast, and, just as the sun was about to disappear behind the mountains on the western side of the sea, we reached Râs Abu Zenîmeh. Here, our boat was anchored and the Arab sailors were awaiting our arrival. This is the traditional point of the encampment of the Israelites "by the sea." [1]

A hasty council was held to determine whether we should continue by camels, four days, to Suez, or take the boat. The wind had continued in the north, and the sailors had been eight days in reaching this place. But the captain informed us that there were generally land breezes at night and that, in his opinion, we could reach Suez sooner by boat than by camels. There was not a house, perhaps not a tent and, at that season of the year, no palatable water in the whole distance. It was a monotonous wearisome route along the coast, to be avoided if possible, and we determined to again trust ourselves to the sea and our Arab sailors.

The cameleers, having unloaded their camels and received their pay, immediately departed for their desert homes, and in a few minutes disappeared into the darkness that had already closed around us. The fire had been prepared, and after dinner we went on board with our effects and set sail. The sea was not rough and the weather was apparently propitious, but as soon as we passed beyond the point we found a strong north wind and waves sufficiently high to make it exceedingly disagreeable in our small open boat.

We continued across the sea, sailing into the wind as much as possible, till about two in the morning when, being near the western shore, we tacked and headed northeastward, expecting to be able to run behind a point ten miles north of that from which we had sailed.

[1] Numbers, XXIII, 10.

We buffeted the waves, tossed and rolled all night with the spray and water coming into our boat and over us and found ourselves at dawn some distance south of our intended haven, near a wall of high rocks, where there was no approach to the shore. The wind grew stronger as the morning advanced and we had no other alternative but to run before it.

In time for a late breakfast we rounded the point and anchored at the place whence we had set sail the previous evening. Had our camels then been within reach, we should have abandoned the sea and re-embarked on the "ships of the desert."

At the end of three more days and nights, after various experiences with the winds and waves, we arrived at Suez. Modern rigged vessels would have had little difficulty in beating against the wind where there was such an amount of sea room; but with a bark belonging to the period of St. Paul the task was not an easy one.

Although we arrived safely and without having to be put upon short rations, we unanimously decided that we would not again undertake a voyage on the Red Sea in an open Arab boat. The trip to Sinai, as a whole, had been most enjoyable and instructive. We had had sufficient desert travel to learn the character of these vast wastes, and something of the mode of life of their nomadic inhabitants.

We had seen nothing of that wild, savage life on the desert, which has often been the theme of romance and of travelers who delight in recounting marvelous tales. In fact the reckless, lawless Arab exists principally in books. I have been assured by those who have made extensive desert excursions and who have lived with Arabs for months at a time, alone or accompanied by only a single servant, that they were in no more danger than that to which they would have been subject in European countries. They added that they never made a display of dress nor of money that would excite cupidity, as there were bad Arabs, as well as bad Christians, who might be tempted to rob or steal.

There are occasional tribal wars to avenge thefts and other wrongs, and in certain localities there are marauding bands, who live by plundering peaceable Arabs and strangers if they happen to meet them unprotected. These, however, are the exceptions; and even these are no worse than our western highway robbers and are quite as merciful as the burglars of our eastern cities.

Generally speaking, the Arabs are a quiet, timid people, living in extreme poverty, in a state of semi-starvation. Like hungry dogs, they seize with avidity the smallest crust or bone left on the sands by the traveler. A full meal is to them a rare joy.

The five thousand Arabs of the peninsula of Sinai would scarcely be able to live by the cultivation of every acre of land that can be irrigated by the water of a brook, spring or well, and by the products of such animals as can be kept in the mountains, were it not for the food brought from Egypt. This consists of beans and dura (*sorghum vulgare*), sometimes called Egyptian maize.

The question arises, how the Israelites were sustained during their sojourn in this country, if it was not by food miraculously furnished. There is no evidence that the physical conditions of the country have materially changed during the last five thousand years. Arabia is, and for an indefinite period must have been, a land of rock, gravel and sand, without sufficient rain to make it other than a continuous desert. According to the Biblical account, the Israelites numbered over two millions. It is difficult to understand how even a hundredth part of this number could have subsisted upon the products of the country. During the dry season, the supply of water for so great a body of people would certainly have been wholly inadequate. If even two thousand people should to-day enter the peninsula, and be cut off from supplies from Egypt and other outside countries, as the Israelites were, it is probable that the greater part of them would die of starvation. For those who do not adopt the conclusion of the interposition of Providence, the whole question of the Exodus is still involved in mystery.

CHAPTER XI

LAKE MENZALEH, PARADISE OF AQUATIC BIRDS

IT was in the heat of summer, the last of May, that I undertook a long delayed trip by the way of Lake Menzaleh to Sân, the site of the Zoan of the Bible and the Tanis of the Greeks. It is a trip rarely made by travelers on account of the time required and the difficulties of reaching this out-of-the-way place. There were a number of routes, all of which required an outfit of tents, provisions, an interpreter and camels or boats. I chose the route *via* Mansûrah, Damietta and Lake Menzaleh. I went from Alexandria to Mansûrah, about one hundred and fifty miles, by railway. This route, for nearly two-thirds of the distance, as far as Tantah, is the same as that to Cairo. From Tantah to Mansûrah it passes through a section of the richest lands in Egypt.

It was at the time of the low Nile and the country, except where recently irrigated, was parched by the dry, hot, south winds and the tropical sun. Clouds of dust accompanied every moving train. The cars were in such a state of dilapidation that, with the windows as closely shut as possible, there was no want of ventilation and after a few hours' ride it was difficult to determine the natural color of the traveler. Notwithstanding this annoyance and the flies, which are an ever present plague, and divers other tormenting insects, there is always the greatest pleasure in traveling by railway in this unique country. The landscape is a continuous plain, but in the foreground are con-

Plowing.

stantly varying scenes of Egyptian peasant life that never lose their enchantment.

It was nearly sunset when I arrived at Mansûrah, wearied by the heat and dust and by constantly viewing the panorama of the day. The station was on the opposite side of the river from the city. The only way of crossing was by a small boat, although as early as the thirteenth century, at the time of the crusades, there was a fortified bridge at this place. I found comfortable lodgings at the house of the U. S. Consular Agent, Mr. Ibrâhîm Doud.

Mansûrah, though a city of thirty thousand inhabitants, then had no hotel. It is on the right bank of the Damietta branch of the Nile and sixty miles from its mouth. It is a town of mediæval origin, historically noted for being the scene of one of the important battles of St. Louis (Louis IX) of France. It was here that this real hero of the Middle Ages gained at great sacrifice of life, in 1250, an important victory over the Saracens. The Crusaders were soon afterwards defeated at the same place and St. Louis taken prisoner. It is this Saracen victory that is said to have given to the place the name of Mansûrah, "the victorious" or, as it has sometimes been rendered, "field of victory."

The next morning, a guide, tent, provisions and other articles necessary for the excursion were procured, the river recrossed and the journey continued by rail to Damietta, five miles from the sea and near Lake Menzaleh.

Damietta, once a prosperous town and one of the principal seaports of Egypt, is now in its decay.

Sand-bars have been formed at the mouth of the river to such an extent that only vessels of light draught can enter and its commerce has been principally transferred to Alexandria and Port Saîd. The numerous minarets and imposing domes of its mosques and the high buildings along the bank of the river still give to the city an appearance of much importance. The architecture of its crumbling buildings attests its former prosperity and wealth. It still has a population of about forty thousand and is visited annually by several hundred small vessels, many of which come from Greece and Syria. It has interesting and well-stocked bazaars and a lucrative, though limited, trade in the rice produced in that part of Egypt and the fish of the neighboring lake.

I had now to obtain a boat, captain and sailors for a trip of forty miles on Lake Menzaleh. There was no scarcity of boats nor of men, but I knew by experience that much time would be required to arrange the details and get the expedition in motion. It was only by securing the kind offices of the Governor, by using much energy and tact and appealing to the authority of the faithful Hassan that a boat was ready late the next afternoon. In the meantime, I was provided with lodgings at the dwelling of one of the principal inhabitants. The tent, provisions, and a large yawl with its sails, to be used if needed, were put on board.

When everything was apparently in readiness and I had embarked, I saw a manifest indisposition on the part of the men to set the sails and depart. There was much loud talk and many menacing gestures, that would have appeared serious to anyone unacquainted with the character and habits of this people. I was simply informed that the men did not wish to leave until the next day, "bookra" (to-morrow).

Never do to-day what can be put off till the morrow should be added to the catalogue of Egyptian proverbs. As is necessary in such cases, I simply insisted on sailing. After more loud talk and threatening gestures, as if to provoke a fight, the difficulty seemed suddenly settled and all came quietly aboard. The sails were quickly spread, and we soon saw the low, sandy shore and the domes and minarets slowly receding.

My company consisted of a native gentleman from Mansûrah, who was acquainted with the country and spoke a little French, a cook, Hassan, the captain and four sailors. The latter were dressed like the common fellah. They were barefooted and barelegged, having, as an outer garment, the blue cotton shirt and on their heads the skullcap and turban. The captain had the distinction of a white shirt. The turban is made by taking about three yards of thin, slazy, white muslin, twisting it into a roll, and then winding it three times around the head over the skullcap and tucking the ends under the rolls in such a manner that it rests closely and firmly upon the head. This rather heavy but picturesque head-gear is the most important item in the fellah's dress, since it protects him from the injurious effects of the sun. It is the ordinary head-dress of the fellâhîn and I never learned, while in Egypt, of a case of sunstroke.

The sun was near the western horizon when we sailed out upon the lake, southeasterly, with a strong southwesterly wind. In the evening it became quite dark and, as there were many low islands and shoal places, we anchored for the night. Soon afterwards, another vessel, of about the same size as the one I had taken, came alongside and also threw out her anchor. I then learned that the Governor had sent this boat to accompany us, of course, at my expense. I did not understand the necessity nor object of this additional vessel, but as the men proved to be very useful and the charges moderate, I made no complaint. The Governor, knowing the lake and the direction of the wind, had concluded that more men than we had might be needed and had wisely sent them.

We were again under motion at the first light of dawn, about four o'clock, the next morning. There was still a strong southerly wind and the boats started off as if for a race. They were open boats of about thirty tons burden with flat bottoms for shallow water. They had immense lateen sails that gave them the appearance in the distance of huge birds with sharply pointed wings flying over the surface of the lake.

It was a beautiful morning with the cloudless sky of an Egyptian summer. The deep crimson that heralded the sun, the yellow light that accompanied it and the clear soft atmosphere, free from the dust of the land, made this early morning sail most enjoyable. It was the more so because there were no waves, although the wind was sufficiently strong to have made an ugly sea, had the water been sufficiently deep to permit an undercurrent.

The lake is very irregular in form, but is approximately forty miles in length and twenty broad and covers an area of from eight hundred to a thousand square miles. It is so shallow throughout its whole extent that it is said that one could wade from one side to the other were it not for the miry bottom. The depth of the water, as I saw it, was generally about three feet. For several miles from the shores it was much less, and generally very shallow. At the time of the high Nile it is somewhat deeper. Many of the low sand-islands then disappear and the narrow low sand-bar, forming the beach between the sea and the lake, is nearly submerged.

The bottom of the lake is covered with a thick matting of coarse grass, which in many places grows to the height of a number of feet. There are some ancient ruins on the islands in the middle of the lake, and it is claimed that the larger part of the surface, now covered with water, was in ancient times, like the bed of Lake Mareotis, rich, highly cultivated land.[1]

In consequence of the shallow waters and grassy bottoms, a continued strong wind, instead of forming waves, moves the waters from one side or end of the lake to the other. The shallow waters near the windward shore disappear, and the shore line advances into the lake, returning again on the ceasing or changing of the winds. The difference thus made in the position of the shore line is sometimes one or two miles.

[1] See Strabo, Book XVII, Par. 21, pp. 240, 241.

As we glided quietly but swiftly over the grassy waters, fish were constantly darting from under the bow of the boat, showing that they were very abundant. We passed between Matarîyeh (situate upon a point of land projecting from the west many miles into the lake) and a group of islands opposite, on the east. Here we saw men wading in the water a long distance from shore and fishing with some kind of nets, their boats being anchored near by.

Matarîyeh is a town of fishermen. It is all fish and fishing. There is no other business. The occupation of the father has been transmitted to the son from generation to generation for centuries, perhaps from the earliest historic periods. These people, with others about the lake, form a race of fishermen. They have angular faces, high cheek bones, haughty mouths, small eyes and stocky forms, very different from the elegant, slender form which is the national Egyptian type.

Egyptologists claim that they are of Semitic origin and some are of the opinion that they are the descendants of the Hyksos or Shepherds. This opinion is based upon a striking physiognomical resemblance between the ancient Hyksos, as shown by the Hyksos statues and other monuments found principally at Sân, and the modern race of Menzaleh fishermen.

There is a saying in the vicinity, "once a fisherman, always a fisherman." There are about four thousand men thus employed. They know no other labor or business. By their situation and condition, they are as closely bound to this service as the Russian peasants formerly were to that of the landed estates.

The right of fishing in this lake is farmed out by the Government for about three hundred thousand dollars per annum. The contract formerly included the forced services of the fishermen at a stipulated small percentage on the money realized from the sale of the fish. It may now be claimed that this labor is not "forced," but these fishermen are compelled to continue the same occupation, on the former basis of percentage, to sustain their miserable existence.

The right of fishing in most of the other waters of Egypt is also farmed out for sums varying according to the amount of fish that can be taken. If fish are caught at any place where there is no such contract, they must be taken immediately to the proper authorities and a tax, amounting to a large percentage of the value, paid to the Government.

Lake Menzaleh is not solely celebrated for its fish. It is the true paradise of the hunter. It fairly swarms with water-fowl of many species. They are so numerous that it is difficult to make even an approximate estimate of their quantity. This lake is the first inland water reached by them, in their journey from the north across the Mediterranean or along its eastern extremity. The mild climate, shallow waters, abundance of fish and other means of subsistence, make it an agreeable winter home for all kinds of aquatic fowl, and many remain through the entire year.

Tall wading birds—the flamingo, with its fire-red plumage, the snow-white spoonbill, the heron, the stork and the crane—indicate by their presence the more shallow waters. The great Dalmatian and other pelicans, the Egyptian goose, the large white-footed goose and the graceful white swan float majestically among the smaller birds in the deeper parts. Legions of different varieties of ducks are to be found in almost every part of the lake.

A competent authority says that the aquatic fowl of this lake consume daily not less than sixty thousand pounds of fish, besides their other food. They are so abundant that, during the winter and until May, the water in many places is literally covered with them. In the distance, they have the appearance of low islands and, when they rise in mass, they fill the air and cover the sky like clouds.

Many years ago myriads of pigeons nested in the great forests of northern New York. Every morning, as they flew away for food, the sky was clouded for one or two hours by their passage and the same thing happened on their return at night. I have seen on a small lake just east of the city of Mexico, near the railway running to Pueblo and Vera Cruz, ducks in such numbers that they apparently covered the waters for some distance.

The gathering of large numbers of birds in uninhabited regions is not uncommon. On Lake Menzaleh, this tendency of the feathered tribes has a most remarkable illustration. By reason of their number, their variety and the beauty of their plumage, the birds of this lake afford a spectacle that is not only unique but that is unsurpassed in ornithological interest. Each group of these many legions has its leader, whose every movement is watched and followed. No bird rises from the water as long as the leader remains undisturbed. The moment he spreads his wings and utters a cry, the whole flock mounts into the air.

The right of fowling, like that of fishing, is farmed out and shooting from a boat is prohibited, but permission to hunt can generally be obtained by foreigners. The fishermen are employed in catching the fowl in nets and in various other ways, and great numbers are secured.

One of the primitive and very curious modes of capture is as follows:

The native arranges for his head a casque, entirely covering it, in the form of a fowl. This is sometimes made from the rind of a water-melon. Selecting a light night, usually when there is a full moon, and a favorable place, he puts himself wholly under water, except the head which is concealed by the casque. Through an aperture, he determines which is the leader of the flock, and approaches him so skilfully that he is able to seize him by the legs, draw him into the water and kill him. If this is done with sufficient celerity and skill to prevent the bird from screeching, the whole flock can be taken, one after another, in the same manner; but on the least screech from the leader, the others quickly take to their wings.[1]

Wild boars of large size and buffaloes are sometimes found in the adjoining marshes.

We had been sailing swiftly all the morning, being obliged to tack occasionally, as our course, after passing Matarîyeh, was southward and almost directly against the wind. The water had for some time been growing shallower, and about ten o'clock we ran aground. We were still several miles from the marshy shore and from the entrance to the old bed of the Tanitic branch of the Nile up which we were to sail a number of miles. Through Hassan I inquired what was to be done, and received the answer, "Wait for the wind to change." This was not very encouraging, as the wind at this season of the year sometimes blows from the south for many days in succession. To wait for a north wind might mean to remain where we were for ten days. Nor did I then understand how this change could aid us.

Perhaps the phenomenon, which to the natives of the lake had always been an almost daily occurrence, was considered too simple and well known to need an explanation. If you ask this class of Arabs for facts or explanations, you rarely get correct answers. There is no bad motive. They simply give you with Oriental politeness such an answer as they think will please. I made it known to the captain that I must be at Alexandria at a certain date and suggested that he should try to work the boat to the west, where I thought there was deeper water.

A sailor, with the end of a long rope in his hand and a short,

[1] This mode of capture seemed to the writer incredible, but it was affirmed at the time of his visit to the lake that it was practiced with great success, where the birds were in the habit of collecting for the night at a point having water sufficiently deep. This manner of securing birds is also confirmed by writers and by a recent letter received by the author from an English clergyman, residing at Port Saîd.

light pole, went over the low bow into the water. He went forward a few rods, pulling the rope after him, thrust the pole into the soft bottom and tied the rope to it close to the ground. While he remained holding the pole in place, the men on board pulled at the other end of the rope, slowly moving the boat forward over the grassy bottom to near the place of the pole. The man then went forward again with the rope and the process was repeated, but little progress was made.

The second boat had left us at an early hour in the morning and gone to Matarîyeh for bread for the sailors, the want of which, as I then learned, was the cause of the angry discussion at the time of our departure. At about eleven o'clock, this boat came over towards us, but further to the west, where I had supposed there was deeper water. When it arrived at a point opposite the one where we had first touched bottom, it also grounded. The men threw out their anchor, took in their sails, and, with their sacks of bread, came over to our boat. No miracle was necessary to enable them to walk on the waters.

With this additional force we moved a little faster. At a little after noon, the men all came on board to take their luncheon of coarse, dry bread. We were apparently still two miles from shore. After finishing their meal, they seemed in no hurry to recommence their work. It was nearly two o'clock and we had probably not advanced more than a mile since running aground at ten. The wind had entirely ceased before noon. Suddenly a light breeze came from the north. Gradually, it grew stronger. It was apparently an ordinary day sea-breeze that had come thus far inland across the lake—about twenty miles. The sails were set, the men went into the water, four on each side, and put their shoulders to the boat. The sails filled and, by wind and man-power, we commenced to move. We advanced very slowly at first, but the wind increased and, within half an hour, the men,

one after another, mounted into the boat and we were soon under
fair motion.

In a short time we had entered the old, narrow, tortuous bed
of the river and were sailing up it at good speed. The water was
shallow and the banks so low and flat that the waves from our
boat washed for some distance over the marshy lands. It was
not long before we were aground again. The help of eight strong
shoulders and a brisk north wind carried us over the shoal, but
we very soon found the water too shallow to proceed farther with
the large boat. The yawl was taken out, the tent and provisions
were placed therein and, with sails set, we pursued our way up
the bed of the stream.

At about sunset, we came to a barrier—a heavy embankment
built across the old river bed to retain for irrigation, during the
dry season, the water that drained from the canals. There was
but little water above the embankment, and none could pass
either way. We pitched our tent and prepared our dinner.

CHAPTER XII

ANCIENT ZOAN

WE started for Sân at early dawn the next morning with donkeys procured in a neighboring village. It was a ride of only two hours. The country was low and marshy and, at the time of the high Nile, flooded. These marshy lands are mostly unfit for cultivation, but produce tall grasses which are of some value since they constitute the only perennial pasturage in Egypt.

The papyrus, once produced in this section in great abundance, has now entirely disappeared. Like its contemporaries, the crocodile and the hippopotamus, it has withdrawn from Egypt to the banks of the Blue and White Nile.

The manufacture of papyrus was for a long period of great importance to Egypt. Commencing early in the reign of the Pharaohs, it continued till the time of the Khalifs. During the Greek and Roman period, Egypt supplied this invaluable article to the whole civilized world and derived from it immense revenues. The rich, wet lands of the Delta, which were once covered with this plant, as with a thicket, are now largely devoted to the culture of rice, indigo and cotton. As a remembrance, we have derived from papyrus our word "paper" and from the Greek form, *biblos*, our word "Bible."

Papyrus served for many other purposes than that of making the paper on which the ancients wrote. It was used for calking their vessels and for sails [1] and rope. The Egyptians, in con-

[1] Herodotus II, Sec. 96.

structing the bridge across the Hellespont for the army of Xerxes, used papyrus cables.[1]   When the storm had broken these and the white flax cables of the Phœnicians, another bridge was constructed of boats.   Over these, cables were stretched from shore to shore, seven-eighths of a mile, each cable being made of two ropes of white flax and four of papyrus.   On these cables, supported by the boats, was constructed the road on which Xerxes' army of seventeen hundred thousand crossed the Hellespont into Europe in seven days and nights.[2]   The lower part of the papyrus plant was also used for food.[3]

The sites of the ancient cities of the Delta are marked by mounds of earth which rise above the surrounding country, sometimes to the height of thirty and forty feet, and which are filled with the potsherds of the successive generations that have inhabited these places.

The mounds of ancient Zoan, or Tanis, are remarkable for their comparative height and extent, covering as they do about a square mile.   Excavations have been made and many valuable monuments secured.   The most important, historically, are those of the Hyksos, the Shepherd Kings.   The grounds where the excavations have been made, on the site of the great temple, are encircled with mounds twenty and thirty feet in height.

The enclosures of the temple were once surrounded by a wall thirty-four hundred feet in length, seventy feet in thickness and forty-five feet in height.   Looking down upon the open space we now see a confused mass of ruins, large numbers of broken pieces of obelisks, columns, statues, pedestals, and parts of fallen walls. These ruins are mostly of red granite.   There are some blocks that are black or of a very dark color.   There is also an occasional piece of sandstone, but the lime-rock of which the temple

---

[1] Herodotus VII, Sec. 34.   [2] Herodotus VII, Sec. 36.

[3] Herodotus II, Sec. 92.

was mainly built long since found its way to the rude, native lime-kiln.

No city is surrounded with more historical mystery than ancient Zoan. It was the capital of lower Egypt during the long reign of the Hyksos, or Shepherd Kings, more correctly "Kings of the Wanderers." After they had been driven out or subdued, the whole of Egypt was again united under one government. Still later, the great kings of the nineteenth dynasty, Seti (Sethos), his son Ramses II (Sesostris), and his grandson, Seti Mineptah, the supposed "Pharaoh of the Exodus," made Zoan one of their capitals, the other being at Thebes.

It was situated upon the Tanitic branch of the Nile, and in the northeastern part of Egypt, not far from the eastern boundary. In consequence of its position, it became a great commercial city. It was also the rendezvous and starting point of the great military expeditions that went out from Egypt in those days and overran western Asia, bringing back as a result of their conquests, or as annual tribute, immense riches in slaves, ivory, gold, silver, precious stones and domestic animals.

It was an important city with numerous monuments during the reign of the Hyksos. In the time of Ramses II, it had its magnificent temple, its obelisks of granite and many other colossal structures of the same material. There were no less than ten obelisks on the sides of the avenue leading to the great temple. A number of these, now broken, and mutilated columns and statues are lying upon the ground where they once stood. Other relics of Zoan, among them statues and sphinxes, in a good state of preservation, are now to be seen at Cairo or in the museums of Europe.

Even in the remote period of the nineteenth dynasty, Zoan was already an ancient town, over two thousand years old. Its temple, rebuilt by Ramses II, dates back at least to the sixth dynasty, thirty-three hundred years before Christ. The town must have been founded soon after the reputed time of the flood, and the numerous Biblical references to it increase, for all Christian people, its historic interest.

"Now Hebron was built seven years before Zoan in Egypt." [1] "Marvelous things did he in the sight of their fathers in the land of Egypt, in the field of Zoan." [2] "How he had wrought his signs in Egypt, and his wonders in the field of Zoan." [3] "The princes of Zoan are become fools." [4] "For the princes were in Zoan." [5] "I will make Pathros desolate, and will set fire in Zoan." [6]

The Land of Goshen, also called the Land of Ramses,[7] was the habitation of Joseph's brothers and of their descendants. They were a pastoral people and it is probable that Joseph had Goshen selected for their occupation on account of its adaptation to their mode of life and, also, because it could be occupied without creating animosities on the part of the Egyptians, to whom "every shepherd was an abomination." [8]

There has been much discussion as to the precise location of the Land of Goshen, the habitation of the Israelites during their sojourn in Egypt. Those who still adhere to the theory of their actual passage through what is now a part of the Red Sea, locate that part of Egypt occupied by them as far south as possible, while others place it in the extreme northwestern part of the country.

It is probable, from all the monumental and philological evidence, that, when their numbers had become great, they occupied the larger portion of all the territory lying in the northern part of the Delta and east of the Tanitic branch of the Nile. This territory included much of the most productive land of Egypt, and was sufficient in extent to have sustained a million of people.

---

[1] Numbers XIII, 22.   [2] Psalms LXXVIII, 12.
[3] Id. 43.   [4] Isaiah XIX, 13.
[5] Id. XXX, 4.   [6] Ezekiel XXX, 14.
[7] Gen. XLVII, 11.   [8] Gen. XLVI, 34.

A large part of this land, once highly cultivated, is now desert and marsh.

In the section bordering on Lake Menzaleh, there was much low, wet land producing an abundance of coarse grasses on which cattle could feed. On the east, it was bounded by the desert, which produced in many places, during the winter season, plants sufficient to sustain a limited number of sheep and goats.

Jacob's descendants, "besides his sons' wives," at the time they came to Egypt, numbered only "three score and six." A small parcel of good land bordering on the desert, where they could pitch their tents like the Arabs of the present day, supplemented by a portion of the wet lands near the lake, was for them the most desirable selection—a very garden, in fact, in comparison with the rough, rocky country from which they had emigrated. It was well adapted to their shepherd-life and to the maintenance of the "flocks and herds" they had brought with them, but was not considered as desirable by the Egyptians.

Zoan, if not actually in the Land of Goshen, was on its border and was the principal city of that part of the Delta. Ramses II also gave to it his name, as appears from hieroglyphic inscriptions on monuments found in its ruins. It is this monarch who is regarded as having been the most severe of all the Pharaohs in his treatment of the Israelites and Zoan must have been one of the principal scenes of this oppression. "Therefore they did set over them taskmasters to afflict them with their burdens. And they built for Pharaoh treasure cities, Pithom and Ramses." [1]

A large portion of the monuments of Zoan were erected during the reign of Ramses II. The immense granite blocks required in this work were cut with rude tools from the quarries of Assuân, transported seven hundred miles, worked, polished and placed in position by the prisoners and bondsmen of Egypt.

There can be little doubt that the Israelites were employed in

[1] Ex. I, 11.

these and a great number of similar works, as well as in lower
grades of labor. They went out of the country understanding
the art of sculpture-writing, as it was then practiced in Egypt,
and were thus capable of recording the laws of Moses on "tablets
of stone." Tablets of the same character, belonging to the same
period, may now be seen in large numbers in the museum at
Cairo.

They were also filled "with the wisdom, the understanding,
and the knowledge of all kinds of workmanship" known to the
Egyptians, "to devise cunning works, to work in gold and in
silver, and in brass, and in cutting of stones to set them and in
carving of timber, to work in all manner of workmanship." [1]
Hence they were able to execute the marvelous works required
in the building of the tabernacle and those of its elaborate and
skilfully wrought furnishings.

As we look upon the broken monuments still at Sân, on the
better preserved ones in the museum of Cairo or upon the other
numerous magnificent works of that period, we imagine that
we see, in the grandeur of their forms and in the elegance of their
execution, the skill and handiwork of the Semitic races and the
result of the toil required by Pharaoh's taskmasters.

Zoan was the capital of that part of Egypt ruled by the Hyksos
at the time of Joseph and, probably, that city was his residence
during the time he served the Pharaoh of that day. If so, it
was there that he "made ready his chariot, and went up to meet
Israel, his father," [2] on the great highway leading to Syria; and
there that, on his return, he presented his father to the great
monarch.

It was "in the field of Zoan" that the Pharaoh of the Exodus,
as a sequel to his and his father's acts of oppression, saw the
wonderful works of the God of the Hebrews. It was here that
the oppressed people gathered for their journey. It was here

[1] Ex. XXXI, 4, 5.   [2] Gen. XLVI, 29.

that Pharaoh manifested his weakness, giving his consent for the departure, when frightened by the execution of Jehovah's judgments, and withdrawing it when the danger seemed to be past. It was here that they finally commenced their flight and here that Pharaoh "made ready his hundred chariots" and "pursued after them."

The Israelites resided in Egypt during its golden period, the era of the erection of the greater part of its finer and more skilfully wrought monuments, the time of the Thûtmosis, the Amenophis and the earlier Ramses. Immediately after the Exodus, as if by divine decree, the national decline commenced. Few new monuments were erected and the old ones, neglected, gradually became impaired, being preserved only by their inherent durability and the clemency of the climate. Only one more great warrior king, Ramses III, was added to the long roll of famous sovereigns.

Most that is known of Egypt, during the seven centuries preceding the conquest of Cambyses, 525 B. C., and his destruction of the greater part of its grand monuments, is the misfortunes, defeats and dethronements of its petty sovereigns, as recorded in the histories of their conquerors.

With its long and glorious history, its beauty and grandeur, its mercantile and commercial importance, what is Zoan to-day? The western boundary of the city was once a great river whose waters were covered with sails, whose banks teemed with the bustling, noisy life of commerce. Crowds of people loaded and unloaded boats. Immense blocks of stone, transported from Syene, were placed on its banks by the simple force of the numbers of slaves and prisoners employed. Multitudes embarked and disembarked amid the awe of marshaled hosts and the pomp of royalty.

It was a mighty city, proud of its elegantly wrought and colossal monuments, haughty in its wealth, strength and power.

To-day it is represented by a small, dirty, miserable village of fishermen of the same race as the fishermen about Lake Menzaleh. Even the sheik's dwelling, the most pretentious in the village, is a miserable abode and the others floorless hovels. Its river was long since filled with its own deposits and is now replaced by the sluggish waters of the draining and irrigating canal, Sân el-Hager, which passes through marshy lands, overgrown with reeds and swamp-plants. The commerce of the once puissant city is represented by an occasional fisherman's boat, and the life and ceaseless whirl of its former business by a semi-weekly market for the sale to the neighboring peasants, under the supervision of an official agent, of the scarcely edible fish caught in the canals.

Its architectural grandeur, the splendor of its colossal monuments, lie buried in its ruins. Nowhere is a deeper sense of fallen greatness, of departed power and splendor experienced. No ruin is more complete, more impressive, and none can give a more vivid suggestion of the inevitable fate that awaits all the works of man.

It was past midday when we returned to camp, and there, much to our surprise, we found the large boat we had left some miles down the old bed of the river the day before. On asking the sailors for an explanation, we were informed that, the wind having continued to blow from the north, the water had risen and they had sailed up for us. On examination, the water was found to be much deeper than the night before. The embankment was such that no water could have come from above.

When all was ready, a rope was fastened to the mast high up, and the eight sailors, transformed into tow-men, put their shoulders this time to the rope and, following the bank of the stream, pulled the boat after them. As we neared the lake, the channel turned to the east, giving us an opportunity to take advantage of the wind. The men came on board, the sails were hoisted and, just at the setting of the sun, we passed out upon the lake, along the very route over which we had come the day before so slowly and with so much difficulty.

There was now an abundance of water. We sailed alongside the anchored boat which had been left behind, put her sailors aboard her and continued our journey. The next day at ten o'clock, we were in sight of the low sand-beach near Damietta, whence we had embarked. The wind, which we had at first supposed to be a sea breeze, had remained in the north. It was a stiff sailing breeze, but by no means a gale, and yet, where we had had plenty of water for sailing on the evening of our embarkation, we were now aground. We were not more than four miles from our destination, but with hard labor, towing and lifting, in the same manner as on the other side of the lake, we did not reach our haven until late in the afternoon.

CHAPTER XIII

ROUTE OF THE EXODUS

A MINUTE description of the trip on Lake Menzaleh has been given to show the effect of the wind on a large surface of shallow water, its arms and inlets, because of its possible aid in correctly interpreting the Biblical account of what has been termed the passage of the Red Sea by the Israelites.

A continued strong wind off a sea or lake always raises the water along the shore, but the receding and returning of a coast line to a degree approaching that witnessed (except in the case of tides) is probably elsewhere unknown. The cause is the shallowness of the water and the grasses which prevent an under-tow. The phenomenon appeared to have a strong bearing upon the theory, then lately advanced by Brugsch Bey (afterwards Brugsch Pasha), as to the point of departure and the route taken by the Israelites at the time of the Exodus.[1]

This theory fixed the point of departure at Zoan or Sân, which has been identified by the inscriptions as Ramses and is claimed to be the Ramses of the Bible. Thence, the route passed east-ward, not far from Lake Menzaleh, to Succoth, Etham and a point before Pi-hahiroth, opposite Avaris (Baal-Zepon), between Migdol and the sea (Mediterranean).

Previous to the excavation of the Suez Canal, Lake Menzaleh stretched much farther east than it does to-day. It formerly

[1] See Brugsch's " Egypt under the Pharaohs ", second edition, Vol. II, page 363.

A View of Port Said and the Suez Canal, with Lake Menzaleh in the Distance at the Right.

extended as far as Pelusium or Sin, fifteen miles beyond its present eastern border, and, probably, in a narrow arm along the coast to and into the ancient Lake Sirbonis. The canal was cut through the sand-beach on the Mediterranean, at the point where Port Saîd is now located, and continued south twenty-eight miles through Lake Menzaleh and its marshes. This part of the lake had a depth of water of from one to three feet.

The canal was excavated with dredges. Immense banks of earth were formed on either side, thus cutting off the flow of the Nile waters, which come into the lake from the irrigating canals. Consequently, all east of the canal became a desert with occasionally impassable marshes. There are now no inhabitants east of the canal, and the sites of the ancient cities and fortified places are only determined by their ruins.

Avaris (Baal-Zephon) was east of Pelusium and about twenty-five miles east of the canal. Pi-hahiroth was a short distance still further east, near the west end of Lake Sirbonis. This lake, in ancient times, extended eastward from this point fifty miles, being separated from the Mediterranean by a narrow strip of sand, which was at no point more than a few hundred yards in width.

From Lake Sirbonis westward to the Damietta branch of the Nile, a distance of about seventy miles, a similar narrow sand-beach separated the sea from lakes and marshes up to the time of the construction of the canal. West of Port Saîd, there is still a similar sand-beach between the sea and Lake Menzaleh. The great ancient highway or caravan route from Egypt to Syria came from the southwest, passing Migdol and Baal-Zephon. It crossed these marshes near Pi-hahiroth at the west end of Sirbonis and continued eastward on the strip of land between the sea and this lake, passing Mt. Casius about twenty-five miles from Pi-hahiroth. All of these shallow lakes and marshes received their waters from the Nile, and were filled with grasses, reeds and other aquatic plants.

Brugsch in his latest notes on the subject did not attempt to fix the exact point of the catastrophe that befell the army of Pharaoh, but indicated that it must have happened, provided his theory was correct, near the western extremity of Lake Sirbonis, or at some point on this lake.

Pi-hahiroth was the "place of the gulfs," or, as the word signifies, "the entrance to the gulfs" on the route to Syria. It was near the point of crossing the marshes to or from the sea-coast. This crossing and Lake Sirbonis were considered by the ancients as exceedingly dangerous and, if their accounts are true, armies have been lost in their treacherous bogs.

The Tanitic mouth of the Nile was a little west of the present city of Port Saîd and the Pelusiac mouth, at Pelusium.

Strabo says:

"Between the Tanitic and Pelusiac mouths of the Nile are lakes and large and continuous marshes, among which are numerous villages. Pelusium itself has many marshes lying around it, which some call Barathra, or water holes and swamps. It is situated a distance of more than twenty stadia (a little over two miles) from the sea. The circumference of the wall is twenty stadia. It has its name from the mud ($\pi\eta\lambda o\hat{v}$) of the swamps. In this quarter Egypt is difficult of access, i. e., from the eastern side, towards Phœnicia and Judea, and on the side of Arabia Nabatæa, which is contiguous, through which countries the road to Egypt lies."[1]

Diodorus, speaking of the Persian King Artaxerxes Ochus' expedition to Egypt, 349 B. C., says:

"When he came to the great lake (Sirbonis), through ignorance of the places, he lost part of his army in the bogs, called Barathra. But because we have before in the first book spoken of the nature

[1] Strabo, B. XVII, C. I, Sec. 21, Casaubon, 802.

of this lake, and the strange things there happening, we shall now forbear to repeat them. Having passed these gulfs he came to Pelusium, the first mouth of the river Nile, where it enters into the sea." [1]

The description Diodorus had given of this lake is as follows:

"The parts toward the east [of Egypt] are partly secured by the river [the Pelusiac branch, long since filled] and partly surrounded by deserts, and by the marshes, called Barathra [τὰ βάραθρα, Gulfs or Pits]. For there is a lake between Cœlo-Syria and Egypt, very narrow, but exceedingly deep, even to a wonder, two hundred furlongs in length, called Serbon [Sirbonis]. If any through ignorance approach it, they are lost irrecoverably; for the channel being very narrow, like a swaddling band, and compassed round with vast heaps of sand, great quantities of it are cast into the lake by the continual southern winds, which so cover the water, and make it to the view so like unto dry land, that it cannot possibly be distinguished. And therefore many unacquainted with the nature of the place, by missing their way, have been there swallowed up together with whole armies. For the sand being trod upon, sinks down and gives away by degrees, and like a malicious cheat, deludes and decoys them that come upon it, till too late. When they see the mischief they are likely to fall into, they begin to support and help one another, but without any possibility either of returning back, or escaping certain ruin; for sinking into the gulf they are neither able to swim (the mud preventing all motion of the body), nor in a capacity to wade out, having nothing firm to support them for that purpose; for sand and water being mixed together the nature of both is thereby so changed that there is neither fording nor passing over it by boats. Being brought therefore to this pass, without the least possibility of help to be afforded them, they go together with

[1] Diodorus, Booth's Translation, Book XVI, page 118.

the sand to the bottom of the gulf at the very brink of the bog; and so the place agreeable to its nature is called Barathrum." [1]

This description is undoubtedly much exaggerated, but it serves with what is written by other ancient historians to give us an impression of the character of this lake and the marshes and quicksands on this part of the route from Egypt to Syria. Milton refers to this dangerous place in the following lines from "Paradise Lost":

> "A gulf profound as that Sirbonian bog
> Betwixt Damiata and Mount Casius old,
> Where armies whole have sunk."

It is very rarely that a European has in recent times passed by this route. Mr. Greville J. Chester, under the direction of the Palestine Exploration Fund, made the excursion in February, 1880. In his report, speaking of Lake Sirbonis, he said:

"I repeatedly tried to get near enough to the lake to dip my hands in the water, but I failed on every occasion. When I got near, and sometimes I got within three or four yards, the treacherous sand gave way under my weight, and I was compelled to retire on pain of being engulfed in the mud beneath." [2]

In the old manuscripts of the Bible the words that have been translated Red Sea were "Yâm Sûph," meaning the "Sea of Sûph." The Hebrew word "sûph," as the lexicographers say, means "weeds, reeds, rushes, papyrus-plant." "Yâm Sûph" indicated a whole navigable region covered with aquatic plants, like Lake Menzaleh, and, according to Brugsch Pasha, than whom there is no higher philological authority on the ancient languages of Egypt and its neighboring countries, was applied

---

[1] Diodorus, Sic. Book I, c. III, p. 35.

[2] Mr. Chester's report was published in the quarterly statement of the Palestine Exploration Fund, in July, 1880.

to the lakes and marshes in the northeast of Egypt. The ark of Moses was made of sûph, that is, reeds or rushes.

The Red Sea was known at the epoch of the Exodus under the name of Yuma Kot and Yuma Sekot, but at no period as Yâm Sûph. In the German Bible of to-day the marginal reading is "Sea of Weeds."

The late Dr. VanDyke, of the American College of Beirût, Syria, was one of the most learned and eminent Arabic scholars. His translation of the Bible into Arabic is used in all Protestant missions in Arabic speaking countries. In a conversation on this subject, he informed the writer that he followed the old version, translating Yâm Sûph into Arabic by words signifying "Sea of Weeds" or "Sea of Reeds," although at that time the question of the passage of the Israelites by any other route than that of the Red Sea had not been raised.

It is also well established that where the word sea alone is used in the narrative it means the Mediterranean. If we take from our version of the Bible narrative the words "Red Sea," there is nothing left on which to base the theory of the passage of the Israelites through the sea now known by that name, and we are free to select such other route as the facts may indicate. The Red Sea is of deep clear water without any growth of grasses, weeds, reeds or rushes.

Assuming that Brugsch is correct in his location of the points mentioned in the Bible, the Egyptians overtook the Israelites when they were encamped beside Pi-hahiroth, the "entrance to the gulfs," "between Migdol and the sea" (Mediterranean). This was a little west of the western end of Lake Sirbonis and in the vicinity of the "dangerous places," the gulfs or pits of the ancient geographers. Even at this day, when the Nile waters have been cut off many years, it is very difficult to approach the ruins of the ancient Pelusium.

Mr. Chester's experiences in visiting this place, a feat rarely attempted, and his description of the extensive marshes lying further east near the lake, partially confirm the statements of Diodorus. He says: "The surface of the marsh, which extends for miles, was covered with drifting sands, through which as through a cake the feet went down. . . . I sank nearly to my knees in the mud."

The shallow lakes, as I have stated, formerly stretched all along the coast and there was an arm or branch of this shallow water extending eastward from Pelusium to the so-called "gulfs," the only point where a passage could be made from the interior to the coast of the sea. Pharaoh, learning the position of his fleeing bondsmen, said, "They are entangled in the land," the desert being on one side, where the army was approaching, and the sea or morass on the other.

The Israelites, on being pursued, "were sore afraid" and "cried out unto the Lord." "Moses stretched out his hand over the sea; and the Lord caused the sea to go back by a strong east wind all that night, and made the sea dry land, and the waters were divided." [1]

A strong east wind, blowing during the night, would have moved the waters of this narrow arm westward and would have left, where in their natural position they were shallow, only "dry land." There was no place in the Isthmus, except along the Mediterranean coast, that an east wind could have had this effect. At neither of the other places, lately mentioned in connection with the supposed discovery of Pithom as possible points of passage of the Israelites—one, near Shalûf, south of the Great Bitter Lake, and the other, between this lake and Lake Timsâh—could an east wind have produced any such result. It would, in either of these cases, have blown almost directly across a narrow body of water.

There was no reason for using the words "caused the sea to go

---

[1] Ex. XIV, 21.

back by a strong east wind," unless this wind had some agency
in producing the result. It certainly could have had no such
agency on the deep waters of that arm of the Red Sea which
comes to Suez, where the Biblical commentators have, until a
recent date, located the point of passage.

The phrases "the waters were divided," "the waters were a
wall to them on their right hand and on their left," and others
of similar character, can easily be explained. Could they not,
they would have but little importance in the minds of those acquainted with the highly figurative character of Oriental languages and with the manner in which the people express themselves.

When the waters were drawn by the east wind out of the eastern branch of the larger body of water lying near Pelusium, as it
now would be out of an arm of Lake Menzaleh, the Israelites,
having no chariots and choosing their locality, could have passed
in safety. The waters were divided when they were so lowered
as to leave where they had been shallow a dry place for crossing.
The "waters were a wall" simply means they were a defence, not
a towering mass. On account of these waters, with their miry
quicksand bottoms, on the right and on the left, the Egyptians
could not approach on either side. They were to the Israelites
a wall of defence.

"In the morning watch," that is, toward morning, the winds
ceased to blow and the waters commenced returning. The Egyptians, who, with their six hundred heavy, small wheeled chariots,
undertook in the night to follow the Israelites, missed their way
in the darkness and were caught in the treacherous bogs of
the "gulfs." "The Lord took off their chariot wheels, and
they drave them heavily,"[1] and, the "sea returning to its
strength,"[2] that is, to the natural depth of the water, the Egyptians were overwhelmed and destroyed as an organized army.

[1] Ex. XIV, 25.　　　　　　　　[2] Id. 27.

The description of the tearing off of the chariot wheels and the difficulty of drawing these clumsy instruments of war applies rather to an army floundering in the mire, than to one suddenly overwhelmed by the falling of walls of water, that had remained piled up on either side, till the moment of the catastrophe, as often represented in old pictures and sermons.

Previous to the approach of the Egyptians, the Israelites may have crossed onto the strip of sand-beach between the sea and the lake, near the east end of which there was in ancient times a fortress. Barred by this obstacle or in obedience to the purpose of God that they should not go by the way of the Philistines,[1] they may have turned south and crossed the lake at some shallow place. In this case, the same results might have been produced by the east wind at the point of their crossing.

Sirbonis was for a long period, beginning, perhaps, with the filling up of the Pelusiac and Tanitic branches of the Nile, a dry lake having only boggy or marshy places. About 1876, a few fishermen from Lake Menzaleh went to this desolate and wholly uninhabited desert region, and cut a channel from the sea to the old lake-bed at its eastern end for the purpose of making a fishing-lake. In ancient times there may have been at this point an outlet to the sea, as there is now from Lake Menzaleh. Sirbonis thus became again, after a long period of dryness, a lake forty miles in length and in some places five miles broad. Like the other coast lakes it is generally very shallow.

Mr. Chester, at the time of his visit, found the lake filled with salt water and, consequently, containing no fresh-water plants, and very few marine plants. He refers to the cutting of the channel and to the fact of the lake having been previously dry, but wholly ignores the consequences of the changed conditions. He assumes that the condition of the lake was the same in ancient times as that in which he found it and that it, therefore,

[1] Ex. XIII, 17.

then contained no fresh-water vegetation, and could not have been the Yâm Sûph, Sea of Weeds, Reeds or Rushes. He even finds fault with Brugsch's map of the lake, because it had been taken from the older charts and was not correct after the refilling of the lake.

He was sent out to obtain facts to disprove the theory of Brugsch Pasha, which startled some of the old school theologians and rendered worthless a multitude of eloquent sermons that had given vivid pictures of the swallowing up of the armies of Pharaoh by the deep waters of the Red Sea. The facts, however, which he gives sustain the opinion of Brugsch as to the general route of the Exodus.

The Israelites did not wait for the reorganization of the discomfited Egyptian forces. "So Moses brought Israel from the Red Sea [Yâm Sûph] and they went out into the wilderness of Shur,[1] and they went three days in the wilderness, and found no water."[2] Shur means a wall and Etham a fortress. Therefore, the wilderness or desert of Shur or Etham is the wilderness of the wall, or fortress. Brugsch says that this desert is on the northeast of Egypt adjoining Lake Sirbonis and the former eastern end of Menzaleh, and that no part of the desert to the east or in the vicinity of the Red Sea was ever known by these names.[3] He also says that his object in what he wrote was only "to direct public attention to the historical consequences of the monumental records, and the writings on papyrus, bearing on the subject."

[1] Or, as it is stated in Numbers XXXIII, 8, the wilderness of Etham.

[2] Ex. XV, 22.

[3] Brugsch Pasha (Dr. Henry Brugsch), lately deceased, was the most learned Egyptologist of his time. His dictionary of the hieroglyphs and his great geography of Ancient Egypt, containing the names of over thirty-six hundred places, on which he labored twenty years, will be a lasting monument of the great work he accomplished. Professor Maspero who took up the work later has now surpassed all his predecessors.

Many criticisms have been made upon Brugsch's essay on the Exodus. One result of the examination and discussion is that all competent persons, who have examined the subject with the light of modern discoveries, have wholly given up the old theory of the passage of the Israelites through any part of what now constitutes the Red Sea.

Objections can be made to any of the routes suggested. No one of the other routes, however, is sustained by evidence as convincing as that adduced by this most candid and conscientious scholar. There is nothing conclusive regarding the question of the route of the Exodus in the supposed discovery of the Pithom of the Bible, the treasure city built by the people of Israel for Ramses. This city is thought to be too far south for the route suggested. The word Pi-tum or Pi-atum was found. Tum or Atum was a god, one of the forms of the Sun-God, who was more particularly worshipped at Heliopolis and in all the eastern part of the Delta. Pi means dwelling or house, and Pi-tum, Pi-atum or Pithom, is the house of Tum. Wherever Tum was worshipped was the house of Tum, the phrase being used in the same way as "the house of God" in Christian countries. The city in question may have been the Biblical city of Pithom, or it may have been simply a place where Tum was worshipped, some edifice or place dedicated to this god.

I have not given the principal facts mentioned by Brugsch, nor have I intended to give any opinion as to the route of the Exodus. I have referred only to such facts as seemed necessary to show the possible bearing on this subject of my experience on Lake Menzaleh. I have done this for the reason that I have seen no reference made in any writings to the extraordinary receding of the coast line and the draining of the arms of these shallow, grassy lakes by a continued strong wind. It is evident that the attention of Brugsch Pasha had never been called to this subject. Certainly, the facts related, considered in connection with the

Biblical narrative, have an important bearing on the question of the route of the Exodus.

There has been no other route suggested which harmonizes the known physical conditions of the country in the earliest historic periods with the Biblical record. All the other routes require the supposition that, at that period, the Suez arm of the Red Sea extended far north of its present terminus. Of this condition we have no proofs and there is no reasonable ground for supposing that it then existed. Such extension, had it existed, would have been directly north. In that case, what agency could the east winds have had in producing the results described in the sacred narrative? What reason could be given for the use of the words "the Lord caused the sea to go back by a strong east wind all that night"? Moreover, this arm of the sea would have been salt water and would not have produced the grasses necessary to constitute a sea of weeds (Yâm Sûph).

The question of the route of the Exodus cannot be considered as solved. The only objection, however, to the northern route is the one based upon the supposed discovery of the site of Pithom. The claims advanced for the other routes are not only founded on improbable suppositions, but are subject to other unanswerable objections.

CHAPTER XIV

CLEOPATRA'S NEEDLE—NEGOTIATIONS BY WHICH IT WAS SECURED

THE idea of securing an obelisk for the City of New York had its origin in 1877. It grew out of the newspaper reports of the work, then in progress, of transporting an obelisk from Alexandria to London. Paris had such a monument already. London was to have one. Why should not New York, the great city of the New World, be equally favored?

It was erroneously stated in a New York newspaper that his Highness, the Khedive of Egypt, had signified "his willingness to present to the City of New York, upon a proper application, the remaining obelisk of Alexandria." Mr. John Dixon, the contractor who transported to London the obelisk now on the Thames Embankment, was the person, it was claimed, to whom the Khedive had thus expressed himself.[1]

Mr. Henry G. Stebbins, then Commissioner of the Department of Public Parks of the City of New York, undertook to secure the necessary funds for transporting and erecting the obelisk in question. Mr. William H. Vanderbilt was asked to head the subscription, but he generously offered to defray the whole expense of the undertaking. After some telegraphic communica-

---

[1] Mr. Dixon afterwards wrote the writer that the report that the Khedive had had any conversation with him regarding the obelisk of Alexandria or had given him any intimation of an intention of presenting an obelisk to the United States, or to the City of New York, was wholly a mistake; that, in fact nothing whatever of that nature ever took place.

tions had been exchanged with Mr. Dixon as to the sum that would be required, Mr. Vanderbilt entered into a written contract with Mr. Stebbins to that effect. Only eight days after the first publication of the erroneous statement, Mr. Stebbins addressed to the Department of State at Washington the following letter:—

"New York, 15th October, 1877.

"Hon. Wm. M. Evarts,
 "Secretary of State,
  "Dear Sir:
   "I have the pleasure to enclose two copies of a letter addressed this day to his Highness the Khedive of Egypt, on the subject of the obelisk to which I had the honor of inviting your attention yesterday.

 "Will you kindly send one copy to the Consul-General of the United States at Alexandria with instructions to await the arrival of an authorized representative of Mr. Dixon, mentioned in letter, bringing with him an engrossed copy of the letter, and upon the arrival of that representative, to accompany him into the presence of the Khedive, or in some other proper way to certify to the authority of the letter, and to the authority of the person bearing it.
    "I am, dear Sir,
     "Yours very respectfully,
     Signed: "HENRY G. STEBBINS."

On the receipt of this letter the Secretary of State, Mr. Evarts, addressed to me the following despatch, enclosing a copy of Mr. Stebbins' letter and a copy of the letter which it was proposed to have delivered to his Highness the Khedive:—

"Department of State,
   "Washington, October 19, 1877.

"No 85.
"E. E. Farman, Esquire, Etc., Etc., Etc.
 "Sir:
   "This department is in receipt of a communication from Mr. Henry G. Stebbins, Commissioner of the Department of Public Parks of the City of New York, relative to the Obelisk which it is understood the Government of the Khedive is willing to present to the City of New York, on due provision being made for its transportation and erection in some public place there. Mr. Stebbins encloses a copy of a letter of which the engrossed original is to be presented to the Khedive by an authorized representative of Mr. Dixon of

London, the engineer in charge of the transportation to England of the obelisk known as Cleopatra's Needle, and solicits the sanction of this Government in the presentation of that letter.

"A copy of the letter of Mr. Stebbins and of its enclosure is herewith transmitted to you. In view of the public object to be subserved you are instructed to use all proper means of furthering the wishes expressed in Mr. Stebbins' letter.

"I am, Sir,
"Your obedient servant,
Signed: "WM. M. EVARTS.

"Enclosures:
"Mr. Stebbins to Mr. Evarts, October 15, 1877, with accompaniment."

Copy of proposed letter of Mr. Stebbins to the Khedive.

"To
"His Highness,
"The Khedive.
"Highness:
"The deep interest excited throughout the civilized world by the removal, under the auspices of your enlightened and liberal Government, of the great obelisk known as 'Cleopatra's Needle,' from Alexandria to England, has been quickened in the United States of America by the intimation conveyed to the people of the City of New York through the estimable Mr. Dixon of London, that your Highness might not be indisposed, upon a proper application to that effect being made, to testify your gracious good will and friendly sentiments towards the American People, by presenting to the City of New York, for erection in one of the great public squares, the companion obelisk which now stands at Alexandria.

"In the hope that such an application may indeed be favorably received by your Highness, an eminent citizen of New York has signified to me his willingness to defray all the necessary costs and charges of bringing this obelisk across the Atlantic Ocean and setting it up in such a situation, there to remain as an eloquent witness alike of the liberal and enlightened spirit in which your Highness administered the affairs of the ancient and illustrious country so happily confided to your sceptre and of your good will towards the youngest of the great nations of the world.

"The generous and public-spirited citizen of whom I speak has requested me in my capacity as a Commissioner, for now many years past, of the Department of Public Parks in the City of New York to lay before your Highness, therefore, through the Honorable, the Secretary of State of the United States of America, this formal application and to say to your Highness that if it shall please you to authorize the removal of the obelisk and its erection here,

I am fully prepared to commission Mr. John Dixon of London at once to undertake the work.

"I am sure your Highness will permit me to say to you, that the successful completion of this work will be gladly and gratefully hailed by the people of New York, and of the United States of America, as a new illustration of the statesmanlike wisdom displayed by your Highness in your patronage of the mighty enterprise which has united the Mediterranean with the Indian seas; and as a new and most interesting bond connecting the Republic of the United States with the Government of your Highness, and with the Egyptian people and Realm.

> "I have the honor to be,
> "Your Highness's
> "Most obedient humble servant,
> Signed: "HENRY G. STEBBINS.

"New York,
"Oct. 15, 1877."

I was much surprised by the Secretary's despatch. I had already received information of the publications in New York relative to the obelisk, but was aware that the question was entirely new in Egypt. Soon afterwards I addressed to Mr. Evarts the following despatch and, at the same time, sent him a private letter in which I made other suggestions as to the course that should in my opinion be pursued.

"No. 196.

> "Agency and Consulate-General of the United States.
> "Cairo, November 24, 1877.

"Honorable William M. Evarts,
"Secretary of State,
"Washington, D. C.
"Sir:

"I have the honor to acknowledge the receipt of your despatch No. 85 enclosing a copy of a letter of Mr. Henry G. Stebbins, Commissioner of the Department of Public Parks in the City of New York, addressed to his Highness, the Khedive, and also a copy of a letter addressed by the same person to you, both relating to the obelisk now standing at Alexandria, which it is desired to obtain and transport to the City of New York.

"On the arrival of Mr. Dixon's Agent, I shall not fail to use, in accordance with your instructions, all proper means of furthering the wishes of Mr. Stebbins.

"I fear, however, that there will be serious opposition to the removal of the obelisk from the City of Alexandria, so much in fact that although the Khedive might personally desire to gratify the wishes of the citizens of New York, he would not think it best to grant their request.

"The obelisk lately removed by the English, having been thrown down many years since, was nearly covered with sand and was not considered of any value to Alexandria. The one now standing, and the monument known as Pompey's Pillar, are the only objects of antiquity remaining in the city that are of sufficient importance to be visited by travelers.

"Should it be impossible to obtain the obelisk at Alexandria, it is not improbable that an application for the one standing at Luxor, or one of those at Karnak would be favorably received.

"The companion of the obelisk removed by the French in 1833, and afterwards erected at Paris in the 'Place de la Concorde,' is within a few rods of the river at Luxor. There are two others at Karnak, two miles below Luxor, and about fifty rods from the river. The removal of one of these might not be impracticable. At least in the case of the failure to procure that at Alexandria, the question might be considered by those in New York, who have taken an interest in the subject.

> "I have the honor to be, Sir.
> "Your obedient servant
> Signed: "E. E. FARMAN."

In the meantime Mr. Dixon had been informed of the steps taken by the parties in New York and of the action of the Department of State. He was much surprised at the manner in which his name had been used. He was directly mentioned in the letter of Mr. Stebbins, which it was proposed should be delivered to the Khedive, as having intimated that his Highness might not be indisposed to present to the City of New York an obelisk. Mr. Dixon, as has been explained above, had never had any conversation with the Khedive upon the subject. He knew enough of diplomatic matters and court usages to understand that it would be entirely out of place for him, a private English citizen, or for his agent, to ask of the Khedive a favor in behalf of the citizens of any country, even his own.

Had the Khedive had any intention or desire to confer a favor upon the people of the United States, he would never have given intimation of the fact to a subject of some other nationality instead of to the accredited representative of our own Government.

Mr. Dixon took immediate measures to inform the parties in New York of their mistake, and, fearing lest I might act on the instructions I had received from the Department of State, he also wrote me the following letter:

> "1, Laurence Poultney Hill,
> "Cannon Street,
> "London E. C., Nov. 16, 1877.
>
> " H. E. The Consul-General of the United States,
> "Egypt.
> "Sir:
>
> " You will, I believe, have received a communication from Mr. Secretary Evarts requesting you to ascertain from the Government of his Highness, the Khedive, whether he would be disposed to sanction the removal of an obelisk to the United States and present one for such purpose.
>
> "This is all very proper but my name has been mixed up with it as though I were purveyor of obelisks to H. H. ! ! I believe it is founded upon a casual remark of mine that if the U. S. wanted an obelisk I thought it possible that one might be obtained. Mr. Vanderbilt offered to defray the expenses.
>
> " You will see whilst a suitable despatch from the United States secretary might have its prayer acceded to, neither my name nor that of anyone else ought to be mentioned.
>
> "I have written to the United States explaining my views and an amended despatch will be sent you. Meantime if you can secure one, well and good, but pray do not mention my name as having suggested it. I shall be glad to co-operate in the novel enterprise, but H. H. has treated me with such consideration that I would not at any price run the risk of offending him as the despatch I allude to would certainly do.
>
> "I have the honor to remain, Sir,
> "Your obedient servant,
> Signed: "JOHN DIXON."

Mr. Dixon's letter, a copy of which was sent to Mr. Evarts, was received immediately after the sending of my despatch to the latter, on the 24th of November.

I expected soon to receive further instructions; but none came, nor any communication on the subject from any source. On receipt of Mr. Dixon's communication, sent to parties in New York, the whole matter of the obelisk was dropped. After the newspaper publications of October, 1877, which I have mentioned, there was a profound silence. No reference to the subject was made in any of the New York journals for more than a year and a half, and then not until my despatches of May, 1879, to the Department of State giving information of the successful termination of the negotiations which I had personally conducted had been received. Neither Mr. Dixon, nor his agent, nor the engrossed copy of Mr. Stebbins' letter ever came.

During my trip with General Grant in Upper Egypt (of which I have written in "Along the Nile with General Grant"), I examined the obelisk at Luxor, and the two at Karnak, with reference to the feasibility of their removal. My conclusion was that the only obelisk in Egypt that we should be at all likely to obtain was the one at Luxor. No one would think of removing that of Heliopolis, antedating Cleopatra's Needle a thousand years and standing where it was originally placed by Usertesen— a solitary monument marking the site of the once famous city of On.

The larger of the two obelisks at Karnak, the largest obelisk known, in fact, stood where it was placed by the woman-king Hatshepsu thirty-four hundred years before. The smaller one near it, that of Thûtmosis I, whose mummy has since been deposited in the Museum at Cairo, had one corner broken. It was also cracked in a manner that would render its removal without further injury difficult, if not impossible. The only other obelisks then in Egypt, except those broken into fragments, were that of Alexandria and that of Luxor.

I informed General Grant of the correspondence relative to procuring an obelisk and asked his opinion as to the propriety of my attempting to obtain one on my own initiative, as the people in New York seemed to have abandoned the undertaking. He

Obelisk of Ramses II at Luxor; Companion of, but Larger than,
That of the Place de la Concorde, Paris.

replied that he could see no objection to my doing so and advised me to procure one if possible.

On the 4th of March, I had an interview with the Khedive at the Palace of Abdîn for the purpose of laying the matter before him. I knew I should not receive a direct refusal. The people of the Orient, especially the better classes, are very polite. They have very little of the brusque, decisive, Anglo-Saxon way of disposing of matters. They seldom give a definite refusal to a request. Courtesy toward a representative of a foreign power would specially require that such a request should be taken into consideration and that a hasty answer should not be given, unless it was a favorable one.

I informed his Highness that the people of the United States desired one of the ancient obelisks of Egypt, and that a wealthy gentleman of New York had offered to defray the expenses of its transportation and of its erection in that city. I mentioned the obelisk of Paris and that of London and the natural desire of our people to also have one in their metropolis. I explained, in the course of the conversation, that our nation was so young and all its works of so recent a date that one of the ancient monuments of Egypt would be much more highly prized in the United States than in England or France. I called attention to the obelisk at Alexandria as the most accessible for shipment, but added that, if his Highness concluded to favor us with such a gift, we should be much pleased with any his Highness might select.

I found the subject entirely new to the Khedive. He seemed, at first, to be surprised at the proposal. However, after various questions and observations, he said that, while it would be a great pleasure for him to be able to accede to my wishes, or to do anything in his power to gratify the people of the United States, the matter would have to be seriously considered. As to the obelisk at Alexandria, he did not think it best even to mention it, since the people of that city would be opposed to its removal.

I did not afterwards make any special mention in the presence of his Highness of the Alexandrian obelisk, although that was the one that was finally given us. As I took leave of the Khedive he said I could call his attention to the subject at some future time.

I immediately sent a despatch to Mr. Evarts informing him of the subject and results of this interview. Other conversations were had with the Khedive regarding the matter, without any definite results. A little later I was present at a dinner given by the Khedive at the Palace of Abdîn and it was on this occasion that the first favorable intimation was given in regard to the obelisk. There were from thirty to forty persons present, among them M. Ferdinand de Lesseps. After dinner the company was conversing in groups. The Khedive, who was constantly shifting his place, seemed in better spirits than was usual for him in those sad days of financial embarrassment. He approached me and invited me to be seated. His first words were, "Well, Mr. Farman, you would like an obelisk?"

I replied that we would like one very much. We conversed some minutes on the subject, without his Highness giving the least intimation of his intentions. Some one came to join us and we rose and, soon after, separated.

A few minutes later I was in conversation with M. de Lesseps. This was at the time the Khedive was about to establish a commission of inquiry to ascertain the amount of the net revenues of the country with a view to determining what rate of interest could be paid on the public debt. There had been an almost total failure of the winter crops in a large portion of Upper Egypt, resulting from the unprecedentedly low Nile of the previous year. This rendered it impossible, in the opinion of his Highness, to continue the payment of interest at the rate of seven per cent on the nearly one hundred millions of pounds of Egypt's indebtedness. He had named, or was about to name,

M. de Lesseps president of the commission. During our conversation the Khedive joined us. M. de Lesseps, turning towards him, repeated something I had just said about the best manner of ascertaining the amount of the revenues. Either his Highness did not hear, or, what is more likely, he did not wish to enter upon the discussion of that subject. Interrupting the conversation he said, "Mr. Farman wishes an obelisk."

M. de Lesseps, who was a fine conversationalist, and always polite, agreeable and quick in his replies, immediately said, "That would be an excellent thing for the people of the United States." Then, after a moment's hesitation, during which time the Khedive seemed to await his further reply, he added: "I do not see why we could not give them one. It would not injure us much and it would be a very valuable acquisition for them."

M. de Lesseps had been so long in Egypt that he considered himself as one of the country, and, in speaking of Egyptian matters, was accustomed to say "we," "us," and "ours." The Khedive simply said, "I am considering the matter" and turned to speak with another person who was approaching.

When I made my dinner call, two or three days afterwards, the obelisk was again mentioned. His Highness said that he had concluded to give us one, but not that of Alexandria, and added that he would take measures to obtain the necessary information and inform me of his decision. He at once called his private secretary and directed him to write a note to Brugsch Bey (afterwards Brugsch Pasha), requesting a list and description of all the obelisks remaining in Egypt, and an opinion as to which could best be spared. I thanked his Highness warmly, and, as I was leaving, he said that within a short time his secretary would inform me which obelisk we could have.

It was not many days after this interview that a reception and ball was given at the Palace. Brugsch Bey and myself happened to meet and, after the exchange of a few words, he said in a rather reproachful tone, "I learn you are trying to obtain an obelisk to take to New York."

I replied, "Why not, they have one in Paris, and one in London and the people of New York wish one also."

He answered: "You will create a great amount of feeling; all the savants of Europe will oppose it. The Khedive has asked me to give a description of the obelisks remaining in Egypt, and to state which one can best be spared. I have sent a description of the obelisks, but I shall not designate one to be taken away, for I am totally opposed to the removal of any of them."

Not desiring to enter into any discussion on the subject, I replied in a conciliatory manner, saying that it was of no great importance, that there were a number of obelisks in Egypt, and that the removal of one would not make much difference. He assured me that I would encounter a great deal of antagonism. This was the beginning of an opposition that was to delay for more than a year the completion of the gift which his Highness had deliberately determined upon.

Had this opposition come from Egyptians of position, who would have had a right to be heard, I should have desisted at once, through delicacy, from all further efforts in the matter. It came, however, wholly from Europeans temporarily residing in Egypt, who, whatever might be their opinions and however well founded their conclusions, had no rights to protect against the United States, and, consequently, were not entitled to be considered. It was purely an affair between Egypt and ourselves, and, as no opposition was made on the part of any real Egyptian, I did not feel bound to yield to the opposition of others nor have any scruples about taking every proper means to overcome it.

About this time I was informed by the English Consul-General that the obelisk at Luxor, the only one I then had hopes of obtaining, belonged to his people. He affirmed that it was given to them at the same time that the one at Paris was given to France, and announced that they claimed it and should object to its being removed by anyone else. The Consul-General admitted that he did not know that they should ever take it, but he insisted upon their right to do so. The Khedive afterwards said to me that it was true that the obelisk at Luxor was offered to the English at the same time that its companion was given to the French. They did not take it, but they objected now to its being given to anyone else. Under the circumstances it would not do to interfere with it.

This was a new and unexpected complication. The Luxor obelisk had been offered to the English by Mohammed Ali, fifty years before, because he did not wish to create any ill feelings on account of his gift to France. It was not then accepted and there was no intention of taking it. Another had in the meantime been accepted and removed to London. It was evident that claim was laid to this simply to prevent its going to the United States.

CHAPTER XV

GIFT OF THE OBELISK

WEEKS passed and no note came from the Khedive. In the meantime his private secretary had informed me verbally that no obelisk had been designated to be given to the United States, for the reason that Brugsch Bey had reported no opinion as to the one that could best be spared. I knew that special objections were being made in the case of each obelisk, that all the European influences were combined against me, and that the English claim to the Luxor obelisk was only one of the results of this combination.

Once afterwards, during the spring of 1878, the matter was mentioned by the Khedive. He spoke of the English claiming the Luxor obelisk and said that he had not yet fixed upon one to be given to us, but that he would do so at no very distant day.

Serious difficulties came upon Egypt about this time. The Khedive was harassed and vexed in many ways. M. de Lesseps, well knowing that he could not do justice to Egypt and at the same time please the Paris bankers, had gone to France without entering upon the duties of the Commission of Inquiry. The Commission had been organized, however. It was composed of persons who had been selected in the interests of the bondholders, and its work progressed with rapidity. Among the measures of economy it demanded was the dismissal of many Government employees, and the Americans in the military service of the Khedive were among the first to be discharged. Without any previous notice, they were informed that their terms of service were ended. They all had considerable amounts of arrears of pay due them, and some of them had disputed claims and demands for indemnity which complicated their relations with the Government and rendered a settlement of their accounts difficult.

I was called upon to aid my countrymen and found myself suddenly thrown into an unpleasant contest. In view of this depressed state of Egyptian affairs and the embarrassments with which the Khedive found himself surrounded, there was no time for him to think of the obelisk and any mention of it on my part would have been discourteous. Therefore, I left Egypt about the middle of July, without again referring to the subject, on a leave of absence, with permission to visit the United States.

Early in October, a few days before I sailed from New York on my return, I had an interview with Mr. Evarts in which I informed him of the state of the negotiations relative to an obelisk. He said he would be very much pleased if I could obtain one, and that he was ready to do anything he properly could to aid me.

On my arrival in Egypt in November, I found a great change in Governmental matters. What was called the Anglo-French Ministry had been formed with Nubar Pasha at its head. It had been organized on the theory of "responsibility." A responsible ministry is responsible, while in power, for the government it administers; but it is supposed to be responsible or accountable to some person, or body of persons. This Ministry assumed to act independently of the Khedive, as the English Ministry does of the Queen. But in England there is a parliament to which the Ministers are accountable, to this extent at least, that they must have its support or resign.

In Egypt there was no parliament, all the legislative as well as the executive power being vested in the Khedive. There was a Chamber of Notables, which was sometimes assembled to vote on questions of extraordinary taxation. This Chamber was convoked in December, 1887, or in January following, but was utterly ignored by the Ministry, which even refused to submit to it a report of the proceedings of the Minister of Finance. The Ministers, according to their theory, were independent of all restraint, and, as it afterwards appeared, no one could rightfully remove them. At least this was affirmed.

Such was the Ministry through which the obelisk was now to come if at all, the Khedive, as claimed, having no authority in the premises.

Mariette Bey, who had spent the summer at the Exposition in Paris, had arrived, and I knew he was making strenuous opposition to the gift. He was then at the head of the Department of Antiquities and his opposition could not but embarrass and delay the negotiations. At one time it seemed likely to wholly defeat the intentions of the Khedive.

On my arrival I paid the customary visit to the Khedive and had frequent interviews with him afterwards, but no mention was made of the obelisk for a number of weeks. He finally signified his willingness and desire to complete the gift, but he did not hesitate to intimate to me what I very well knew, that the matter of the obelisk was in the hands of the Ministers.

Though I had little faith in any long continuance of the existing state of things, I took occasion to bring the matter of the obelisk before his Excellency, Nubar Pasha, whom I had never seen until my late arrival in Egypt. He had been in disfavor with the Khedive and had resided in Europe since 1875, being recalled to head the Ministry at the instance of certain European Powers.

I found that he already understood the question, not through the Khedive, but through those who were opposed to the gift. He took a fair view of the matter, however, and said that, if the Khedive had expressed his intention of giving us an obelisk, it should be considered as a "*fait accompli*," and that there was no reason why the Ministry should oppose it. He promised to see the Khedive, learn exactly what had been done, and then carry out his Highness' wishes. He added, however, that if it were a new and open question, he should oppose it.

Not long afterwards he informed me that he had seen the Khedive, and that his Highness said that he had promised an obelisk and desired to have the promise fulfilled. His Excellency added that he would take the necessary measures for that purpose.

About this time Mariette Bey laid before the Council of Ministers a memorial on the subject, in which he made strenuous opposition to the removal of any of the obelisks of Egypt, and particularly set forth the sacredness of the obelisks at Karnak and Heliopolis. It was this memorial and the declarations of Mariette that afterwards determined which obelisk should be given us. He undoubtedly thought that there would be sufficient opposition from other sources to prevent the removal of the obelisk at Alexandria; that the English would take care of theirs at Luxor; and that, if he could prevent the selection of either of those at Karnak, or the one at Heliopolis, the project would be defeated.[1]

In February Nubar Pasha informed me that the English claimed the obelisk at Luxor and that Mariette Bey was so strongly opposed to the removal of those at Karnak and Heliopolis that he had determined to give us the one at Alexandria, Cleopatra's Needle. He at the same time prepared and handed his clerk a memorandum of a despatch to the Minister of Public

[1] Previous to the time of his being employed by the Egyptian Government, Mariette Bey took to Paris the finest collection of antiquities that has ever been removed from Egypt. A large, and the most valuable, part of the collection was obtained only by long and strenuous diplomatic pressure and by keeping the secret, during the negotiations, of what had been found. The collection, numbering about seven thousand objects, is still in the Museum of the Louvre.

Works who represented France in the Ministry, asking him to institute the necessary formalities for its delivery. Whether this despatch was ever sent I do not know. Two or three days afterwards, events happened that threw Egypt into intense excitement and compelled Nubar Pasha to retire from the Ministry.

A large number of Egyptian officers and soldiers had been discharged, without receiving their arrears of pay. It was also just at this time that we were getting the details of the famine in Upper Egypt during the previous months of November and December, and the public feeling had become very hostile towards what was known as the European Ministry. This state of excitement culminated on the 18th of February in a street attack by the discharged officers upon Mr. Rivers Wilson and Nubar Pasha, as they were leaving their departments to go to their noon-day meal. The officers demanded their arrears of salaries and, on payment being refused, took the Ministers back to the Department of Finance and held them prisoners until information was conveyed to the Khedive who came personally to their relief. It was then only with great difficulty, and after some shots had been fired, that order was restored.

Nubar Pasha resigned the next morning. The English and French Ministers, supported by their respective Governments, retained their places and, after thirty days of diplomatic negotiations, the Ministry was reorganized, but under such conditions that the two European Ministers could virtually control the Government. This reorganized Ministry was not destined to last long. Turns of the wheel of fortune were frequent in Egypt and they generally happened when least expected. It is called a country of surprises, and there is an Oriental proverb, according to which only what is intended to be provisional is lasting. An Arab does not finish his house through fear that some accident will befall it or its occupants.

The new régime was supposed to be permanent. Telegraphic

lines had been freely used and the combined diplomatic wisdom of two great European Powers called into action. Conditions were formulated and imposed that were designed to insure the immovability of the Ministers. When the work was completed, it was supposed that there was at least one unchangeable institution in Egypt. The reorganized Ministry was henceforth to be an immovable fixture in the governmental machinery. But the Arab proverb held good and the structure which rested on laborious negotiations lasting thirty days, endured just eighteen. On the 7th of April occurred what was called the "*coup d'état*" of the Khedive, Ismaîl Pasha.

The action of the new Ministry was such that the Khedive soon afterwards claimed it to be necessary, for the safety of the country, that he should again take the Government into his own hands and form a Ministry composed wholly of Egyptians. He requested Cherîf Pasha to form and take the presidency of a new Ministry. The trust was accepted and the Ministry was formed. Once more the Khedive was the real as well as the nominal chief and head of the Government, but the diplomatic and political circles of Europe were thrown into a state of excitement. At Paris, where the feeling against the Khedive was the most intense, his dethronement was loudly demanded.

I had known Cherîf Pasha since the time of my first arrival in Egypt. He was admitted by all parties to be a noble, honest and just man, who never entered into intrigues or speculations. In his youth he had received a good European education. He had commenced his career as an army officer and risen to the rank of colonel, and afterwards had had experience in every department of the Government. Always frank and sincere, he enjoyed more of the confidence of the people than any other person the Khedive could call into his service.

It was not many days before matters were again running smoothly so far as the local Government of Egypt was concerned.

The only difficulties were in Paris and London, where potent influences were at work against his Highness. In Egypt, the native public sentiment was one of hostility to being governed by foreigners. As a result of this sentiment, there arose about this time a faction styling itself the "National Party," having for its motto "Egypt for the Egyptians." It was small in numbers and to a large extent necessarily secret in its action, but its feeling of antagonism to "foreign rule" was in accord with that of the native population.

A number of European Governments were at this time, in consequence of some real or supposed interest, claiming a share in the Government of Egypt, and vying with each other for a preponderance of influence and power. The Government of the United States, having no political purposes to carry out in this country, did not assume the right to interfere with its Government. It was, consequently, able to keep itself free from all political complications. Under these circumstances, there was naturally the kindest feeling among the Egyptians toward our Government and people.

Cherîf Pasha was conversant with the negotiations relative to the obelisk. Though the new Ministry had been organized on the same theory of "responsibility" as the one it replaced, I had good reasons to believe that his Excellency would not put any obstacles in the way of the fulfilment of the expressed intentions of the Khedive.

About a month after the so-called "*coup d'état,*" political affairs became entirely quiet, and it seemed for the moment as if the European Powers were to acquiesce in the new order of things. A convenient opportunity occurring, I suggested to Cherîf Pasha, that I would like to have the matter of the obelisk terminated. He said he would take the first opportunity to talk with the Khedive and that his Highness' wishes, whatever they were, should be carried out. Some days afterwards when I was calling upon him for another purpose he told me that the question of the obelisk had been considered and had been practically decided in my favor, but that he desired to speak to the Khedive once more on the subject. He added that he should see him that evening and if I would call on the morrow at eleven o'clock, he would give me a definite answer. This I was led to understand would be a favorable one. The next day I went to the Ministry at the hour designated, but was informed that Cherif Pasha was at the Palace, and probably with the Khedive.

On my return to the Consulate I stopped to visit the Pasha who held the position of Keeper of the Seal, and who had rooms in one part of the Khedive's residence. I found there two of the princes, brothers of the late Khedive, Tewfik Pasha. We entered into conversation, and coffee was served according to the universal Oriental custom. In a few minutes Cherif Pasha came in, and, after the usual salutations, had a few words with the Keeper of the Seal in their own language. Starting to leave, he gave me an invitation to accompany him, and, bidding good morning to the others, we went out together. On shaking hands with Cherif, I noticed that he was much agitated, and I suspected that there was important and perhaps alarming news from the Cabinets of Paris and London. As soon as we were in the hall, his Excellency commenced a conversation, saying that he presumed I had been to see him, that he regretted not having been at the Ministry, but that he had been detained by important business with the Khedive. We had passed through a long hall and down a stairway and were just going out of a doorway near which both of our carriages were awaiting us when the Pasha said, "It is the obelisk at Alexandria that you prefer, is it not?"

I replied that that one was more conveniently situated for removal than the others.

"Well," said the Pasha, "we have concluded to give it to you."

After thanking him, I said that I ought to have something in writing, confirming the gift, to send to the Secretary of State at Washington. I said further that, though we had always talked of it as a gift to the United States, it was understood that it was to be erected in New York, and that I had been thinking it would be better to give it directly to that city, as otherwise there might be some complication requiring an act of Congress.

Cherîf replied, "We give you the obelisk, do as you wish with it." After a moment's reflection he added:—"Write me a note indicating what you wish to have done. State that all the expenses of removal are to be paid by the United States, or by the City of New York if you prefer. Hand the note to my Secretary-general and tell him to prepare an answer confirming the gift, in accordance with the suggestions you give, and to bring it to me for my signature."

Two hours later I handed to the Secretary-general of the Department of Foreign Affairs, at the same time informing him of what the Pasha had said, a letter of which the following is a translation from the French:—

"Agency and Consulate-General of the United States at Cairo, May 17, 1879.
"Excellency;

"Referring to the different conversations that I have had the honor to have with your Excellency in which you have informed me that the Government of his Highness, the Khedive, is disposed to present to the City of New York, to be transported and erected there, the obelisk of Alexandria, I should be pleased if your Excellency would have the kindness to definitely confirm in writing the gift of this monument.

"It is understood that its transportation is to be effected at the expense of certain citizens of the said City of New York.

"I beg to assure your Excellency in advance of the warm thanks of my Government for having thus favorably responded to the representations I have made to the Government of his Highness the Khedive, in accordance with the instructions that I have received on this subject.

"I have every reason to believe that the monument which is thus soon to be transported to and erected in the City of New York, will always be a souvenir and a pledge of the friendship that has ever existed between the Government of the United States and that of his Highness, the Khedive.

The Obelisk, Known as Cleopatra's Needle, as It Stood at Alexandria, Showing the Nearly Effaced Hieroglyphics on the Land Side.

"I beg your Excellency to accept the renewed assurance of my high consideration.

Signed: "E. E. FARMAN.

"To his Excellency Cherîf Pasha, Minister of Foreign Affairs and President of the Council of Ministers."

The next day I received the following reply which I have translated from the French.

"Cairo, May 18th, 1879.

"To Mr. Farman, Agent and Consul-General of the United States.

"Mr. Agent & Consul-General:

"I have taken cognizance of the despatch which you did me the honor of writing on the 17th of the current month of May.

"In reply I hasten to transmit to you the assurance, Mr. Agent & Consul-General, that the Government of the Khedive having taken into consideration your representations and the desire which you have expressed in the name of the Government of the United States of America, consents, in fact, to make a gift to the City of New York of the obelisk known as Cleopatra's Needle, which is at Alexandria on the sea-shore.

"The local authorities will therefore be directed to deliver this obelisk to the representative of the American Government, and to facilitate, in everything that shall depend upon them, the removal of this monument, which according to the terms of your despatch is to be done at the exclusive cost and expense of the City of New York.

"I am happy, Mr. Agent & Consul-General, to have to announce to you this decision, which while giving to the Great City an Egyptian monument, to which is attached as you know, a real archæological interest, will also be, I am as yourself convinced, another souvenir and another pledge of the friendship that has constantly existed between the Government of the United States and that of the Khedive.

"Be pleased to accept, Mr. Agent and Consul-General, the expression of my high consideration.

Signed: "CHERÎF."

It will be seen by these notes that the obelisk was given directly to the City of New York, and not, as is stated in the inscription on a claw of one of the crabs upon which it now rests, to the United States.

On the 22d day of May I sent Mr. Secretary Evarts, the following telegram:—"The Government of the Khedive has given to the City of New York the obelisk at Alexandria, known as Cleopatra's Needle." I also, on the same day, forwarded to him a despatch enclosing copies of the notes that had been exchanged between Cherîf Pasha and myself.

The obelisk was secured, but the complications in the affairs of Egypt continued. On the 27th day of June the Khedive abdicated in favor of his son, Mehemet Tewfik Pasha, who, on the same day, was proclaimed Khedive of Egypt.

The experiment of a European Ministry was not tried again. Cherîf Pasha was continued at the head of the Administration during the summer, but early in the autumn what was known as the Riaz Ministry was formed.

The final negotiations by which the obelisk was secured had been conducted so quietly that the first public information in Egypt that the gift had been made came from New York through the medium of English newspapers. Very little was then said upon the subject by any of the local journals, but as soon as the Riaz Ministry was organized an attempt was made, through the influence of certain Europeans, to have the action of the late Government reversed. The matter was two or three times considered in the Council of Ministers, and commented upon by the European press of Egypt. The Ministers, however, finding that the gift had been confirmed in writing, by an exchange of official notes, decided that it was too late for them to take any action in the matter. Lieutenant-Commander Gorrings arrived in October, 1879, to effect the removal of the obelisk, and the necessary orders were given to the local authorities of Alexandria for its delivery.

On the receipt of my despatch of the 22d of May informing him of the successful termination of the negotiations, Secretary Evarts wrote me a private letter, and at the same time sent me an official despatch, dated June 13th, 1879. In the latter he said:—

"I have to acknowledge the reception of your despatch of the 22nd ultimo, with its enclosures in which you have informed the Department that the negotiations entered into to procure an Egyptian obelisk for the City of New York have been successful, and that the Government of his Highness the Khedive has generously presented to that city the obelisk known as Cleopatra's Needle.

"It is a source of great gratification to this Government, that through the generosity of the Khedive this country is soon to come into the possession of such an interesting monument of antiquity as Cleopatra's Needle.   You are therefore instructed to inform his Highness that the great favor he has conferred upon this Republic by making this gift is highly appreciated and that it is felt that such a rare mark of friendship cannot but tend to still further strengthen the amicable relations which have ever subsisted between the two countries and will cause the memory of the Khedive to be long and warmly cherished by the American people.

"The historical account of the obelisks of Egypt, which your despatch contains has been read with interest."

It must not be supposed that the obelisks and other ancient monuments of the country are slightly prized by the educated Egyptians.   On the contrary, they are highly valued and guarded with great jealousy.   Considering all the circumstances, the Khedive could not have furnished a stronger proof of his respect for the Government and people of the United States than this gift of Cleopatra's Needle.   I have abundant evidence of the great admiration he had for our institutions, though he knew that nothing of the kind was possible in the Orient.

The other obelisks that have been removed from Egypt were obtained under circumstances entirely different from those now existing.   They were for the most part removed by the Roman conquerors. Only two, besides Cleopatra's Needle, have been taken away in modern times, that of Paris and that of London. The latter was given to England in 1820, at a time when Egypt was in a condition entirely different from that of to-day. Furthermore, this obelisk had been lying for centuries nearly buried in sand and rubbish. It was much injured, and, in comparison with the standing obelisks, little prized. Yet it was considered a gift worthy to be bestowed upon his Majesty, George the Fourth, in return for favors and presents received from him by Mohammed Ali Pasha, then Viceroy of Egypt.

The obelisk now at Paris was given to France ten years later, in 1830, on account, it is claimed, of services rendered to the Government of Egypt. It stood at Luxor, then a small village of mud huts, situated six hundred miles up the Nile and inhabited by a few hundred natives.

There were three other obelisks standing in this vicinity and many colossal ruins, the most magnificent and interesting in the world. The place was at that period, however, seldom visited by Europeans, and the removal of one of its obelisks was not an event to create any opposition. Yet the monument was considered an important embellishment of the city of Paris.

The European press of Egypt, commenting in the fall of 1879 upon the subject of the removal of Egyptian monuments, laid great stress upon the fact that the London and Paris obelisks were both given on account of services and favors rendered by the Governments of the countries to which they were presented, while there was no pretence of any such consideration for the gift of Cleopatra's Needle to the City of New York.

This only proves that the courtesy was prompted by the respect and kindly feelings of a sovereign towards a government and a people who had always been his friends, and who had no selfish designs to further against him, his subjects or his country.

In the acceptance of the obelisk the City of New York assumed a solemn obligation toward future generations, towards all of those millions of the citizens of the Republic who shall in the coming centuries visit the great metropolis. That obligation is to preserve the monument which has been placed in its keeping. It has come to us through thirty-five centuries, and, after all the vicissitudes through which it has passed, is still in a fair state of preservation. It would now be a shameful negligence, as reprehensible as wanton destruction, on the part of those having the custody of this noble monument, to allow it to be unnecessarily injured for the want of that provident care which prudence demands should be bestowed upon it.

The injuries it has already received are generally supposed by those who have only slightly examined the subject to have resulted from its having stood for a long time near the sea. This is a mistake. It was not the sides facing the sea that were injured. I have elsewhere shown that these injuries could only have been produced by the alkalies of the soil in which the obelisk probably lay for several centuries, or by fire. It is probable that the principal injuries were caused by the latter agency.

It is well known that polished granite successfully resists all atmospheric influences in cold as well as in warm climates. But when this polish is once removed, and a rough uneven surface is presented, certain atmospheric and climatic influences are injurious.

CHAPTER XVI

THE REMOVAL OF THE OBELISK AND MASONIC EMBLEMS

CLEOPATRA'S NEEDLE is a single shaft of red granite from the quarries of Syene, now Assuân, at the First Cataract of the Nile, seven hundred miles from the Mediterranean. It is sixty-eight feet ten inches in height and seven feet ten inches by eight feet two inches at its base. It tapers gradually upwards to six feet one inch by six feet three inches, terminating in a pyramidion seven feet high. Its weight is about two hundred and twenty tons. It stood upon the sea-shore at Alexandria, fifty feet from the water line, with its base buried in sand and earth that had been accumulating for centuries.

The base of the obelisk, when uncovered, was found to be considerably rounded. It rested on two copper supports cast in the form of sea-crabs and placed under opposite corners. Under a third corner was a stone, but the fourth corner was unsupported. This left a space between the obelisk and its pedestal of eight inches. There was a thin iron wedge wholly oxydized on the top of the stone support. The bodies of the two crabs were about twelve inches long, measuring from the head back, and they were sixteen inches broad and eight inches high. Each, when entire, weighed over five hundred pounds. Bars of the same material as the crabs ran from their upper and lower surfaces into the obelisk and the pedestal. These bars were over three inches square and nine inches long, forming dowels which

Placing the Obelisk in the Hold of the Steamer *Dessoug*
at Alexandria.

held the obelisk securely in its place. The dowels were surrounded and made firm in the mortises with lead.

Originally, there were four crabs, the two missing ones having been removed by the natives for the metal. The remaining crabs were much injured. The claws and legs of one had been removed. The other had only one leg left and even this was broken in turning the obelisk to a horizontal position. It is probable that the crabs were placed under the obelisk as supports at the time of its reërection by the Romans, on account of the rounded condition of its base. One writer conjectures that the form of the crab was chosen to satisfy the superstition of both the Egyptians and Romans.

The obelisk rested upon a pedestal formed of a single block of Syenitic granite tapering upward in about the same proportion as the obelisk. It was seven feet high, averaged nine feet square and weighed forty-eight tons. The substructure on which the pedestal rested was four feet nine inches high and the under surface of its lowest step was only eighteen inches above the level of the sea.

At the time of the erection of the obelisk at Alexandria, a little over nineteen hundred years ago, the surface of the earth at this point was lower than the lowest step of the pedestal. There was a gradual accumulation of sand and gravel to the height of seventeen feet, burying the steps, the pedestal and finally the base of the obelisk. During the same period, there has been a marked change in the relative position of the land and sea. Tombs cut in the rocks overlooking the sea are now partly submerged and constantly washed by the waves. The height of the obelisk, measuring from the base of the lower step, was eighty-one feet two inches.

Lieutenant-Commander Gorrings, U. S. N., was granted a leave of absence to enable him to remove the obelisk to the United States. He was accompanied by Lieutenant Seaton Schroeder, now Captain, and late Governor of Guam, who was a valuable assistant. Heavy constructions were made in the United States to aid in the accomplishment of the work.

When the excavations were finished, the obelisk was encased with planks, and stone piers were erected to support the constructions used in turning it to a horizontal position. These constructions consisted of steel frame-works on two opposite sides of the obelisk, similar in form to the iron piers of a bridge, on the top of which were placed bearings for trunnions. Heavy plates, with trunnions cast upon them, were fastened to the sides of the obelisk by means of long bolts or rods passing from one to the other through their projecting edges. Four pairs of heavy rods ran from the trunnion plates downward and through the ends of heel straps that passed under the obelisk. These straps were double-channeled and fastened to the rods by nuts. When the base of the obelisk was pushed by means of hydraulic jacks from the supports on which it rested, its whole weight was sustained by the rods and, thus supported, it was swung to a horizontal position, turning on its improvised trunnions like a mammoth cannon.

Through an error in the computation of the weight of the upper and lower parts, the trunnions were placed too low, making that part of the obelisk above them heavier than that below. The obelisk, when once started, swung very quickly and struck with great force upon the nest of planks that had been erected to receive it. Happily, it was not broken, though the great throng of people present were startled by the crashing of the planks. It was a fortunate escape from a serious accident to the noble monument. A similar nest of planks was placed under the other end of the obelisk. After the pedestal and foundations had been removed, it was gradually lowered by means of hydraulic jacks to a caisson constructed to receive it.

The caisson was pushed into the sea, towed around the ancient island of Pharos and into the harbor. Here, it was placed with the steamer *Dessoug* in a floating dry-dock. The dock was closed, the water pumped from it and the obelisk run into the steamer through a hole made in its side near the bow. The ways on which the obelisk was moved were made of heavy rails of channel iron on which cannon balls were used as rollers. To prevent any injury to the obelisk and cover its uneven surfaces, similar rails of channel iron were placed, inverted, under the obelisk and over the balls. On the arrival of the steamer in New York the same means as those used in Alexandria were employed in unshipping and erecting the obelisk.

The *Dessoug* did not leave Alexandria until the 12th of June, 1880, eight months having been employed in lowering and shipping the obelisk with the aid of the most approved modern appliances which had been previously prepared for this special purpose. Six months more, after its arrival in New York, were required for its unshipment and reërection.

When we compare this work with that accomplished on the banks of the Nile thirty-five hundred years ago, we are unable to find words to express our astonishment at the skill of the ancient Egyptians. The most perfect and beautiful of the existing obelisks is one of those that stand at Karnak. Its weight is nearly twice that of Cleopatra's Needle. According to hieroglyphic inscriptions on its base, this immense monolith was cut from its native bed at Assuân, transported one hundred and forty miles and erected on the pedestal where it now stands, in seven months. The work appears to have been hastened in order that the erection of the obelisk might "commemorate an anniversary of the queen's coronation." We can excuse the satisfaction, the pride, the egotism of the wonderful woman, Queen Hatshepsu, over her marvelous achievement, as expressed in the following inscription which she had chiseled on the pedestal of the obelisk:

"This is what I teach to mortals who shall live in centuries to come, and who shall inquire concerning the monuments I have raised to my father. . . . When I sat in the palace and thought upon him who made me, my heart hastened me to erect to him two obelisks of electrum whose tops should reach the sky before the august gateway between the two great pylons of king Thûtmosis I. . . . When they see my monuments in after years and speak of my great deeds, let them beware of saying 'I know not, I know not why it was determined to cover this monument with gold all over.' It is thus that it hath been done, that my name may remain and live forever. This single block of granite has been cut at the desire of My Majesty between the first of the second month of Pirît of the Vth year and the 30th of the fourth month of Shomû of the VIth year which makes seven months from the day when they began to quarry it."

If we credit the ancient records, there were formerly obelisks of twice the weight of the largest now existing. The broken statue of Ramses II, at Thebes, weighed nearly nine hundred tons. Herodotus mentions a temple of Latona in the sacred enclosure at Buto, Egypt, forty cubits square, "made from one stone" and, for its roof, another stone laid over it, having a cornice four cubits deep.[1] A stone which I saw cut, but still remaining in the quarry, at Baalbec, weighs one thousand tons; and there are in the walls of the temple of that place three stones each weighing nearly one thousand tons. That part of the wall which contains them is of unknown antiquity, but it is probably contemporaneous with some of the great monuments of Egypt, the ruins of which abound with stones of gigantic size.

We know from the ancient drawings and hieroglyphic writings that colossal statues were drawn on sledges and that obelisks were sometimes transported by boat on the Nile or in the canals. By what means the great obelisks were placed on their pedestals

[1] Her. II, 155.

Cyclopean Walls, Baalbec, Syria

with the greatest precision, and without in the least marring the sharp edges of their bases, is still left wholly to conjecture.

Obelisks were originally made with a flat base which rested directly on the pedestal. Many of them were thrown down at the time of the Persian invasion and remained on the ground five hundred years, till the Roman conquest. Cleopatra's Needle, originally erected at Heliopolis, was removed to Alexandria in the reign of Augustus Cæsar. Either while lying at Heliopolis or in its removal, the corners of its base were broken off, leaving the lower surface slightly rounded.

The bronze crabs appear to have been placed under its four corners that it might rest more securely on the pedestal. The crabs were discovered in 1877 by excavations made by Mr. Dixon at the time of the removal of the companion of Cleopatra's Needle to London. Copies of inscriptions then found upon the remaining leg of one of the crabs were published by Dr. Neroutsos Bey, an antiquarian of Alexandria, and the crabs and base of the obelisk were recovered with earth.

The inscriptions, as then published and subsequently copied by Lieutenant-Commander Gorrings, inserted by him in his book and inscribed on one of the crabs now under the obelisk, erroneously gave the date of the erection of the obelisk at Alexandria as the year eight of the reign of Augustus Cæsar, 23–22 B. C., instead of the year eighteen, 13–12 B. C. This led to much discussion by antiquarians and historians, both in Europe and America, in consequence of its contradiction of what was supposed to be a well established historical fact, namely, that Barbarus (Publius Rubrius) was not at that time the prefect of Egypt, though he was the prefect ten years later. This fact had been established by a Greek inscription found on the ruins at Philæ, which read, "To the Emperor Cæsar, the August, the Savior and Benefactor, in the 18th year. Under the auspices of Publius Rubrius Barbarus."

In 1883, the question was submitted by the authorities of the Metropolitan Museum of Art, where the crab had been deposited, to Columbia College, and by the president of the College to the professor of Greek, Augustus C. Merriam. After a long and exhaustive research, being unable to reconcile the facts of history with the inscriptions as published, the professor had the leg of the crab cleaned of its oxydation. Besides bringing clearly to view some of the Greek and Latin characters that had been supplied in the reading, he found that in the Greek inscription the date was the year IH (18) of the reign of Cæsar, instead of H (8), and in the Latin inscription XVIII instead of VIII.

The correct reading of the inscription is as follows:—

L IH ΚΑΙΣΜΡΣ
ΒΑΡΒΑΡΟΣΑΝΕΘΗΚΕ
ΑΡΧΙΤΕΚΤΟΝΟΥΝΤΟ(Σ)
ΠΟΝΤΙΟΥ

The Latin L represents the word year and is used on nearly all of the dated Egyptian coins of the Greco-Roman period. I alone would be ten, IH, eighteen. The whole inscription may be translated: "In the year eighteen [of the reign] of Cæsar, Barbarus erected [or dedicated] [this monument], Pontius being the architect."

The Latin inscription was on the inner side of the claw and much injured, some of the letters being wholly effaced. The date and the other essential parts, however, were legible. The full inscription, restored, is as follows:

Ψ

ANNO XVIII CÆSARIS
BARBARVS PRÆF
ÆGYPTI POSVIT
ARCHITECTANTE PONTIO

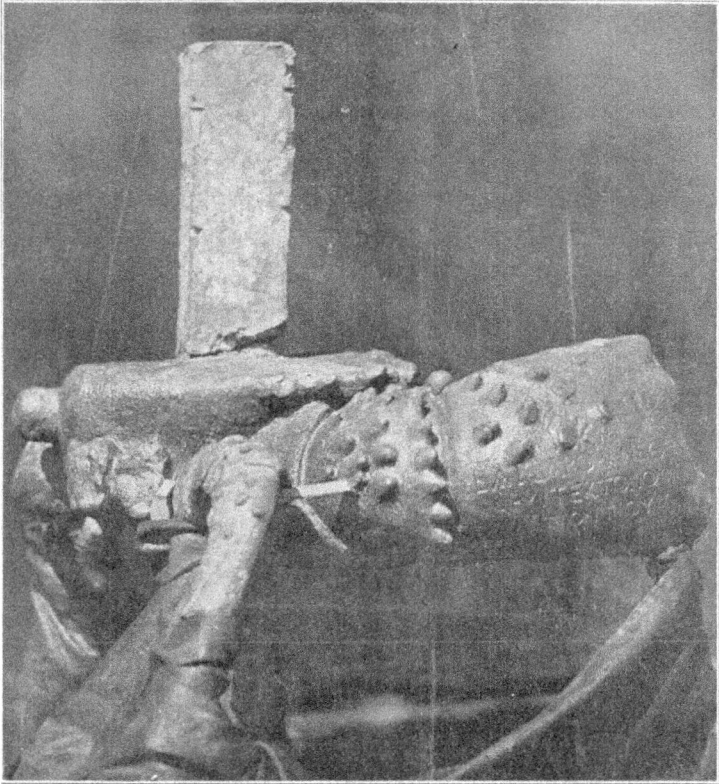

Remaining Part of One of the Bronze Crabs Which Supported the
Obelisk, Showing Greek Inscription. The Upper
Part Is One of the Dowels.

Professor Merriam was of the opinion that the Greek letter Psi (Ψ) in the upper corner was the initial of the engraver. The inscription may be translated as follows:

"In the year eighteen [of the reign] of Augustus Cæsar, Barbarus, prefect of Egypt, erected [this monument] by the architect Pontius (Pontius being the architect)."

The foundations of the pedestal consisted principally of large blocks of limestone. The whole structure below the pedestal and above the lower surface of the lower step was fastened together with "iron dogs" protected with a covering of lead, in the same manner as iron similarly used is protected at the present day. The iron was of an excellent quality and in a marvelous state of preservation, even where it had been somewhat exposed to atmospheric influences. The entire structure was a magnificent piece of work and showed that the architect, Pontius, would have been entitled, even at this day, to a position in the first rank of his profession.

In this structure were found emblems which have been regarded by many Free Masons as an important discovery relating to the history of their order. Others have taken an entirely different view. The foundations were, with the exception of four pieces, of light-colored gray limestone. On removing the pedestal, there was found under its easterly corner a large block of finely polished Syenitic granite in the form of a cube, except the height was less than the side measurement. I was present at the removal of the first tier of stone. Directly below the granite cube and on the same plane with the lower step, was another piece of granite, the upper part of which was cut in the form of a builder's square. Its long arm was eight feet six inches by one foot seven and a half inches and its short arm four feet three inches by one foot seven and three-fourths inches.

Between the arms of the square was a piece of pure white limestone, four feet long by two wide and nine inches deep. On one side of the square and touching its short arm was an irregular piece of granite, its upper surface very rough, its angles all different, and having, consequently, no two of its sides parallel. On the other side of the stone forming the square was a large block of limestone with its upper surface about four inches below that of the square. It was covered with a thin stone, on the removal of which an iron trowel and a lead plummet were found.

The trowel, which was the shape of a flattened spoon and eight inches long by five wide in its broadest part, was wholly oxydized. The handle was four inches long and three-eighths to one-half of an inch in relief. Spaces had been cut in the limestone block in which these objects had been imbedded in cement. These symbols—the square, the trowel, the plummet, the two granite blocks, the one rough and the other finely finished (the rough and the finished ashler), the white stone and the relative positions in which they were found—are claimed by some members of the Masonic Fraternity to be strong evidence of the existence in the Roman period of an order of Free Masons from which the modern orders have sprung. So many concurrent items of evidence certainly tend to prove that these objects were designedly placed as emblems in the structure. But the presence of all but the trowel and the plummet might be wholly accidental, and these might well be placed by the workmen in so famous a structure as symbols of their occupation without any reference to an organized order.

Alexandria had been a large city for over two centuries. It had recently suffered severely from battles fought within its walls and contained many ruins. These were used as far as practicable in new constructions and probably furnished the material for the foundations of the obelisk. There was nothing unusual in the form of any of the pieces, except that of the square. This stone, when taken out, was found to be twenty-five inches thick, having the part between its two arms cut out and lowered to the depth of nine inches. This space was filled with other stone, including the white block. When it was first discovered, only the upper surface of the form in a square could be seen. The lower part of the stone had the form of a rectangular parallelogram. Taken by itself, the natural inference would have been that it was a part of a large water-basin (from the court of a temple or palace), such as was common in the Greco-Roman period, and that one side and one end had been taken off, by accident or design, leaving the bottom and the other side and end as originally made.

The inside of the rim of the basin, if it was a basin, had, at its junction with the bottom, three small mouldings or beads and, on the outside at the bottom, the edges instead of having sharp angles were grooved.   There was nothing in the appearance of the stone to indicate that it was cut in the form of a builder's square for the purpose of being placed in the obelisk foundation. Its resemblance to a square, when it was in place and the space between the arms was filled, may have suggested to the workmen the idea of adding the trowel and plummet.

CHAPTER XVII

HISTORY OF OBELISK AND INSCRIPTIONS

CLEOPATRA'S NEEDLE comes to us from the golden period of Egypt's history. It was taken from the quarries of Syene, brought down the river six hundred miles, and erected at Heliopolis during the reign of Thûtmosis III, the most brilliant and famous sovereign of the long line of the Pharaohs. The central columns of its inscriptions are devoted to his praise.

Ahmosis, the founder of the eighteenth dynasty, having expelled from Egypt the last of the Hyksos, or "Shepherd Kings," who had ruled the Delta of the Nile for five centuries, led his victorious army as far as Sharuhen, a town near the southern boundary of Palestine which was subsequently allotted to the tribe of Simeon.[1] He afterwards built, to protect his country from further invasions, a series of fortifications on his eastern frontier, not far from the present line of the Suez Canal. He restored peace and order in the interior of his empire and subjugated certain tribes in Nubia that had refused to pay their customary tribute. Contenting himself with the laurels he had won, he turned his attention to the restoration, extension and embellishment of the temples which had been neglected during the long reign of the foreigners.

Thûtmosis I, the second in succession after Ahmosis, was a great warrior and carried his conquests much farther than his predecessor. He led his victorious army through Palestine and

[1] Joshua XIX, 6.

northern Syria to Naharaîm, the "land of the two rivers," which extended from the river Orontes far beyond the Euphrates, and returned to his capital, Thebes, "covered with glory" and "laden with booty." He enriched Egypt by his conquests and by the wealth he afterwards constantly drew from Syria and his southern provinces.

After a short life, he was succeeded by his son Thûtmosis II. Thûtmosis II ruled in the right of Hatshepsu, his half-sister and wife, who was in fact the real sovereign. She was, through her mother, more nearly of purely divine descent than her husband, but it had required a miracle, wrought at her birth, to purify her blood of the taint inherited from one of her maternal ancestors who was not of the royal family.

The kings of Egypt claimed descent from the gods and received homage as divine beings from their subjects. Hence the purity of the royal blood was of the first importance. The king was the "son of Râ." His father was the "son of Râ," and his grandfather and great-grandfather and so back through all his ancestors to the god himself. There were no other earthly families of divine descent with whom to contract marriages. Brothers and sisters intermarried and it was only their children who were of pure royal blood. The male child had the right of succession if he was of the same mother. It sometimes happened that a prince whose mother was only a common woman of the harem succeeded to his father's government, and those whose ancestors were wholly unknown, by success in war or by other means, became *de facto* rulers. These were not regarded by the priests and people as legitimate kings, and they often sought to legitimize their reigns and establish the succession in their children by marrying princesses of the divine blood. They made their wives queens and ruled in their right. The king also often associated with him in his government one of his children, when yet a mere child, because through its mother it was more nearly of the pure royal blood than the father. These means were not always considered sufficient to purify the blood and establish the legitimacy of the reigning family. This could only be done by a miraculous interposition of the ancestral god. Râ, the Sun-god, condescended to become incarnate in the earthly father at the moment of conception and thus the offspring became divine, a "son of Râ." Besides that of Hatshepsu there are two other instances recorded in Egyptian history of the miraculous infusion of the divine essence into the blood of royal families, viz.: that of Amenôthes III, the son of Thûtmosis IV, and of Ptolemy Cæsarion, the son of Julius Cæsar. These inventions of the priests were believed by them to be political necessities.[1]

Thûtmosis I also reigned in the right of his wife. His mother was a mere concubine. To legalize his *de facto* government and continue the divine succession he made Hatshepsu his associate when she was a child.

Thûtmosis II died, after a short and uneventful reign, at the age of thirty. He left one son, Thûtmosis III, whose mother, Isis, was a woman of low birth. He was then a child, but his aunt, Queen Hatshepsu, proclaimed him her successor and continued to rule in his name, as she had previously done in the name of her husband. This nominally dual government continued upwards of sixteen years and ended at a time and in a manner of which the monuments give us no account. It was a prosperous, peaceful reign in which Egypt continued to amass wealth, build and beautify temples and erect other magnificent monuments.

Thûtmosis III was about twenty-five years old when he became sole ruler. He immediately entered upon his glorious career of conquests. About a hundred years had elapsed since the expulsion of the "Shepherd Kings," during which period

[1] Maspero's "Struggle of the Nations," M. L. McClure's translation, demy quarto ed., pp. 236, 237.

the foundations of the empire had been firmly laid. But it was left to this ruler, to whom we are indebted for our obelisk, to raise Egypt to the highest rank among the then existing nations. Including the time he was associated with Hatshepsu, he reigned nearly fifty-five years.

His whole reign was a succession of victorious campaigns, which extended the boundaries of the empire and brought to Egypt a constant flow of gold, silver, horses, cattle, sheep and other useful animals, and all the forms of personal wealth known to the commerce of that period.

From the twenty-third year of his reign to the fortieth, he conducted against the Asiatic nations fourteen campaigns. He made long marches in strange and hostile countries, crossing rivers, mountains and deserts, taking by siege and storm stronghold after stronghold and, finally, destroying or subjugating every tribe and people who dared to resist the victorious and beloved son of the god Amon. In the language of the hieroglyphics, he extended his boundaries in the south to the remotest lands of inner Africa; in the west, beyond the tribes of the Lybian desert and along the shore of the sea; and, in the east and north, to the land of the "two rivers" and the "four pillars of heaven."

He was acknowledged by his contemporaries to be the conqueror and ruler of the world and was regarded by his faithful subjects with reverence and awe as a divine being. Under his rule, Egypt became the central point of the world's influence both in commerce and war. His long reign and the immense resources at his disposal, arising from the annual tributes of the conquered countries, enabled him to carry out his early conceived plans for increasing the number and enlarging and decorating the temples of the gods of Egypt, of whom he considered himself an emanation and a part.

It was in this and the immediately succeeding reigns that Egyptian art reached its highest degree of perfection. The centuries that have passed have left us, in most cases, only heaps of ruins; but enough remains to give us a full knowledge of the marvelous monuments of this period. Whether we consider the grandeur of the original conceptions, the grace of the massive forms, the completeness and symmetry of the structures, the elegance and effectiveness of the ornamental designs or the fineness, beauty and fidelity of their execution, we must conclude that the artists of the sixteenth century before our era produced master works that have never since been surpassed. It was Egypt's golden period in power and glory, in war and commerce, in wealth and art, and even historians and poets were not wanting. Indeed, it is to these we are indebted for the very full knowledge we now have of this wonderful people.

Among the monumental works of Thûtmosis III, his obelisks occupy a prominent place. That of St. John Lateran at Rome is one of his, though it appears from its inscriptions to have been finished and erected some time after his death by Thûtmosis IV. It has been somewhat shortened, but it is still one hundred and five feet in height and is the largest existing obelisk, except the unfinished one lying in the quarry at Assuân. It weighs five hundred tons and that of Assuân over seven hundred. It was one of a pair erected in front of the temple of Amon at Karnak. The inscription says: "The king has raised these immense obelisks to him (Amon) in the forecourt of the House of God."

The remaining part of an obelisk now at Constantinople was also his work, and has been attributed to the early part of his sole reign. Like the other Egyptian obelisks, it is of rose-colored Syenitic granite, and its inscriptions were carved in the elegant style of the period. The king here tells us of his Asiatic conquests: "King Thûtmosis III passed through the whole extent of the land of Naharaîm as a victorious conqueror at the head of his army. He placed his boundary at the horn of the world, and at the hinder water-land of Naharaîm."

Cleopatra's Needle and its companion now in London were originally erected by him at one of the gates of the Temple of the Sun at Heliopolis, probably toward the end of his life, about fifteen hundred years before Christ. He restored and beautified the then ancient temple and, according to the inscriptions, built a wall around it in the year forty-seven of his reign.

Heliopolis was sometimes called the city of obelisks from the number of these monuments it contained. It had been a city of obelisks for a long period previous to the time of Seti I, and yet this monarch is spoken of on the monuments as "having filled Heliopolis with obelisks to illumine with their rays the Temple of the Sun." The obelisks, or, at least, their inscriptions, were gilded with gold or other metals. An inscription on the Temple of Amon at Karnak describes certain objects dedicated by the king, Thûtmosis III, to this god. Among them was a "beautiful harp, inlaid with silver and gold, and blue, green and other precious stones," a statue of the king, giving his exact likeness, "such as had never been seen in Egypt since the days of the Sun-god Râ," and "obelisks on which silver, gold, iron and copper were not spared and which shone in their splendor on the surface of the water and filled the land with their light like the stars on the body of the heavenly goddess Nut."

The obelisks stood in pairs at the gates of the temple, to which long avenues, with rows of sphinxes on either side, conducted. Heliopolis was not only one of the oldest cities of Egypt, famous for its monuments and the worship of the bull Mnevis, but for many centuries it was the seat of Egyptian learning. Many Grecian philosophers came to Heliopolis, during its later years, to add to their store of knowledge from the wisdom of its priests.

The long and glorious history of Heliopolis was suddenly ended by the Persian invasion, 525 B. C. From that time, though the priests afterwards restored the worship of the Sun-god, incarnate in the sacred bull Mnevis, the city has remained deserted.

According to Herodotus, Cambyses, the son of Cyrus, when a youth of ten years, promised his mother that when he became a man he would "turn Egypt upside down." The promise was loyally kept. We have no history of the details of the destruction of the sacred city and can only judge of what was done by the cruel and sacrilegious character of the Persians and the condition in which it was afterwards found by Greek and Roman travelers. When Strabo visited it, five hundred years later, 24 B. C., twelve years before the erection of our obelisk in Alexandria, he found only a deserted city, but the faithful priests, tenaciously clinging to the old religion, were still worshipping in the ruined temple. He says:

"Here in Heliopolis, upon a large mound, one sees the Temple of the Sun where the bull Mnevis is kept in a sanctuary. He is regarded as a god, as the Apis is at Memphis. In the front of the mound are lakes fed by the neighboring canal. The city is now wholly deserted. Its ancient temple, built in the Egyptian style, bears numerous marks of the fury and sacrilegious spirit of Cambyses, who ravaged the holy buildings, mutilating them with fire and violence. In this manner he injured the obelisks. Two of these monuments that were not greatly damaged were taken to Rome. There are others of these obelisks, both here and at Thebes, now Diospolis, some standing, much eaten by fire, and others thrown down and lying on the ground."

From this description, the cause of the rounding of the base of Cleopatra's Needle and the injured condition of its sides is evident. It and its companion were probably lying on the ground at Heliopolis from the time of the Persian invasion until they were removed by the Romans to Alexandria. They were not only thrown down and otherwise injured by Cambyses, but they suffered from the alkalies of the soil and the fires of the natives who prepared their food beside them for five hundred years.

The Obelisk, Cleopatra's Needle, in Central Park, New York.

Heliopolis is but an hour's drive from Cairo. The first object seen is its solitary obelisk in the distant fields. There are a few low mounds in the vicinity and occasional ruins protruding from the soil. These and the lone obelisk are the only marks of the site of the once famous city. This obelisk is the oldest of the large obelisks that have been discovered. It was erected by Úsertesen I of the twelfth dynasty, nearly a thousand years earlier than the time of Thûtmosis III. Centuries before Abraham was born, even before the recorded time of the flood, the priests of On (Heliopolis) read the deeply cut inscriptions on this obelisk that we read to-day. The same inscription is repeated on each side. The translation is as follows:—

"The Hor of the Sun,
 The life for those who are born,
 The king of the upper and lower land,
 Khepher-ka-ra.
 The lord of the double crown,
 The life of those who are born,
 The son of the Sun-god Râ,
 Usertesen.
 The friend of the spirit of On,
 Ever living,
 The golden Hor,
 The life of those who are born,
 The good god,
 Kheper-ka-ra,
 Has erected this work,

 In the beginning of the thirty years cycle,
 He the dispenser of life forever."

Úsertesen was one of the great kings of the twelfth dynasty and had a prosperous reign of forty-five years, including ten years in which he was associated with his father. In the third year of his reign, after counseling with the high officials of his court, he ordered the "raising of worthy buildings to the Sun-god Râ." He either restored or enlarged the temple, which was already ancient even in that remote period. When the great gate was finished, he erected at its entrance a pair of obelisks, of which the obelisk now standing was one. Its companion was often mentioned by the old Greek and Arab writers, and remained standing till A. D. 1160, when it fell and was broken.[1] The pyramidions of these obelisks were covered with copper caps, which, according to these writers, were of great weight and value. They also had figures carved upon them.

The New York obelisk, before its removal from the sacred city of Heliopolis, had long outlived its own civilization. It had passed through the whole of Egypt's golden period. It had looked down upon the boy Moses, as he went daily, with the noble youths of the land, to receive instruction from the priests of the Temple of the Sun; and Moses, on his part, beheld with admiration the then golden hieroglyphs, that so long puzzled the wise men of modern times, but which he read as a student reads his Latin. It had beheld the chosen people of God in the days of their oppression and witnessed the excitement at the time of the Exodus—the hurrying to and fro of the priests of the temple and the groups of the people in the public places of the city discussing the great event.

It had afterwards watched for eight centuries the passing of the generations during the reign of the Pharaohs, and had looked down not only upon these monarchs, but upon all the long lines of scholars who came to seek knowledge in this famous city of learning. It had then mutely witnessed the conquest of the

[1] De Lancy in his notes accompanying his translation of Abel-ul-Latif, from the Arabic into French, cites at length the statements of these writers relative to this obelisk.

Persians and seen the city of On and its temples destroyed, and itself and many of its companion obelisks become victims of the vengeance of the sacrilegious soldiers of Cambyses.

Afterwards, lying upon the ground, where it had been left by the Persians, it had seen Plato in his daily walks pursuing his study of philosophy and astronomy. It had then beheld the coming of Alexander the Great into its surrounding ruin and desolation and his warm reception by the people as their deliverer from the yoke of the Persians; and later, the three hundred years' reign of the Ptolemies.

On the coming of the Cæsars, it had left the ruin and decay of its inland town and been transferred to the busy seaport of Alexandria. Here, standing upon the seashore, a beacon to mariners for nineteen hundred years, it watched the rolling waves and the coming and going of the ships on the one side and the kaleidoscope of human events on the other.

Rebellions and insurrections, invasions and conquests; the struggles between paganism and Christianity, between Christianity and Mohammedanism and between the different dynasties of Arabs and Turks; the successive reigns of Sultans, Khalifs and Mamelukes; the conquest of Napoleon and the land and sea battles between the English and French were all seen by this ancient monument while standing at Alexandria. What it is to see during the coming centuries, in its new home within a metropolis that had not even an existence when it was three thousand years old, can only be related by historians to be born in the distant future.

The ancient Egyptians had a literature far surpassing that of any other of the early peoples. Only a small part of it has come to us. Many hundreds of inscriptions, however, have been preserved on stone and papyrus. The more they are studied the greater is the admiration of the scholar. Some of these inscriptions are historical; others relate to religious beliefs.

Of all the Egyptian writings, the inscriptions on the obelisks are the least interesting. They are devoted to the boastful self-praises of the kings and the affirmation of their descent from the gods. Those on the pyramidion and the central columns of the New York obelisk were inscribed by Thûtmosis III. Nearly three hundred years later, Ramses II used the vacant space on each side of the central column. He was not only famous for his numerous and great works, but he was also the great appropriator of the works of his predecessors for the record of his own name and fame. The two outer columns which he inscribed on each face of the obelisk tell us of his abundant years, his great victories, and that he is the son of the Sun-god Râ, the issue of his loins.

Four hundred years later, Osarken I placed close to the outer edge of each face, near the base of the obelisk, inscriptions informing succeeding generations that he was the king of Upper and Lower Egypt, and a descendant of the Sun-god. This king, under the Bible name of Zerah, was defeated by Asa in a great battle in the south of Palestine.[1]

On the east face of the pyramidion, Thûtmosis III is represented as a sphinx couchant on a pedestal, holding in his hands two vases and in the act of offering a libation to the hawk-headed Ra-Harmachis, the Sun-god of On (Heliopolis). Thûtmosis is here called, "The Good God," "Lord of the Two Lands" (Upper and Lower Egypt), "Men-Kheper-Ra," and "The Bull of Victory arisen in Thebes, son of the Sun, Thûtmosis." Under the vases in the half-effaced inscription may be read, "Giving Wine."

The central column of hieroglyphs, that of Thûtmosis III, on the east face of the obelisk, is translated as follows:

[1] II Chron. XIV, 9–13.

Banner-name

"The crowned Horus
Bull of Victory
Arisen in Thebes.

.

"The lord of the Vulture and Uræus crowns
Prolonged as to kingdom,
Even as the sun in the heavens.
By Tum lord of On begotten,
Son of his loins, who hath been
fashioned by Thot,
Whom they created in the great-temple
With the perfections of their flesh,
Knowing what he was to perform,
Kingdom prolonged through ages,
King of Upper and Lower Egypt
Men-kheper-ra (Thûtmosis III),
Loving Tum, the great god,
With his cycle of divinities,
Who giveth all life stay and sway,
Like the sun forever."

Central column, north face.

Banner-name

"The crowned Horus
Tall with the southern crown
Loving Ra.

.   .   .   .   .   .

"The king of Upper and Lower Egypt,
Men-kheper-ra (Thûtmosis III),
The golden Horus, content with victory,

Who smiteth the rulers of the nations—
Hundreds of thousands;
In as much as father Ra
Hath ordered unto him
Victory against every land,
Gathered together;
The valor of the scimeter
In the palms of his hands
To broaden the bounds of Egypt;
Son of the Sun, Thûtmosis III,
Who giveth all life forever."

Inscriptions of Ramses II

Translation of the south column of the east face.

Banner-name
"The crowned Horus,
Bull of victory
Son of Kheper-ra.

.   .   .   .

"The king of Upper and Lower Egypt
User-ma-ra (Ramses II).
The chosen of Ra, the golden Horus
Rich in years, great in victory,
Son of the Sun, Ramses II,
Who came forth from the womb
To receive the crowns of Ra;
Fashioned was he to be the sole ruler,
The lord of the Two Lands,
User-ma-ra (Ramses II),
The chosen of Ra, son of the Sun,
Ramessu Meiamun (Ramses II),

The Hieroglyphics on the Four Sides of the
Obelisk in Central Park, New York.

Glorified of Osiris
Like the Sun life-giving forever."

North Column.

Banner-name
"The crowned Horus
  Bull of Victory
  Loving Ra.

.   .   .   .

"The king of Upper and Lower Egypt
 User-ma-ra (Ramses II),
 The chosen of Ra,
 The Sun born of divinities,
 Taking the Two Lands,
 Son of the Sun,
 Ramessu Meiamun (Ramses II);
 The youth
 Beautiful for love,
 Like the orb of the Sun
 When he shines in the horizon,
 The lord of the Two Lands,
 User-ma-ra (Ramses II),
 The chosen of Ra,
 Son of the Sun
 Ramessu Meiamun,
 Glorified of Osiris,
 Life giving like the Sun forever."

There are also some nearly effaced hieroglyphics at the bottom
of the obelisk. They have been translated as: "Life gracious-
god, Ramses II." This phrase is repeated several times at the
bottom of each face.

The other inscriptions on the different sides of the obelisk are of the same character and to a large extent repetitions of those of which the translations have been given.

On two sides of the pyramidion, Ramses III, as a sphinx couchant, is represented as offering libations to the Sun-god, Ra-Harmachis (the rising sun) and on the other two sides to Tum (the setting sun).

CHAPTER XVIII

WHAT EGYPT HAS DONE FOR ENGLAND—THE SUEZ CANAL

Soon after my first arrival in Cairo, the remnant of the Khedivial army, which had met with disastrous defeat in an attempt to invade Abyssinia, returned to Egypt. The facts of the losses of the campaign had till that time been mostly concealed.

In August of the previous year, the Khedive had sent to Massowah two thousand men to invade Abyssinia for the purpose of obtaining redress for continued grievances. It was claimed that the Abyssinians, in their raids in search of booty, crossed over their border into the Sudân, driving off cattle and committing other depredations. The Khedivial troops were met by King Johannes with an army of natives, claimed to have numbered thirty thousand, and were almost wholly annihilated. Only about thirty men escaped the massacre.

As soon as it could be prepared, an army of sixteen thousand men was sent to retrieve the lost prestige of the Egyptians. It was under the nominal command of Prince Hassan, a youthful son of the Khedive, who had received a military education in England, but the real commander was Ratif Pasha, who had acquired some distinction by his services in the Sudân.

General Loring accompanied him in the position of adviser. According to the account which the General personally gave the writer, the Khedive, in his presence, enjoined Ratif Pasha to follow strictly his advice in every military movement.

General Loring was a resident of Florida. When only a lad he ran away from home, went to Texas and engaged in the war then being carried on by the people of that state, under General Sam Houston, against the Mexicans under Santa Anna. He served as an officer under General Scott in the Mexican War, and distinguished himself at the storming of one of the gates of the City of Mexico, where he lost an arm. He was afterwards engaged in our Indian wars on the western frontier and, at the commencement of the War of Secession, was a colonel in our army. He resigned his commission, entered the Confederate service, became a General, and was a good fighting officer, but never achieved more than a moderate success.

Some years after the close of this war, being out of employment, he entered the Khedivial army with the rank of a general. He claimed to have been engaged in seventy-five battles. He was a very agreeable and interesting gentleman, but he had the hot Southern blood and an ungovernable temper, and this peculiarity contributed not a little, according to the opinion of high Egyptian officials, to the disastrous results of the Abyssinian campaign.

The Egyptian army, after some days' march into the interior, was met by the Abyssinians and defeated with great loss. General Loring's advice was completely ignored. According to his views, if it had been followed, the army would have been successful. The more recent experiences of the Italians, however, clearly prove that the invasion of Abyssinia is a difficult task. The success of the English in 1868 was due to discords among the Abyssinians and the want of a centralized governing power.

The second Egyptian defeat was not as disastrous as the first one, nor even as that suffered by the Italians. The Abyssinians themselves met with severe losses, and the Egyptian Government was enabled to withdraw its army, and re-establish peace on what was called "honorable terms."

The Khedive probably sent his first small expedition to Massowah with the intention of taking and holding a small province lying between that place and the Sudân. No less ambitious a design than the conquering of Abyssinia, or a considerable part of it, would have prompted the sending of so large and expensive an expedition as the second. In addition to the loss of life, the cost was over $5,000,000. The army was transferred from different parts of Egypt to Suez and thence by water over one thousand miles to Massowah. All of the provisions of the commissariat and, to a large extent, the means of their transportation into a physically difficult and hostile country, without roads or civilization, were also shipped from Suez.

The Khedive had already conquered and added to his possessions an immense extent of territory in Central Africa. His name was a power from the mouths of the Nile to its sources in the Albert and Victoria Nyanzas, a distance by the way of the river of over three thousand miles.

Over all this territory he held undisputed sway. His word was law; and the life and liberty of six millions of people in Egypt proper, and as many more in the Sudân and Central Africa, were subject to his arbitrary will. The Abyssinian campaign was the first check to his grand schemes of territorial aggrandizement, and his disappointment can easily be understood.

It would be assuming too much good nature and too gentle a disposition in an Oriental potentate to suppose that he was in good humor on learning the real facts. His native officers, to avoid their own disgrace, put the blame upon the Americans, thereby very much increasing for them the difficulties of getting a settlement of their accounts, when they were discharged two years later.

Accusations were especially made against General Loring and Colonel Dye. No one had fought more bravely, nor done more to save the Egyptians from defeat, than the latter. Yet, when no facts could be found to sustain any other charge, an order was issued for his arrest and trial before a court-martial for having struck with his hand one of his inferior native officers. The state of feeling was such that the Colonel came to the Consulate-General, demanding protection, and remained there several days. After I had had several interviews with the Khedive, the matter was dropped and, on the Colonel's discharge two years afterwards, I obtained for him an indemnity of five thousand dollars on account of a wound received in the Abyssinian battle, from which he was still suffering. The same amount was obtained for Colonel Colston also on account of loss of health in the Sudân.

After long and tedious negotiations, the accounts of all the Americans who had served as officers in the Khedivial army, about forty in number, were satisfactorily settled and paid.

In Egyptian finance, the Abyssinian War was "the last straw that broke the camel's back." During the organization of the company for the construction of the Suez Canal, after M. de Lesseps had sold all that was possible in Europe of the capital stock of 200,000,000 francs, there still remained unsold 177,642 shares out of the whole number of 400,000. Saîd Pasha, then Viceroy of Egypt, subscribed, in the name of his Government, for all of these remaining shares a sum amounting to over $17,500,000.

At the time of the preparations for the second Abyssinian expedition, the financial situation of Egypt became serious. Not only was ten, twelve and even fourteen per cent interest paid on the amounts received on loans, but as high as two per cent a month was paid on temporary loans and for carrying overdue obligations. Up to this time the Khedive had not defaulted in his payments, but he found it difficult to procure the means necessary for his expensive Abyssinian campaign. In his embarrassment, he was negotiating for a loan on the pledge of his canal shares as security for its payment.

The French bankers thought they had within reach an opportunity for another rich, usurious contract. Ten and twelve per cent interest was demanded. There was an attempt to form a syndicate in Paris to make the loan. The amount to be raised was large and the procuring of the money difficult. Some of the bankers whose aid was asked had affiliations in London. Acting under the influence of their London associates they "threw cold water on the undertaking" and retarded the negotiations. Application was made to the French Ministry for aid. It was argued that the securing of the Suez Canal shares was a transaction of such national importance that the Government should not only lend its influence but should aid financially.

It was expected by those attempting to form the syndicate that, through the loan, they would become the owners of the stock, and that the loan would in effect be a purchase. M. Decazes, then the French Minister of Foreign Affairs, was courting the English. He was very desirous of their friendship, on account of the strained relations between France and Germany, and did not wish in any manner to take the risk of offending them. Through his diplomatic representative in London, he informed Lord Derby, the English Minister of Foreign Affairs, that there was a report that the Khedive was negotiating with a French financial company for the sale of his Suez Canal shares and asked if England would have any objection to such sale. The prompt answer was, "Certainly England would be opposed to these shares becoming the property of a French company."

Disraeli saw and quickly seized the opportunity. He counselled with the Rothschilds and they agreed to furnish the money, take the stock and wait the future confirmation of the purchase by an act of Parliament. Within less than three days, the Suez Canal shares were the property of England and the certificates in the possession of the English Consul-General in Cairo. Disraeli acted without authority, but, in the eyes of the English, he was in the position of a General who, by disregarding or acting without orders, has won a great victory. The act of Parliament was easily obtained. The commissions of the Rothschilds in this transaction, in addition to the interest on the money loaned, amounted to half a million dollars.

Disraeli said to the Khedive, through his diplomatic representative in Cairo, "We will buy the Suez Canal shares, advance the money, and require only the payment of five per cent interest on the amount of the purchase money during the period for which the interest coupons and the right to dividends has been taken by the Canal Company." This was half the minimum rate of interest Egypt was then paying. The Khedive caught at the alluring offer and the purchase was completed before the French had had an intimation of the negotiations. Egypt then had remaining 176,602 shares of its canal stock. These were transferred to England for £3,976,583. It was a *"grand coup"* for Disraeli, but a death blow to the Khedive, the most serious political as well as financial mistake of his life.

In the settlement of one of M. de Lesseps' claims, the interest and dividend coupons of these bonds had been cut off and transferred to his company for the intervening time up to 1895. During the remainder of this period, Egypt agreed to pay and did pay to England, five per cent per annum on the money advanced for the canal shares, that is, about $1,000,000 per annum.

A year later than the end of this period, November, 1896, these shares were worth in London £23,841,270. In dollars, the amount paid was $19,256,661, and the value at the time named was $115,391,746, leaving England a net profit of $96,135,085— a sum equal to the original cost of the canal. England had also received up to that date two per cent more annual interest on the money advanced than she paid on her own obligations. Since that time, the net income of the canal has been so largely increased that the price of the stock has risen in the market to nine times its par value, which would give England a profit of over $130,000,000 besides the high rate of interest and, since 1896, the dividends she has received. According to a statement published by the House of Commons in 1884, this difference of interest which was figured at one and one-half per cent had already liquidated nearly $500,000 (£99,414) of the debt created on account of the purchase of these canal shares.

This immense pecuniary profit is only a small part of what England has gained by the transaction. She has gained Egypt itself with its Central African provinces and the Sudân, territory sufficient for an empire. From the moment of the purchase, she regarded the canal as an English possession and, "to protect her interest," it was necessary from an English standpoint to control the country through which it passed. From that time on, this has been her purpose. In every move on the diplomatic chess-board, this purpose has been kept in view by England's controlling statesmen. Nor have there been any scruples about the employment of means that would aid in its realization.

France, since the time of the conquest in Egypt of the first Napoleon, had tried to maintain a preponderance of political influence in that country. England had been her constant and powerful rival preventing the realization of her ambition.

France, through one of her citizens, had obtained the grant of the Suez Canal franchise. A French company, by the aid of the then powerful Napoleon III, succeeded in constructing the canal against the wishes and the strong active opposition of England, both in Egypt and at Constantinople. The French, on the completion of this great work, believed that they had obtained a permanent advantage over the English. Marseilles was to become a Liverpool and France was to maintain a dominating influence in the land of the Nile.

England soon learned that the canal, contrary to her former opinion, was of much more importance and benefit to her than to all other nations. From the time of her full realization of this fact, it is not improbable that she had her eyes on the Khedive's canal shares. Absolute secrecy was necessary for success; otherwise, the French would have protested, and either made the purchase or prevented the sale. When the opportune moment arrived, no time was lost.

It has been said by those who assume to have a knowledge of the facts that M. de Lesseps was in the secret and privately aided the English in the purchase. This may have been true, though it is not probable. It is claimed, on the other hand, that he was very active in his efforts to form the French syndicate for the purchase of the stock. His interest, however, at that time, was in the revenue and the consequent value of the stock. He foresaw that, if the English were interested, the business of the canal and its revenues would be increased. It is certain that he never manifested any hostile feelings against the Khedive on account of this transaction. The French people, however, never forgave his Highness. Nothing that he did afterwards pleased them.

M. de Lesseps was undoubtedly correct in saying soon after the purchase that it would be an advantage to the company. The English interest, thus acquired, became, in fact, a valuable aid in augmenting the revenues of the canal. This arose not so much from the increase of tonnage passing through the canal on account of the purchase as from England's aid in fixing and maintaining the tolls. Without this interest, England would not have remained silent while paying tolls on her immense tonnage transported through the canal, in consequence of which the price of the stock has increased to nine times its par value. She would have long since found "just cause" of complaint and demanded and enforced reduction.

There are other reasons for the phenomenal rise in the value of the canal shares. The canal nominally cost about $91,000,000. Of this sum 200,000,000 francs were realized for stock, 100,000,000 were borrowed and 124,000,000 were wrongfully taken from

Egypt by and as a result of an award of Napoleon III. There was an interest account which made up the balance of the nominal cost of the canal. Of the capital from which the canal was constructed, Egypt paid for her canal shares 88,801,000 francs of principal which, added to the 124,000,000 mentioned, make 212,801,000 francs. All the other stockholders paid for their stock only 111,101,000 francs. Thus Egypt furnished of the capital stock, in dollars, 40,000,000 and all the other stockholders 22,000,000. The 124,000,000 francs ($24,000,000) were taken from Egypt in a manner that cannot be too severely characterized. It was a disgraceful national fraud.

The Suez Canal project, with all its disastrous consequences to Egypt, was a legacy to Ismaîl Pasha left by his immediate predecessor, Saîd Pasha. The original grants for the construction of the canal and the various privileges mentioned in them were made "subject to the ratification of his Imperial Majesty the Sultan." They had no validity without such ratification. "As to the work of excavating the canal, it was to be commenced after the authorization of the Sublime Porte." The work, however, was commenced in the spring of 1859, without the authorization of the Porte, and was continued under these conditions for four years.

On the granting of the first concession, England commenced at Constantinople and Cairo strenuous opposition to the whole scheme of the canal. One of the arguments presented to the Sultan was that, under the guise of workmen, regiments of Zouaves would be introduced into and take possession of Egypt. To obviate this objection, which the Sultan made at the instigation of Lord Palmerston, M. de Lesseps had inserted in a second act of concession a clause providing that "four-fifths of the laborers should be Egyptians."

In one of the acts of concession, the canal company was ceded the right to excavate a canal to conduct fresh water from the

Nile to the Suez Canal. It provided, furthermore, that, in case of the construction of such a canal, Egypt was to "abandon to the company" all the then unoccupied desert lands that might be irrigated by its waters with the right of the navigation of the canal and other privileges—all of which grants were subject to the ratification of the Sultan.

When M. de Lesseps was ready to commence work, he said to the Viceroy that there should be an agreement as to the price to be paid the laborers. An agreement was made fixing the price for adults at fifteen cents a day, for those under twelve years of age at twelve and a half cents, with an allowance of five cents a day to each class for food. It was the children that to a large extent carried the dirt out and emptied it on the banks.

The pay would have been adequate had it been for work in the cultivated parts of Egypt and near the villages of the laborers, but, under the conditions which actually prevailed, it was a mere pittance.

The canal was constructed across the desert at a distance varying from fifteen to sixty miles east of the cultivated land. During the first four years of the work, not only the provisions but the water for the use of the laborers were conveyed across this strip of desert on camels. Sixteen hundred camels and upwards, furnished by Egypt, were constantly employed for this purpose. During the same period, twenty to twenty-five thousand people were furnished by the *corvée*, or forced labor, to work on the canal. These were replaced, at periods of one to three months, by fresh levies.

According to information obtained from those who were cognizant of the facts, even the small sums agreed upon for the laborers were, for the most part, not paid to them, but to the Viceroy, Saîd Pasha. In proceedings afterwards instituted, it was admitted that nearly a million dollars (4,500,000 francs) of the small amounts due to these people, a large proportion of whom were children, had not been paid to anyone. What is more, it was never paid. It was offset against interest on damages claimed for not continuing to furnish the *corvée* laborers.

The Viceroy, Saîd Pasha, and M. de Lesseps had, in their younger days, been friends when the father of the latter was the representative of France in Egypt. The acts of concession were "To my devoted friend of high birth and elevated rank, M. Ferdinand de Lesseps." The Pasha was a man of moderate mental capacity and during the last years of his reign in delicate health. The influence over him of the vigorous, polite and ever fascinating M. de Lesseps was nearly unlimited. This accounts in a large degree for some of the remarkable conditions under which the work of the canal was carried on until after his death.

During the time the work was being done under the acts of concession, void, by their very terms, on account of not having been approved and ratified by the Sultan, the English Ambassador at Constantinople had been ceaseless in his efforts to throw obstacles in the way of the enterprise. As an argument to induce his Imperial Majesty not only passively to withhold his ratification of the concession, but to intervene actively and stop the work, he claimed that a French colony would be established on the desert land to be irrigated by the fresh water canal, the excavation of which had been commenced by the canal company, and that this colony would put in jeopardy his sovereignty in Egypt. It was also claimed that the *corvée* laborers were cruelly treated and were dying like flies.

The question of the French colony on the then desert lands was disposed of by the canal company. It is probable that intimations of the Sultan's apprehension were communicated to M. de Lesseps by the French Ambassador at Constantinople and that these had their influence. There were other weighty reasons for the company's action. Its funds were nearly exhausted and it was evident that it would be unable to construct a fresh water canal of sufficient capacity to meet its needs. It was also evident that the value of the desert lands, if they could be utilized at all, would not exceed the cost of putting them in a condition for cultivation.

Ismaîl Pasha had become Viceroy and it was with him that negotiations were thenceforward to be conducted. It had been learned that the canal, to give sufficient water, instead of connecting with an irrigating canal near Zagazig, must be continued to Cairo. Under the claim that the company's ownership of this canal might lead to complications with the people along the line and with the Government, the company proposed to renounce their right to construct it, and persuaded the Viceroy to accept this renunciation and undertake the work himself. The company at the same time retroceded to Egypt the land granted to it which it was supposed could be irrigated by this canal.

A few days later, April 6, 1863, the Sultan, in a despatch, communicated to the parties interested the condition on which he would ratify the concessions, viz.: that the clause in one of the acts stipulating "that four-fifths of the laborers employed in the work on the canal should be Egyptians" should be abrogated. This condition was accepted by all the parties interested.

The Viceroy, therefore, in obedience to the Sultan, discontinued furnishing laborers by the *corvée*. The concessions having been made subject to the ratification of the Sultan, and the retrocession of the lands and of the rights of constructing the fresh water canal having not only been made voluntarily, but on the initiative and in accordance with the expressed wishes of the company, the Viceroy believed, and had good reasons for believing, that the matter was closed. He had not then fully learned all the lessons of diplomacy. M. de Lesseps was an adept in that line, a most accomplished diplomat.

The company needed and must have more money or its enterprise would be a failure. The work had not progressed far enough to permit loans sufficient for its continuance. Saîd Pasha had saved the company from failure at an early day by taking the stock that could not be sold elsewhere, thus adding to the company's available assets 88,801,000 francs. Why should not Ismaîl, in the commencement of his reign, do even better? It was during the American War of Secession. Cotton was high and Egypt was supposed to possess untold wealth. Certainly, in a country where events often produce the most unexpected results, the chances of success were worth the trial.

The attack was begun.

First: a large claim was made for damages for not furnishing the *corvée* labor.

Second: another, for the desert land that had been retroceded.

Third: another, for the amount that had been expended on the abandoned canal.

Fourth: another, for the amount that it was estimated it would cost to complete the canal.

Fifth: still another, for the value of the water which the completed canal would furnish.

The Viceroy was alarmed, but his objections were wholly disregarded. The French Consul-General and M. de Lesseps were persistent in their demands. Finally, the whole matter was submitted to Napoleon III as sole arbiter. He was then the all powerful monarch of Europe. The Viceroy had absolute confidence in his Imperial Majesty, and no suspicion of disastrous results.

The award was quickly prepared by French attorneys and signed by Napoleon. It astonished the jurists of all Europe, and, had it not been of so serious a character, would have been regarded as a judicial curiosity.

His majesty awarded the company 38,000,000 francs damages on account of the withholding of the *corvée* labor.

He found further that the company could not be considered as having retroceded the land and the benefits they would have received from the fresh water canal, except on the supposition that it was to be reimbursed for these lands and the benefits they would have received under the concession. On this finding, he awarded the company: 30,000,000 francs for 60,000 hectares of desert land (about 120,000 acres) that it was assumed could be irrigated by this canal; 10,000,000 francs that the company claimed to have expended on the canal including some interest on damages; and 6,000,000 francs, on account of water that the company had thought might be sold to outside parties.

The whole award amounted to 84,000,000 francs.

It was also decided by the award that the company was entitled to all the benefits it would have derived from the canal, had it been constructed at its own expense, such as tolls, right of navigation and the use of all the fresh water needed for the success of its enterprise. The amount of water to be received was fixed at 70,000 cubic metres per day. The canal was necessarily large and nearly 100 miles in length. It was constructed at a cost of 50,000,000 francs and was to be perpetually cleaned and kept in repair by Egypt. The canal company was to receive its waters gratuitously. Egypt was to pay the company 30,000,000 francs, for the worthless land it was supposed might be irrigated with its waters, 10,000,000 francs on account of labor done on the canal and certain interest on supposed damages, and 6,000,000 francs for water that it was expected the company could sell to other parties! That is, Egypt gratuitously gives the company the right to construct a canal and to receive the benefits therefrom. She gives also certain lands that might be irrigated with its waters. The project is abandoned by the canal company and the land is retroceded unconditionally. Egypt, however, must construct the canal at her own expense, and the canal company is to receive not only the benefits of its waters, but also compensation for all the lands it might have irrigated, had not the company otherwise used its waters!

But the end was not yet in sight. The wonderful success of this attack on the treasury of Egypt only encouraged the making of others. The company had forgotten some of its "just claims." A second attack was prepared. The second claims were, like the first, utterly groundless. That was of no importance. They were claims, and a claim made at that time by one who had as a supporter the great and all powerful Napoleon III must be considered as an obligation. A Frank could never be considered in the wrong. This non-Christian people had not then learned all the righteous ways of the enlightened and superior Christian nations. The 84,000,000 francs and the 50,000,000 francs to be expended on the fresh water canal for the use of the company were not enough to meet its needs. The pound of flesh was not sufficient.

Among the newly discovered "just claims" was a large one for buildings for the Egyptian laborers, so-called "hospitals and barracks," which were now asserted to be useless to the company because of the discontinuance of the *corvée* laborers. This was, in effect, an admission that the company was to have no more work done by hand-labor, that is, that the Egyptians were not to be employed. The fact was, that at the time of the award the part of the labor which could be performed by the Egyptians, in their simple way of removing the earth, had been nearly or quite completed.

The canal was to be twenty-six feet deep and seventy-two

feet wide at its base, with a water line varying from two hundred
to three hundred feet in breadth. The banks formed by the
earth removed were on either side very high. In the dry dig-
gings, this earth was dug up by adults and carried up the steep,
high banks to a great extent by *corvée* children. But a large
part of the distance was not dry land. From the Mediterranean
side, the canal was constructed thirty-four miles through the
shallow waters of Lake Menzaleh and its marshy lagoons.
These waters were one to three feet deep. The roadstead excavated in this lake at Port Said was nine hundred feet wide
and on a narrow strip of sand beach separating the lake from
the sea. Near Suez, there were also extensive marshy lagoons.
In other places, as soon as the sandy top was removed, infiltra-
tion commenced. The water was pouring into the unfinished
channels. The Egyptians were good swimmers, but the children
could not dive into the water and bring up the soft mud from
the bottom. The balance of the work must be done with dredges.

This condition had been foreseen and the necessary provisions
made. The dredging machines had been ordered and constructed
and were already at work when the award was made. Yet one
of the arguments supplied to Napoleon by the French attorney,
on which his labor award was based, was the alleged increased
cost of the work if done by machinery.

Diplomacy has many tortuous and mysterious ways. In this
case, the French Ambassador at Constantinople was able,
through the powerful influence of Napoleon, to delay the decision of the Sultan relative to the *corvée* for four years, until
there was no longer any use for this kind of labor. When this
time arrives and the *corvée* work on the canal must necessarily
be ended, the Sultan, in the interest of humanity and his solicitude for the well-being and happiness of his subjects, orders the
discontinuance of *corvée* labor!

Another of the forgotten "just claims" was for the right of

fishing in the famous fresh water canal! This would have belonged to the canal company had it constructed the canal under its grant. Though it had renounced its rights to do so, and the work was to be done by the Egyptian Government at its own expense, Napoleon had decided that by this renunciation it had not renounced its rights to the benefits that would have accrued under the original concession. On this basis, one of the items of damages of his Majesty's award was 6,000,000 francs for water that might have been sold. Then why should not Egypt pay for the right of fishing in these prolific waters? Fishing rights are regarded in Egypt as valuable and the Government derives from them revenues amounting to a considerable sum. In the French advocate's imagination the stream would be alive with piscatory species. These would increase like the fish on the shore of the Sea of Galilee and be brought forth in the simple nets of the natives in miraculous quantities.

It is unnecessary to follow further the details of these claims. The Viceroy was badly frightened. He was in the condition of a vanquished army ready to submit to any terms of surrender. A settlement was agreed upon. Happily, it was to include a release of all claims of the company of every nature against Egypt. To be thus freed from further "discoveries," the Viceroy agreed to pay 30,000,000 francs. To this was added 10,000,000 francs for a piece of property for which the company had paid, a short time previous, 1,800,000 francs. In round numbers, these last two items of spoil amounted to $8,000,000.

The Egyptian Government had no money with which to pay this little peace offering. Nothing is easier, says the bland M. de Lesseps. On the item of 30,000,000 francs we will ask no money. We will take it in the interest coupons of your canal stock (discounting them, of course, at the regular rate of interest which was then about ten per cent). We will only just ask you to throw in the right to dividends on the stock. The canal shares bore interest at the rate of five per cent from the time of their issue. This was to be paid before dividends could be made. The canal was then not completed and there were no revenues and consequently no dividends; neither would there be for a number of years. To these propositions, the Viceroy perforce assented. The discount computation of the coupons was made and 125,000,000 francs of the coupons taken to pay the 30,000,000. This took the coupons up to 1895.

This is a brief statement of one of the many schemes of "spoiling the Egyptians." No greater fraud was ever successfully perpetrated, and this upon a people to whom the perpetrators were sending missionaries to teach them Christianity.

In addition to furnishing the *corvée* labor for four years and paying the sums we have stated, Egypt furnished for the use of the company large numbers of camels for which little was paid.

Including the benefits of the *corvée* labor furnished, the amounts paid on the various claims, the costs of the sweet water canal and the gratuitous labor and use of the camels, Egypt, by the most conservative estimate, paid in addition to the cost of its canal shares at least one-half of the original cost of the canal. This estimate is not that of the writer alone, but of such men as Riaz Pasha, who was for a long time at the head of the Egyptian Ministry under the Anglo-French control, and of others equally capable, and cognizant of the facts.

If the canal had been constructed under normal conditions by paid voluntary labor, and the company had constructed its own fresh water canal, the cost would have been very largely increased. The fresh water canal would have cost the company double what it cost Egypt. As to the desert land, it was of no value whatever.

From the account given, one of the principal causes of the

rise in the value of the canal stock will be readily seen. The interest coupons for over thirty years, which were to have been paid annually, had been taken off from over seven-sixteenths of the stock and transferred to the company. This alone lessened the fixed charges against the company $1,000,000 per year during this time. The right to dividends to the year 1895, twenty-five years from the opening of the canal, had also been surrendered. Thus, during this period, less than nine-sixteenths of the stock, about $22,000,000, received the full benefit of what would have cost under normal conditions at least $100,000,000, in addition to the bonded indebtedness of the company. The stock that received all these benefits was in amount only about one-fifth of the amount of the actual cost of that from which it received its revenue. Since 1895, $40,000,000 of stock has enjoyed these benefits.

Had it not been for the aid voluntarily given and forcibly taken from Egypt, the canal could not, at that period, have been constructed. The enterprise would have proved a disastrous failure, not as appalling, perhaps, as that of the Panama venture, but certainly similar to that.

For all its loss of life and outlay of money, Egypt has received no benefit. The canal is not only a real, but a great damage to her commerce. Formerly she had an immense overland trade, which is now entirely lost. Heavily laden ships are constantly passing through the canal in the desert east of her cultivated lands, with no more benefit to Egypt than their passage through the Mediterranean.

The conditions under which we are completing the Panama Canal furnish a marked and characteristic instance of the difference between our manner of treating the small Powers of America and the treatment of Oriental non-Christian countries by the European Governments. After paying the French for the work they have done, we pay $10,000,000 for the right of

control of sufficient lands to enable us to complete the canal
and insure its maintenance and use. We demand no assistance
of *corvée* labor, nor damages for refusal to furnish it. We do
not ask Panama to construct at great expense a feeding-canal
(as Egypt constructed the indispensable fresh water canal) to
give us all the water it furnishes, and then to pay us not only
for all the land this water might irrigate, if we had not already
appropriated it to other uses, but for all the water which might
have been sold—to say nothing of making claims for the right
of navigation and fishing in its waters.

England is in no way accountable for the extortions practiced
upon Egypt during the time of constructing the Suez Canal, but
the benefits of the spoils are hers, to a very large extent, and
she has no intention of returning any part of them to the people
who were despoiled. Nearly all the commerce of the canal is
English and to the English accrue many millions of dollars of
benefits annually in addition to the $130,000,000 advance on
her canal stock.

Egypt's first loan was made to obtain money for the Suez
Canal Company. She has paid interest, generally at a very
high rate, on this indebtedness for about forty years, and is
destined to continue these payments for a long, indefinite period.
All these burdens of an oppressed people arose from concessions
that appeared perfectly innocent. It was expressly provided
that the canal was to be constructed wholly by the company,
without cost to Egypt. Such is the fate of weak nations.

CHAPTER XIX

THE TRAGEDY OF ISMAÎL SADIK PASHA

Soon after my arrival in Egypt a characteristically Oriental event occurred in Cairo. I was returning from Europe to Egypt in October at the expiration of a two months' leave of absence. On the same steamer, came Hon. G. J. Goschen, M.P., late member of the Cabinet of Mr. Gladstone, and M. Joubert of Paris. They came as representatives of the English and French bondholders. Their mission was to arrange a settlement with the Khedive, Ismaîl Pasha, more favorable to his creditors than that which had been offered by his Highness. The Khedive claimed, what everyone at all conversant with the country knew to be true, that five per cent interest was all he could pay. This did not satisfy the bankers of Paris and London who had been receiving ten and twenty per cent, and often more, on their Egyptian loans.

Egypt had received for the sale of its bonds an average of only sixty per cent, in round numbers, of their face value. On the last issue in 1873 of £32,000,000 it had received only a little over fifty per cent, or £17,000,000. This issue of bonds was forced upon the Khedive by a threat of exposing his financial condition. On a basis of six per cent interest, three-fourths of the nominal debt had in 1876 been paid.

According to official documents, the correctness of which has never been denied, Egypt had paid in 1882 the whole of the principal of the money actually received on its loans and interest at the rate of six per cent per annum. Yet this indebtedness remained and still remains at the nominal amount of $500,000,000. On this amount of indebtedness, three-fourths of which, at that time, was made up of usury, Mr. Goschen insisted, with the moral support of his Government, on the payment of interest at the rate of seven per cent per annum. He also asked for the formation of a commission of European controllers authorized to collect the revenues of the country and pay this interest direct to the bondholders. As Egypt is wholly an agricultural country, having no manufacturing establishments, the interest demanded would require an annual tax of between six and seven dollars on each acre of land, besides enough to meet the other large burdens of the country. A considerable part of the lands are not very productive and from them such a high rate of taxes could not be realized. This would increase the amount necessary to be obtained from the better classes of lands.

Mr. Goschen was an ex-banker and broker and well fitted for his mission. It was a firm to which he belonged that negotiated the first loan to Egypt made by the Khedive to pay the indebtedness incurred on account of the Suez Canal. Because of his high position as a member of Parliament and a late member of the English Cabinet, he was selected by the bondholders for this work. The Khedive regarded him as a representative of her Majesty's Government and did not dare to refuse his persistent demands, though the money to comply with them could be procured, if at all, only by using the means employed by Sadik Pasha. When the English obtained full control, they found it necessary to reduce the interest to about one-half of the amount demanded by Mr. Goschen.

Ismaîl Sadik Pasha was at the time of Mr. Goschen's visit the Egyptian Minister of Finance. He was known as the

Mufettish, because, previous to being Minister, he had been the Mufettish of the Khedive, that is, one of the superintendents or managers of his private estates. He was the Khedive's foster-brother. Although belonging to the fellah class, and having a very ordinary education, speaking only Arabic and writing it poorly, he and the Khedive as boys were much together. From his childhood, he had been his Highness's protégé. He became first his secretary and, on arriving at manhood, one of the managers of his estates. In 1869 he was made Minister of Finance, a position which he held till his tragic death.

He was a man of much natural ability, an astute and sagacious manager and had great influence over the Khedive. No one ever did the work assigned him, that of raising revenue, with greater tact or success. Being himself a fellah, he was able to ascertain the incomes and accumulations of this class. Then, applying the theory of autocratic law, that the fellah was only the steward of the Khedive to whom he, his family and all he possessed belonged, Sadik proceeded, in the name of his Highness's Government and clothed with all the authority of the supreme tax imposer and collector, to obtain any surplus that might remain after the payment of the regular taxes. These were equivalent to rental rates, but if anything remained and was not forthcoming, he was not scrupulous as to the use of any means by which it might be obtained.

In default of his demands being complied with, crops were taken, and, if money or valuables were supposed to be concealed, as was often the case, imprisonment and the daily bastinado were resorted to until the last shilling and the last treasured heirloom, and, in some cases, all that could be obtained on mortgages was pressed from the poor victim.

The bastinado is a common means of punishment in the East. It consists of throwing the victim upon the ground on his breast, sometimes putting him in stocks, and applying a leathern whip

to the soles of the feet. It is said to produce the most ex-
cruciating pain, but does not leave serious wounds. The fellah
will often submit to this mode of punishment for an unlimited
time, rather than give up his treasures. He sometimes does this
on the theory that if he yields what he has, he will still be
whipped on the supposition that he has more. Generally, what
he may have has been accumulated by little savings from long
and severe toil. He is the more tenacious from the fact that he
well knows that, when the wolf appears at his door, he has no
reliance for aid, except on the few sovereigns he may have
buried beneath the dirt floor of his cabin.

Sadik was horribly cruel in the numerous modes of extortion
which he practiced, partly to enrich himself, as was shown by
his accumulated wealth, but principally to meet the pressing
demands of the creditors of the Government. His eminently
bad qualities did not, however, prevent him from foreseeing the
difficulties of the future and he was inexorably opposed to the
plans of Messrs. Goschen and Joubert. Perhaps he was tired
of the cruel methods to which he was obliged to resort to replenish the constantly exhausted treasury. He well knew that,
even by these methods, the ever increasing wants of the Government could not be supplied, for Egypt's accumulations of the
past had already disappeared to a large extent, having gone to
enrich the usurers of London and Paris, and replenish the
treasury of the Sultan.

Henceforth, there would be only the annual crops of the country with which to meet increasing demands, and the amount thus
obtained, even with the strictest economy, would not be sufficient to sustain the Government and pay more than five per
cent interest on the public debt. I know he used to say in those
days, when urgent demands were made by creditors, that the
money could not be obtained, that one might continue to whip
the fellâhîn, but it would not bring the money because they did

not have it, and could not get it. Mr. Goschen had been previously informed that the Mufettish was opposed to the paying of the high rate of interest demanded by the bondholders and that he would be the greatest obstacle to his obtaining the agreement which was the object of his mission. On his arrival, he met the Khedive and called upon all the Ministers, except the Mufettish whom he entirely ignored. He also informed the Khedive that he would have nothing to do with his Minister of Finance.

Nearly a month passed in fruitless negotiations, but the Khedive under the pressure of the English and French Consuls-General began to weaken, thinking, probably, that it was best to yield for the moment and find means afterwards to extricate himself from the difficulty. In the meantime some excitement had been produced in the provinces and Sadik was accused by the English and French of attempting to create an insurrection. Whatever the real facts may have been, they will probably never be known to the public. English agents reported that Sadik had threatened the Khedive. There is not the least probability that these reports were true.

Sadik sent in his resignation and, in his letter, warned the Khedive against the proposed Goschen-Joubert contract, the responsibility of which he refused to accept. Because of this and the reports made to him, the Khedive became very angry, but, with his accustomed ability for acting well his part, he concealed his wrath. The next day he matured his plans and yet appeared in his accustomed good humor. He passed the evening, according to those who saw him, in pleasant conversation and even joviality with those who were gathered at Abdîn. He was in the habit of taking his siesta after his midday meal and of sitting up very late at night, until twelve and even one and two o'clock. He rose early in the morning and ordinarily took a drive immediately afterwards.

On the second morning after the receipt of Sadik's resignation, his Highness arose at the usual time and sent for Sadik to accompany him in his morning drive. This he had frequently done, when he had some important matters concerning which he wished to converse with his Minister. Sadik, little thinking, probably, of anything but friendliness, obeyed the summons and came to the palace. The two left Abdîn together in an open carriage, smoking and talking as usual, crossed the Great Bridge at Kasr en-Nîl and, turning into the boulevard, drove to the palace of Gezîreh. They mounted the steps and entered the magnificent hall, which I had entered on my first visit to the Khedive. The door closed behind them and with it all certain knowledge of Ismaîl Sadik Pasha, the all powerful Minister, who for seven years, so far as the people were concerned, had exercised an authority in matters of taxation equal if not superior to that of the Khedive, and had, by his cruelty, become a terror to the fellâhîn. The Khedive immediately came out of the palace, re-entered his carriage and was driven back to Abdîn.

Several versions have been current at different times as to what happened to the ex-Minister, perhaps none of them correct. According to the official account, a special Council of Ministers was immediately called, of which Cherîf Pasha and Tewfik Pasha, afterwards Khedive, were members. By this Council, Sadik was tried for treason, convicted and sentenced to banishment with close confinement at Dongola. This trial was private, without the presence of the prisoner, and he had no knowledge of the proceeding. In fact, as this Council was held the next day after the arrest, it was very probable that the prisoner was already beyond being affected by any decision it might make. Formerly, in Massachusetts, perhaps still, a civil process was commenced by the issue of an execution. In this case, it is supposed that the execution preceded the judgment.

Dongola is a small town of Nubia, on the left bank of the Nile, about one thousand miles from Cairo, and the principal place of a small province of the same name. It was said that other prisoners had been banished to this place to work in the mines. There were, however, no prisoners there and no mines that had been worked within the memory of any living person. It was well understood in Egypt that banishment to Dongola meant secret capital punishment by strangulation, poisoning, or some other Oriental mode, and no one was deceived by any official declarations.

The prisoner in such cases disappears and is never afterwards heard from, as was the case in the time of Louis XI and other Kings of France. The prisoner in France entered a mysterious dungeon, "*oubliette*," and was forgotten. In Egypt, he was supposed to have started on a voyage up the Nile, but nothing was ever heard from him afterwards.

A steamer left Cairo the night after the arrest of Sadik and ascended the river to the First Cataract, ostensibly to convey the prisoner. A second steamer continued the voyage to the Second Cataract and, thence, a small caravan went to Dongola. No one was allowed to visit these steamers while they were ascending the Nile, and the whole proceeding was surrounded with as much mystery as possible.

Sadik had the rank of Mushir, which entitled him to a trial at Constantinople. The Sultan, on learning of the affair, directed the Khedive to send him the prisoner. The journey to Dongola required about thirty days, and the Khedive waited for a report from that place, which was to the effect that the Mufettish, having taken to excessive drinking on the voyage, had died soon after his arrival, The certificate of a physician, purporting to have been made at Dongola and certifying death from this cause was afterwards produced. This was the official death.

As to the real death, there were several statements current in Cairo soon after the event. The one most generally credited was that the prisoner was kept in the Gezîreh palace during the day of his arrest; that, the following night, he was taken on board the steamer we have mentioned, which immediately started on its trip up the Nile; that, at a short distance above the city, he was strangled, placed in a weighted sack and dropped into the river, the steamer continuing on its voyage as we have stated. All the particulars were given in detail, even to the name of the Pasha in charge of the steamer.

In 1879, when Ismaîl Pasha had been sent away, and the English and French had obtained full control of the finances of the country, a large number of names of persons who had received pensions from the Government, generally very small, were dropped from the rolls.

Among the pensioners whose cases were thus summarily disposed of was an Arab of Upper Egypt, one Ishak Bey. He was a soldier at Cairo at the time of the disappearance of the Mufettish and of large and powerful physique. He had lost a thumb and enjoyed till this time a small pension. Whether he had other disabilities that would have entitled him to this aid from the Government, I do not know. On the discontinuance of the pension, he gave and continued to reiterate a new account of this mysterious tragedy.

Mr. J. C. McCoan, an English writer with whom I was well acquainted in Cairo, gives this version of Ishak Bey's story:

"About an hour after Sadik's arrest he, Ishak Bey, was summoned into a room in which Sadik was confined and there found Prince Hassan and the prisoner already stripped of his clothes. The Prince whispered to him an order to kill the Mufettish either by strangling or preferentially by another method of acute painfulness, which would leave no marks of violence. He adopted the latter and having thrown the victim on his back endeavored with his left hand to smother his cries, while with his right he did his deadly work. Although a slight man, Sadik in his agony struggled with a strength almost equal to that of his murderer and, getting the Arab's left thumb in his mouth, bit it clean off. That on the following night, the body, wrapped in canvas and heavily weighted, was carried on board the waiting steamer which started up the river into which the corpse was flung a few miles above Cairo."

Prince Hassan was then Minister of War and I remember his occupying Gezîreh after my return from Europe that year. I called upon him according to custom and he came out of the building occupied by the harem, crossed the garden and received me in the palace.

There is, however, much doubt about the truth of Ishak Bey's story. At the time of its first relation, the ex-Khedive, Ismaîl Pasha, and his son, Prince Hassan, were in exile. Those who then controlled Egypt lent a willing ear to every statement in any way injurious to Ismaîl and hastened to publish it in Europe. Arabs are always ready to make such statements as they believe will please their hearers and Ishak probably hoped for and perhaps received some reward. The assertions that he found the prisoner naked in the presence of Prince Hassan, that he was ordered single handed to commit the murder, or that he could have accomplished the object, had he been so ordered, are all highly improbable. All the stories agree in stating that Sadik's body was thrown from the steamer into the Nile, a little above Cairo, on the night after his arrest. It matters little as to the precise manner in which he was killed, or the place of his death.

The motive for this act on the part of the Khedive is as mysterious as the details of the deed. Sadik had been the Khedive's life-long friend, confidant and, so far as known, faithful servant. Many conjectures have been made, but no satisfactory explanation has been given. Some claimed that there was a real conspiracy, others, that the victim possessed compromising facts that he might reveal against the Khedive and still others publicly stated that Mr. Goschen was morally responsible for the deed. That he was pleased to have the ex-Minister out of the way of his financial scheme, there is no doubt.

The next day after the arrest, the English Consul-General, Mr. Vivian, in a despatch to his Government speaks of the tragedy "as one of those dramatic incidents peculiar to Eastern life." He adds, "He was the greatest stumbling-block to any chance of financial reform or administration and his fall, however it was brought about, can only be regarded as a great public benefit." The same day, he reported the probable success of Messrs. Goschen and Joubert, "which had for some time been doubtful in consequence of the hostile attitude of the late Minister of Finance." As a matter of fact, the Goschen-Joubert proposition was agreed to the next day.

It is quite true, as I stated at the time in my report to Secretary Fish, that there were no regrets for the Mufettish. There was joy at his removal and people cared little whether it was just or in what way it was accomplished.

In an interview that I had with the Khedive the day after the arrest, I found him very much excited. It was the only time I ever saw him when he seemed to have lost control of himself. He was apparently very angry with the Mufettish. He told me how he had raised him up from a common fellah to the most important position in Egypt and said that he had undertaken to incite a rebellion. He detailed what he claimed to be some of the facts which he had learned from the governors of the provinces and the heads of the religious organizations. Having already some knowledge of the methods of autocratic Oriental Governments, I concluded from the temper of the Khedive that the ex-Minister was already dead, though nothing was said indicating that such was the fact.

As a sequel to the disposal of the Mufettish, came the confiscation of his estates. In his wealth, we have a marked illustration of the wonderful opportunities and privileges of a favorite minister of an autocratic ruler. Perhaps we have also a case in which the accumulated wealth of such a favorite has been the cause of his fall.

Foucquet, the Finance Minister of Louis XIV, lost the favor of his sovereign in consequence of the wealth he had amassed and the splendor of his palaces and festive entertainments. He ended his days in a dungeon after nineteen years of imprisonment.

No one can say to-day whether the wealth of the Egyptian Minister was one of the causes of his tragic end. The positions of such servants of royalty are always precarious and, the greater the wealth, when confiscation is permitted, the greater the danger.

In this case, we have a man from the lowest class in Egypt, who commenced life in poverty and squalor, and who never had any apparent means of accumulating wealth, except his official position. Yet, at the age of fifty-five, after having spent immense sums in Oriental extravagance, he left a fortune of from $10,000,000 to $15,000,000. He had thirty thousand acres of choice Nile lands, three large, magnificently decorated and furnished palaces, hundreds of female slaves, large amounts of valuable jewelry, securities and other personal property.

I had an opportunity of passing through his palaces previous to the removal of the furniture. They were on adjoining lands. As you approached, nothing could be seen from the streets but the high walls that surrounded the gardens and buildings. The entrances were by large porte-cochères, which contained lodges for eunuchs and guards. Each palace was separated from the others by a high wall, so that the view from one to the other as well as that of the streets was obstructed. There were no communicating passages, except by a small door through the wall, presumably for the convenience of the master. The buildings were large, and contained, I should judge, two hundred rooms. The appointments were all princely and excelled in Egypt only by the palaces of the Khedive.

Here lived the Mufettish in luxurious splendor, with his wives and female slaves, the latter numbering, according to the most conservative statements, not less than three hundred. Very few of these ever went outside the garden walls, and all were always closely guarded by eunuchs. Among the inmates of his harem, there were said to be many of the handsomest young Caucasians and Georgians. White slaves of this class are very costly, and the favorites are gorgeously dressed and adorned with jewels.

The harem has its well defined aristocracy. The wives and favorites are served by slaves, generally colored, who are often treated by their mistresses with great cruelty. The worst acts of cruelty, of which I heard while in Egypt, were those of women towards their slaves. All children born in the harem are legitimate and have equal rights as heirs. The mother, on the birth of a child, is raised to the rank of a wife.

The slaves of the Mufettish were absorbed by the other harems of Cairo—those of the Khedive, Pashas and Beys— the Khedive, of course, having the first choice if he desired. A large number of them were said to have been sold. If so, the sales were privately made and the secret kept. They disappeared, but under what conditions the public never knew, and the numerous reports were mere conjectures.

A few days later, there was a sale at auction of such furniture and jewels as had not been otherwise disposed of. The Khedive, according to report, pocketed the proceeds of the confiscated estates and thus ended a drama that at the time attracted much attention in Egypt and Europe.

The principal actors are now dead,—the Khedive, his son Tewfik, afterwards Khedive, Prince Hassan and Cherîf Pasha. There is, however, no authentic evidence that any of these persons except the Khedive, Ismaîl Pasha, were responsible in any degree for what happened. As Ismaîl was an Oriental ruler in whom were centered all governmental powers,—legislative, judicial and executive,—we cannot say, not having full knowledge of the facts, that his course was criminal, however much we may condemn such arbitrary modes of procedure in cases of persons accused of crime.

In judging the acts of people of different nationalities and different systems of morals, religion and government, we must take into consideration their laws and the criminal procedure to which they have always been accustomed. Christian governments do not hesitate, for the benefit of the example, when it is thought necessary or when their sovereignty is in question, to resort to the most summary executions. Even to establish a questionable authority, there have been numerous cases within a century of Christian governments sacrificing large numbers of people, summarily, in the most cruel manner, and without even the form of a drumhead court-martial.

On the arrival in Egypt, in 1882, of the English attorneys who had been generously employed by Mr. Wilford Scawen Blunt to defend Arabi Pasha and his associates against a charge of treason, Riaz Pasha refused them access to the prisoners. This he claimed would be contrary to Egyptian law.[1] Neither would he allow any communication with them, not even the conveying to the prisoners the information that the attorneys had arrived in Egypt and were ready to enter upon the preparation of their defense. It was only after long negotiations and the intercession of noble, high-minded Englishmen that any

[1] He was then Prime Minister and continued to hold that position a long time under the English régime.

communication was permitted between the attorneys and their clients.

When the question was raised of their having a fair trial, as had been stipulated on their delivery by Sir Garnet, now Lord Wolseley, to the Government of the Khedive, Riaz replied: "What is the use of a trial, when we all know that they are guilty?" Such a proceeding was entirely superfluous according to his ideas of justice. He would have had a secret court-martial, without the annoyance of the presence of the accused, sitting only long enough to draw up the necessary judgments, and a secret execution of the prisoners before the dawn of the following morning.

The only crime of these prisoners consisted in being loyal to their own people instead of being wholly subservient to the foreign domination which was being forced upon the country.

The strangest part of this remarkable history is that Riaz was sustained by the whole English Jingo Party in Egypt. They brought every possible influence to bear to prevent the chiefs of the National Party from having the benefit of counsel at their trials. The pressure of the Gladstone Ministry, supported by the better classes in England, prevailed in the case of Arabi and his friends.

The investigation showed that he was not guilty of the so-called massacre of the 11th of June, 1882, nor of the burning of Alexandria, nor of treason in any legal sense. As Minister of War, he had obeyed the orders both of the Khedive and the Sultan in opposing the English, and the Government accounts were found to have been kept with the strictest honesty.

To avoid the scandal a public trial would certainly have caused, without losing the benefit of an example of the danger of any opposition to the English Government, arrangements were made for banishment to the island of Ceylon, instead of hanging, and with this both Riaz and Arabi had perforce to be content. In this connection, we might refer to the cruel, illegal executions, sometimes of innocent victims, indulged in by the populace in our own country, which are more summary and often more barbarous than the acts of any Eastern potentate These barbarities are tolerated and find numerous apologists among us, while we boast of our Christian institutions and our advanced civilization.

There occurred in Egypt in June, 1906, an incident which shows the extreme measures sometimes employed to maintain the principle of the inviolability of the governing authority.

A body of English soldiers were on the march from Cairo to Alexandria. Five of the officers set out for a small village, four or five miles from their camp, where they were certain to find pigeon-shooting. A rural Egyptian village consists of a collection of sun-dried brick huts placed closely together. On some of the rude dwellings cotes are built by the natives in which pigeons are reared in large numbers, giving the owners small incomes. To some of the older people this is a chief means of support. There are only a few villages where there are pigeons in any considerable numbers and naturally one of these was chosen by the officers. For the same purpose, and to the displeasure of the people, they had visited this village the preceding year.

Lord Cromer in one of his reports says: "The standing instructions to the army of occupation are that no pigeon-shooting is to take place without the consent of the local Omdeh.[1]" In this case such consent was not obtained, as the Omdeh was absent. The shooting, however, was not abandoned or even delayed. The officers separated into two parties and began to shoot the tame pigeons which were flying close to the village. Two of the officers chanced to stand near a threshing-floor where wheat was being threshed; and presently it was discov-

---

[1] Village chief.

ered that the wheat was on fire. On hearing the screams of a woman and the alarm of fire the natives quickly gathered and the fire was extinguished without serious loss.

As to the origin of the fire no evidence was offered during the trial that afterwards took place, except the testimony of the wife of the owner of the wheat, a woman twenty years old. She gave the following testimony: "I was on the threshing-machine [1] and my husband was collecting the threshed corn [wheat]. Suddenly a shot hit the threshing-machine and set it on fire. Another shot hit me in my leg. I fell and do not know who fired the shots." The machine was charred by the burning of the wheat.

There were two physicians who made the official examinations for the trial. One was an officer, a member of the shooting party, and the other a native village physician. According to their report, used as evidence on the trial, this woman had "about sixty shot wounds," "many of the shot were still in the flesh," and "the skin on the parts affected painful and swollen." It is important to note that the villagers had no firearms; these are a luxury not permitted to the natives.

At the time of the burning of the wheat, or immediately after, its owner, the husband of the wounded woman, attempted to wrest his gun from the officer who had been shooting near him. Others who had come at the alarm of fire came to the aid of the native. The gun was discharged, as was later claimed, by accident. On the trial it was argued that the woman might have been shot at this time; though there was no evidence tending to prove that this was the fact. The struggle for the gun continued, and according to the testimony certain of the officers

---

[1] A rude sled drawn by animals and having rollers between the runners set with short irons, or with disks, so that the wheat is not only threshed by the treading of the animals, but the straw is at the same time cut finely so that it can be eaten by camels. See the accompanying illustration.

Threshing-Machines, with a Mound of Unthreshed Wheat in the Background.

who had been shooting on another side of the village hurried
to the scene of the incident. They then shot two or three times,
one witness said four times, into the crowd of natives, variously
estimated to have numbered from thirty to one hundred. Three
of these persons were wounded, one of them being as it happened the Sheikh-el-Ghaffir [1] and another a ghaffir. The testimony of both of these persons was taken on the part of
the prosecution, and no accusation was made against them.
The Sheikh-el-Ghaffir in his evidence said that "the shot that
wounded him came from another Englishman," that is, one of
those who had come up after the crowd had gathered, and not
the officer who was struggling to keep possession of his gun.
He added, "No aggression against the officers was committed
until I was injured."

As none of the officers in their evidence deny this shooting
or give any explanation concerning it, one must assume that a
correct version was given by the Sheik. On the part of the
officers the chief claim was that the wheat or straw could not
have been set on fire by the shooting.

Whatever the exact facts may have been, the husband of the
wounded woman and the natives who had been suddenly
brought together by her cries and the alarm of fire naturally
believed from what they saw and heard that the officers had set
fire to the wheat and wounded the woman. They became excited, beside themselves, furious. One of the officers testified
that the natives who were struggling for the gun "were in a
state of excitement and fury." In this not unnatural obsession
of rage they followed the officers after they had been disarmed
or had given up their guns, beating them with sticks and throwing at them sun-dried brick and dried mud. There is no doubt
they were rough to brutality after the manner of infuriated
mobs; though apparently nothing happened which might not

[1] Chief of the guards or watchmen.

have taken place in any labor riot in the United States. One officer had a broken arm and other members of the party were badly bruised.

Two of the officers escaped and hastened to camp for soldiers. The abuse of the other three continued. They were taken back to the threshing-floor and seated not far from the wounded woman. There was no interpreter at hand. The natives pointed to the woman and one of them drew his hand across his throat in a manner that might have been taken as a direct threat to kill the officer. Surrounded by this excited and furious body of natives, and powerless to communicate with them, the Englishmen were certainly in an awkward and even dangerous position. However, there were no further hostile acts.

It was excessively hot, and one of the two officers who had attempted to return to their camp had a sunstroke and died twenty-four hours later. As to the cause of death, the court found "that a blow had caused a concussion of the brain, and though it was not sufficient in itself to cause death it weakened him and thereby made him to be quickly affected by sunstroke and so contributed to his death."

Under a Khedivial decree which the English had previously obtained providing for the trial of offenses against the army of occupation, a special court was organized for the trial of fifty-nine natives accused of having taken part in the assault upon the officers. This court consisted of three Englishmen and two natives. One of the natives was a judge of the native court whose official position was dependent upon the will of the English authorities. The other native was designated in the proceedings as the Acting Minister of Justice. With him, however, as one of the English members of the court, was the English Acting Judicial Adviser.

The Khedive has for his adviser the English Consul-General, who instructs his Highness as to his duties and thus becomes the absolute ruler of Egypt. The other high native officials also have their English advisers whose duties are to instruct the natives as to what they shall do and to see that they carry out these instructions. Thus, while nominally the principal officials are natives, in fact, they have only the powers of subordinates subject to removal for the slightest disobedience to the commands given them by their English advisers.

The court thus organized listened for a part of two days to the reading of the evidence (*procès verbal*), which had all been previously taken,—for the most part wholly *ex parte*, without the presence of the accused or of any one representing them. In fact, some of the parties were not arrested till the testimony had been closed. All the evidence taken, that on which the conviction was afterwards based, was merely in the nature of that taken in the United States before the issuing of a warrant of arrest. Orders were issued from time to time for the arrest of such persons as were shown to have been present and taken part in the affray.

The prosecuting attorney was then heard. Afterwards, when the trial had in fact been ended, counsel was permitted to speak in behalf of the prisoners. The English representative (Lord Cromer having left Egypt) triumphantly reported to his Government that "the defense broke down completely, and all that their counsel could say on behalf of the prisoners practically amounted to an appeal for the mercy of the court"!

The five members of the court, after "due deliberation," rendered a judgment condemning twenty-one persons: four to death by hanging; two to penal servitude for life, one of whom was the husband of the wounded woman; one to penal servitude for fifteen years; six to penal servitude for seven years; three to fifty lashes and labor for one year; and five others to fifty lashes.

The judgment was without the right of appeal or approval

by any higher authority. The sentence of the persons condemned to be hanged and those to be flogged was publicly executed the following day at the village of the riot. The native "medico-legal expert" certified that the hanging and flogging had been "properly performed." Thus ended the judicial tragedy.

There was no attempt to identify the person who struck the deceased officer and no more properly admissible evidence given against the four persons condemned to death than against many others. They were designated with others as ringleaders who had excited the riot. The proof to establish this fact was hearsay and as follows: The official who took the testimony directed a person who was not present and knew nothing personally of the incident to ascertain and report what he could learn relative to the affair. Among other items of his report, which was rendered verbally and not on oath, was the statement that certain persons were the ringleaders, the authority cited being the Omdeh of the village. The Omdeh was also absent at the time of the attack upon the officers, but upon being asked if he had made these statements, answered in the affirmative. To the inquiry as to the source of his information, he said: "I was told this by the inhabitants." The English official in his report attempts to justify the admission of this and other hearsay evidence, alleging that it was in accordance with French procedure.

As might be expected, the action of the court was loudly condemned by all nationalities represented in Egypt, except the English. Complaints were made in Europe and a report of the whole proceedings was called for, and presented by the English Ministry to Parliament. The evidence that was read before the court on which the prisoners were convicted and such other facts as the Ministry thought politic to make public were printed in two Parliamentary papers on Egypt, Nos. 3 and

4 (1906). The account that I have given is taken wholly from these official documents.

However abhorrent this whole procedure may appear from information based on the official reports, it would appear much more abhorrent should we accept, as the true version of the facts, information received from native sources and from Continental residents of Egypt. Because of the unrest it produced in Egypt the cry was at once raised of Moslem fanaticism, and more English troops were demanded. The Egyptians were said to be ungrateful for all that had been done for them, and even to hate their English benefactors!!

It is not probable, however, that the Englishmen who were responsible for this remarkable procedure intended to do injustice to any one. In its severity and injustice it probably has no parallel in the modern judicial annals of any civilized Christian country. Yet this was thought to be demanded by English interests, and by the necessity of sustaining English prestige and authority. In their opinion this terrible exhibition of power, this spectacle of hanging and flogging, was necessary as an example. The natives must learn the danger of molesting those whom the Government of his Majesty, the King of England, had placed over them, regardless of the right or wrong of either party. They viewed the affair wholly from an English standpoint. The slave must not return the blow, however cruelly and unjustly he may be chastised by his master. If he does, the master may kill him to maintain his authority, without incurring any penalty of the law.

On the route between the English camp and the village there was found late on the day of the affair the body of a native with his skull crushed. No investigation seems to have been made as to the manner in which he came to his death.

CHAPTER XX

REIGN OF THE BONDHOLDERS

YIELDING to the diplomatic pressure instigated by the bond-holders, the Khedive consented to the appointment of European comptrollers for the different financial departments. Not satisfied with these concessions, the foreigners soon demanded and obtained control of the Ministry, leaving his Highness only the shadow of power. Important economies were promised in obtaining consent to this last demand. Native officials were dismissed and their places filled by highly paid strangers, unacquainted with the language of the country, and, in a great number of cases, incompetent for any duty except that of drawing their salaries.

The English Consul-General kept his Government well informed as to all that took place. On the 12th of July, 1877, he wrote as to the payment of the coupons then due:

"The money required, £2,074,975 ($10,000,000), was fully paid yesterday. But I fear these results may have been achieved at the expense of ruinous sacrifices to the peasantry by forced sales of growing crops, and by collecting taxes in advance. All this must be wrung in some shape or other from the country already crushed by taxation. Meanwhile I fear the European administration may be unconsciously sanctioning the utter ruin of the peasant creators of the wealth of the country, for which I hold that Englishmen are incurring a serious responsibility."

This and other despatches of similar import did not in the

least lessen the pressure of London and Paris, though they did cost the Consul-General Disraeli's displeasure and his ultimate removal.   •

On the thirtieth of November, 1878, he reported to his Government as follows: "The treasury is empty, the troops and the Government employees are many months in arrears of pay, and among the latter class the greatest distress and misery prevail." He should have added that the hundreds of foreign sinecure employees were promptly paid, each month, their high salaries.

In speaking of the situation at the beginning of 1879, an English writer who made no secret of his pride in England's good fortune in capturing Egypt, says:

"The new year opened with no improvement in the Egyptian situation.   The oppressive fiscal methods of the old personal régime were still in full operation; yet the treasury was empty, and the unpaid native officials, the army, and the local creditors were all suffering and clamoring as of old.   Only the legion of European functionaries were content, receiving their fat salaries punctually in full.   Indeed, if there had been no other grounds of complaint against the new system, the very number of these foreign half-sinecurists, and the fact that they were so paid, while native employees, and all ranks of the army were left many months in arrears, were enough to account for the popular discontent which found freer and louder voice each day."

In the face of these facts and of the starving thousands in Upper Egypt caused by the low Nile, English journals at the time (and English writers ever since) attributed the national discontent to the Khedive, claiming it was "all of his fomenting."

For the year 1877, out of the £9,543,000 of revenue, £7,473,909 went as interest to the bondholders and nearly £1,000,000 to pay England the interest on the Suez Canal shares and the Turkish tribute, leaving only a little over £1,000,000 for all the expenses of the Government, including the army and the high-paid foreign employees. Substantially the same conditions were true of 1878.

It must be remembered that there were no municipalities in Egypt, and that all the expenses of the country, including those of the cities, towns, dikes and canals, schools, etc., were paid, if at all, from the Government Treasury. With the sum remaining for current expenses, about one-fourth of what was absolutely necessary, the Khedive was asked to be responsible for the public security and the regular working of the Government and was treated as a criminal because he could not succeed.

I watched closely the finances of Egypt from the time of my arrival and know that the Khedive, whatever his previous sins may have been, did his utmost, after the beginning of 1876, to alleviate the financial situation. There was no building of palaces, no extension of railways, nor of telegraph lines, no purchase of steamers, no personal expenses greater than those of the petty princes of Europe, or greater than the private fortune of the Khedive, before he became Khedive, would have permitted.

It had been persistently claimed, contrary to the assertions of the Khedive, that the revenues of Egypt properly applied were amply sufficient to enable the Government to pay seven per cent interest on its indebtedness. The European Ministry on coming into power soon learned that this was not true. They immediately sought other resources to enable them to fulfill their promises to the bondholders, who had secured them their lucrative positions. If these promises could be kept, bonds that had been bought at from fifty to seventy cents on the dollar, would be worth their face value. First, they demanded the vast estates belonging to the Khedive and his family.

Ismaîl Pasha, before he became Khedive, was the wealthiest and most thrifty prince in the Orient. He had inherited a large property, consisting of buildings in Alexandria and Cairo, and of lands, principally plantations of sugar-cane in Upper Egypt. These estates were well managed and productive. With his vice-regal throne he also had large inheritances. He undoubtedly had the mania of acquisition, and, on his accession to the absolute sovereignty of Egypt, his landed estates increased very rapidly. Within ten years, they amounted to nine hundred and fifty thousand acres. A part of this was acquired by purchase, but much the larger portion was reclaimed from the desert by the construction of irrigating canals, leveling the ground, and otherwise preparing it for cultivation.

In the acquisition of these additional lands, and the putting of them in a state of cultivation, the Khedive incurred an indebtedness, in excess of the net profits of all his estates, of $43,000,000. Some idea can be formed of the value of these estates from the fact that they constituted nearly one-fifth of the lands of Egypt, and produced annually more than a million of acres of crops. Upon this property there were fifteen sugar factories, well constructed and in excellent condition, containing fifty mills for crushing the cane; two old factories not in use, and the machinery and the other materials for the construction of three more. There were also two hundred and fifty miles of railroads with forty locomotives and a proportionate amount of other rolling-stock, all constructed and principally used to transport cane to these factories. The presence of these railroads did not obviate the necessity of employing large numbers of camels. I have seen lines of camels miles in length conveying cane to the railway stations.

A large part of these estates had been previously conveyed by the Khedive to members of his family. On the demand of the European Ministry they were all conveyed, with the personal property pertaining to them, to the State to aid in relieving it from financial embarrassment. Some of these lands were subject to a mortgage of forty-three million dollars, the indebtedness previously mentioned, but over four hundred and fifty thousand acres were unencumbered. Thus was terminated the ownership of what was, when all owned by the Khedive, the most valuable individual landed estate in the world. The gift also included large amounts of property in Cairo and Alexandria.

Among the early official enterprises of the English member of the Ministry was a trip to London to obtain a loan, to be secured by a mortgage on the unencumbered part of these lands. He had an interview with the Rothschilds. This was their opportunity. Why should they not profit by it? Egypt wanted money. The security was ample and the interest high. The only question was how much blood they should take. As to the Minister, he was ready to consent to any terms they might think expedient to name. A contract was concluded, therefore, by which this banking house undertook to market, at seventy-three per cent, £8,500,000 of bonds to be secured by a mortgage on the unencumbered estates conveyed by the Khedivial family to the Egyptian Government. These estates were to be put under the management of English and French comptrollers, and in case the revenues were at any time insufficient to pay the interest and principal of the loan, as they should become due, the deficit was to be paid by the Egyptian Government. These bonds were worth, at the time of their issue, their face value, and would have been gladly taken at that figure by the creditors. That it might appear that they were acting as brokers, the Rothschilds stipulated that they should receive for their services three per cent of the proceeds of the sale, which amounted to the modest sum of $900,000. The bonds were nominally put upon the market, but were all immediately taken by the Rothschilds and such friends as they chose to favor. By this transaction, Egypt lost $12,000,000. This sum, to say the least, was needlessly thrown into the coffers of the rich bankers of London. The bonds of this loan are known as the "Domanial," those of the domain. The interest has been promptly paid, and from the sale of lands the larger part of the principal. The bonds remaining, if any, can be sold at a premium.

Notwithstanding the promises made to the Khedive, when he gave these vast estates to the Government, that the floating debts should be paid, and that he should thus be relieved of further annoyance from the financial situation, these debts remained unpaid. The proceeds of the loan, as fast as received, were applied by the Franco-English control to the payment of the high interest on the bonds. It was the creditors holding these bonds that the European Ministry specially represented.

The discontent of the people increased and the opposition became daily stronger against the inundation of the country by foreigners, who had already obtained possession of the most important official positions and were fast filling the minor ones.

The soldiers of the Egyptian army were discharged and the officers, twenty-five hundred in number, placed on a detached list. The pay of both soldiers and officers, during nearly the entire period of the bondholders' control of the finances, was one to two years in arrears. The officers had been educated for the military service and knew no other way of obtaining a subsistence. They and their families were in a deplorable state of destitution. The people became intensely excited. Notwithstanding all that the Khedive and his family had given to the Government, the national debt continued rapidly increasing. There were disturbances in Upper Egypt and incipient rebellion in Cairo, all arising from the sufferings of the people caused by the oppressive taxation insisted upon by the European Ministry, and the taking of nearly all the proceeds to Paris and London to pay six and seven per cent interest on what was claimed to be Egypt's indebtedness. The Khedive was held responsible for the good government of the country and the peaceable conduct of its inhabitants without the least means being allowed him with which to alleviate their sufferings.

Thus commenced, either with premeditated design on the part of the Franco-English Ministry, or through their administrative inability and excessive zeal in the interest of the London and Paris bankers, the political disturbances which culminated three years later in the forcible opposition of an oppressed people under the lead of Arabi Pasha. This situation was foreshadowed by the Khedive in a statement made to the writer in the presence of two of his colleagues at the time of the first civil disturbances. He said: "I can govern the people without a soldier, but a Ministry of foreigners or of a different religion can only govern them with military force." The experiment of thus governing has not been repeated since the first disastrous failure.

There was no amelioration in the governmental conditions. With every change of the Ministry, the two European Governments assumed more powers, until the only duty of the Khedive was to sign such decrees as might be prepared by the European Ministers. According to their pretensions, he was wholly subject in the affairs of the Government to their dictation. This too, in spite of the fact that they had not had legislative, executive or governmental experience and lacked the ability that their positions required. It would have been more dignified for the Khedive to have revolted in the first instance, as the Sultan did when the Powers asked him to establish a European control at Constantinople. His answer was laconic, but it left no doubt as to his Majesty's meaning. He replied, "I may be the last of the Khalifs, but I will never consent to become a second Khedive."

The Egyptian policy of England and France was then dictated by the bondholders. An early, positive and firm refusal to permit them to interfere in the internal affairs of the country, instead of trying to please them with continual concessions, would have saved the Khedive his throne. Each new concession only increased their demands, until he virtually abdicated his sovereignty. It must have been known at London that the Government could not continue under the conditions imposed. It is not probable that Disraeli intended that it should. He was already waiting and watching for an opportunity to rid himself of the French alliance, which the English hated from the beginning, and into which they had entered to prevent the French from obtaining control of Egypt.

Both the French and English Consuls-General opposed the action of the European Ministry, but the bondholders in Paris succeeded in having the French Consul-General promptly recalled. The English bondholders were not immediately successful in getting rid of the English Consul-General, but the political designs of Disraeli and the financial interests of the Rothschilds and other bankers demanded the sacrifice. Even a future member of the House of Lords was not permitted to stand in their way, and a few weeks later the English Consul-General, Mr. Vivian, was also recalled. He was an only son of Lord Vivian, who was of a very old and honorable family, but, in politics, a member of the Liberal Party.

Mr. Vivian afterwards represented his Government in several countries, became Lord Vivian on the death of his father and died while Ambassador at Rome. The English member of the Ministry accomplished his purpose, but his administration was such an evident failure that the time of his own departure was not long delayed. A wise administrator, like the present English ruler, Lord Cromer,[1] might have retained his position

---

[1] Since the writing of the above, Lord Cromer has resigned and has been succeeded by Sir Eldon Gorst as British Agent and Consul-General at Cairo, who thereby becomes the real ruler of Egypt.

indefinitely and been highly beneficial to Egypt. The Government had, however, been placed by the European control in the worst possible condition, and this furnished a plausible excuse for the drastic measures soon to be taken.

The Egyptian question in the early days of the Khedive's embarrassment, for those not in the secrets of diplomacy, was wholly one of finance,—how bonds that had been bought for fifty cents on a dollar by bankers and syndicates in Paris and London might be made worth their face value. Many of these bonds had been placed in the hands of those in power, or in positions of great political influence, where, to use an American phrase, "they would do the most good." Thus it turned out, especially in Paris, that relatives of cabinet officials and members of Parliament were large holders of Egyptian securities. These officials were ready to aid in procuring any measures that would be likely to increase the value of their holdings.

At the time of England's first official interference in Egyptian finance, there were nearly a score of Governments, in different parts of the world, that had failed to meet their liabilities, and who were owing English creditors many hundred millions of dollars. Yet the English Government had never officially aided one of these creditors in collecting their claims. On the contrary, it had always given them "the cold shoulder." Not only did it refuse them aid, but plainly informed them that if they wished to loan their money where it would be secure, they must loan it at home, and be content with the English rate of interest. If they loaned it abroad, taking foreign securities, they did it at their own risk and must not expect any aid from their Government in enforcing the payment of their demands, just or unjust. This had been the settled policy of England. It did not undertake to resolve itself into a sheriff's *posse comitatus* for the purpose of enforcing the collection, in foreign countries, of the securities purchased by its adventurous citizens. England had never given official aid in the collection of claims arising from voluntary contracts, such as the loaning of money, or the buying of foreign bonds. Such aid could only be given in the collection of claims arising from the wrongful acts of Governments or their citizens, or their wrongful neglect.

It is quite evident from these facts, as well as from the sequel to this Egyptian drama, in which Disraeli, for a time, became the principal promoter, that he had, after the purchase of the canal shares, other than purely financial objects in view. This was the more apparent from the fact that the demands sought to be collected were notoriously usurious, to such an extent, that not nearly one-half of the amounts claimed was justly owing. It is not probable that, in the whole enormous list of foreign bonds held by Englishmen against defaulting states, any were more unjust than the Egyptian. While France and England were apparently harmoniously engaged in forcing the payment of interest on Egyptian bonds, and the Shylocks of Paris and London were pocketing the plunder, these two very Christian powers were watching each other with most intense jealousy, each striving for preponderance of power and each afraid the other would obtain some political advantage. Thus the strife continued until the final acts of the drama, the bombardment of Alexandria, Tell el-Kebîr, and the permanent military occupation of Egypt by the English.

The burdens of the fellâhîn under the last years of the Khedive had been excessive. He had been constantly threatened with the loss of his crown unless the excessive interest was paid, and had made the most desperate efforts to accomplish the impossible. The taxes under the European Ministry were not diminished, but rather increased. I have written a detailed account of the acts of the bondholders' reign, but space will not permit its insertion in this narrative.

Cupidity grows on being well fed. After the acquisition of

the Khedivial estates, worth at least seventy-five million dollars above the encumbrances, search was made for other means of increasing the amounts that could be drawn from Egypt. I will only mention two or three of the principal of these sources of increased revenue. One is what was known as the Moukabalah. Under a decree of the Khedive all persons who should "pay into the treasury a sum equal to six years of their land tax were to be relieved in perpetuity from one-half of their taxes, such taxes to be computed on the basis of the land-tax then paid, the taxes thus lessened not to be increased in the future, in any manner nor for any reason." Over seventy-eight million dollars had been paid into the treasury under this decree, many mortgaging their lands to raise the money.

The European Ministry proposed the abolition of the Moukabalah and the repudiation of all claims made under it. This would, as claimed, increase the annual revenue five and a half million dollars, sufficient to pay the bondholders an additional one per cent per annum.

Another source of revenue was to be derived from increasing the tax on that class of lands known as the Ouchouri. The average annual land-tax on all the cultivated lands of Egypt was already five and a half dollars per acre. On the Ouchouri lands, lower taxes were paid than on the other lands in Egypt. They had been reclaimed from the desert, during the last seventy-five years, at great expense in leveling and constructing canals. At first, it was agreed by the Government that they should be free of taxation. They were afterwards taxed, according to the old Moslem law, a tenth of their gross income, giving them their name, Ouchouri, one-tenth. The taxes were later increased under various pretexts till they were about half of those of the other lands known as the Karadja, or conquered lands. In consequence of this immunity from a part of the taxes, this land sold for about double the other lands.

The Ministry proposed, under a pretense of equalizing taxation, to raise the tax on these lands, placing them on the same basis as the Karadja. This was to add immediately to the annual revenues seven hundred and fifty thousand dollars, the amount to be largely increased as soon as appraisals of their products could be made.

There was also an indebtedness of the Government of over nine million dollars which had been paid into the treasury under agreements for perpetual annuities. This, it was proposed to wholly repudiate. These reforms, as they were called, with others equally just, were all embodied in a decree which the Khedive was asked to sign. When objections were made by the people and the Khedive, he was accused by the reformers of fomenting discontent. After the removal of the Khedive, these measures, slightly modified, were imposed upon Egypt. A small interest was made payable on the money advanced under the decree known as the Moukabalah.

Under these conditions, the Khedive determined to make one supreme effort to save his sovereignty and rid his people of the foreign control. The Consuls-General were invited to assemble at the Khedive's palace to receive from his Highness an important communication. All of the Great Powers of Europe, the United States, Spain, Holland and Denmark were represented.

We were received by the Khedive in the presence of Cherîf Pasha, a committee of the Chamber of Notables, and certain Ulemas. His Highness appeared at first considerably agitated, but proceeded to say, that it was impossible for the Government of the country to continue under the existing conditions, that a financial plan had been prepared by the European Ministers that destroyed acquired rights and annulled laws that were regarded as sacred; that the plan would be injurious to the country, and unjust to a large number of its inhabitants; and that so strong an opposition had been created among the people that it was necessary for him to yield to their wishes and form a new Ministry.

Cherîf Pasha explained the situation more at length. He stated that the National movement had originated in the Chamber of Notables which had been in session all winter, and was finally dismissed without any realization of what they considered their just demands, and that the country could no longer support the present administration. The next morning a new cabinet was formed, with Cherîf Pasha at its head, from which the European Ministers were left out.

CHAPTER XXI

DETHRONEMENT OF ISMAÎL PASHA

THE Anglo-French bondholders' reign had been suddenly suspended, never to be resumed in the anomalous form in which it had been commenced. It might be characterized as the English reign, for, while it had nominally been Anglo-French, the English influence had latterly prevailed to such an extent that the French influence was scarcely felt. This preponderance was so marked that some of the French residents were quite as much rejoiced as the natives at what they termed the Khedive's *coup d'état*.

The whole movement was popular, and its popularity arose largely from the utter failure of the attempt at governing (in the interest of foreign creditors) by an irresponsible Ministry which had little knowledge of the country and none of the language, customs, laws and necessities of its people. The foreign Powers were fully aware of this failure and of the political mistakes for which they were responsible. This, they could not be expected to admit. European Powers claim infallibility for all their acts in the Oriental non-Christian countries and, however great their mistakes, or those of their agents, they always insist that they were in the right.

There was at that time scarcely a precedent in history for their interference in the affairs of Egypt under the pretense of securing the payment to their citizens of claims arising from money that had been loaned. Supposing that in the case of any one of the many refusals of our individual Southern states to pay their indebtedness the others had attempted a forced collection, what would have been the result?

In the case of Egypt it was not repudiation that was involved, but a mere question as to the rate of interest. Notwithstanding the low price at which the Egyptian bonds had been sold, twice as high a rate of interest was claimed on them as was paid by the English Government. This amount was more than Egypt could pay; and the source of all the trouble, was the attempt to compel the Khedive to do what was impossible, even after the despoiling of the Khedivial family and the people.

At the very time of the making of the exorbitant demands I have mentioned, the thousands who had died of starvation or from the result of insufficient food in Upper Egypt had scarcely been buried. These deaths were the direct consequence of the exaction of high interest.

An English gentleman [one of the commissioners who went up the Nile about the month of February of this year (1879) to carry provisions to the people and to ascertain their condition] reported that the number who had died of starvation and as a result of the want of sufficient food was not less than ten thousand, and that many more would be added to this number in consequence of diseases contracted by their privations and sufferings. He added that all this was the direct result of poverty arising from over-taxation. The scenes witnessed by the first travelers who ascended the Nile that winter were appalling.

For this famine and all its ghastly work, the English and French Governments were directly responsible, and this after having been previously informed of the conditions of the country and the approaching want of food supplies. The famine occurred in Upper Egypt, the nearest section of the stricken region being three hundred and fifty miles above Cairo. They were the most densely populated rural districts in the country. Their extreme northern portions had a population of from one hundred to one hundred and seventeen persons for each one hundred acres of land, and the remainder a population of one hundred and seventy-nine persons to each one hundred acres.

In April, 1878, the question of the payment of the May coupons on the bonded indebtedness was under consideration. It was well known that large portions of these districts were as dry as the desert, and that no crops had been produced upon them in consequence of the unprecedentedly low Nile of the previous year. Wheat was then one of the principal products of this part of Egypt. It is one of the winter crops and is generally produced by the natural overflow of the river.

The famine did not occur till about the beginning of the year 1879, though the low Nile was in 1877. It was so low in the summer and fall of that year that no crops were produced the next winter in large portions of Upper Egypt. Where there were crops, they were sold to pay taxes and exported. The earliest crop following the rise of the Nile in the summer of 1878 was a kind of bean that was not sufficiently advanced until about the month of February, 1879, to give any relief. It was during a few weeks previous to this time that the famine occurred. Those who actually died of starvation were mostly old or feeble people and women and children. It was a poverty famine like all others of the present day. With modern facilities of communication and transportation, there is always an abundance of food that can be obtained by those having the means necessary for its purchase.

There was not sufficient money in the treasury to pay the May coupons of 1878, that I have mentioned, the deficiency being about $6,000,000. The Khedive said these coupons could not be paid in full. The French Consul-General, acting under instructions from his Government, and seconded by the English Consul-General, also acting under instructions, but against his personal judgment and wishes, demanded their payment. The matter had been well considered. The facts were notorious, and had been reported to these Governments. The Khedive even begged the Consuls-General not to insist, calling renewed attention to the inability of the people to pay their taxes and the destitution that would necessarily result from such a drain upon their resources. The answer of the French Consul-General was, "You must pay."

The English Consul-General reported to his Government, that, as the English and French Governments required that the coupons should be paid, the Khedive said he would do all that lay in his power to meet them, at whatever cost to the country; but that the responsibility for the consequences would not rest with him. The fiat went forth to raise the money. The tax collectors used extraordinary methods, but, after the last piaster that could be forced from the poor fellâhîn had been obtained, there was still a deficiency of over $2,000,000. This was raised by the sale by the Government of the taxpayers' unharvested wheat, then still green in the fields, and by pledging the personal property of the Princes, the sons of the Khedive.

The coupons were paid the day that they became due, and the wheat was afterwards exported to Europe to reimburse the money advanced. A score of men at Paris, who received early private information of the effect of the French Consul-General's declaration to the Khedive, made fortunes by the rise of Egyptian bonds. The result for Egypt was the famine of the following winter. Not enough was realized from the sale of the wheat to pay the deficit. After various payments, a judgment was finally taken against the Princes for the balance, about $120,000.

A little before this, the expense of maintaining an army in

Turkey had been added to the burdens of the country. The Khedive was required to send a body of troops to take part against Russia in the Turco-Russian war. His Highness hesitated a long time, even after the troops were ready to embark, and only sent them forward under the diplomatic pressure of England. Monsieur de Lex, the Russian Consul-General in Egypt, who at the time gave the writer full information as to the negotiations, tried in vain to induce the Khedive to withhold them.

In the end, the Khedive did not dare to disobey the demands of the Sultan, supported by England. About thirty thousand troops, including those that had been previously sent to aid against Servia, were clothed, equipped, sent across the Mediterranean and maintained in Turkey about a year. They came back to Egypt just at the time of the demand of the payment of the May coupons of 1878.

Notwithstanding all the burdens imposed upon the country, and the mistakes, if we forbear using harsher terms, of the bondholders' reign, there was no abandonment of aggressive projects. The French took the lead in a new movement, namely the dethroning of the Khedive. The old enmity caused by the sale of the canal shares to England had latterly been much increased by the constantly augmenting preponderance of English influence in the Orient.

This hostility being thus aroused, nothing less than the blood of the Khedive could satisfy a Frenchman. " *Une revanche éclatante* " was what they publicly demanded at Paris, and what, in their hearts, they had desired from the moment of this sale. They attained their object, but sacrificed thereby all the political influence they had acquired in Egypt by nearly a century's strife. The strong head of the Government being removed, conditions inevitably and quickly followed that made the road easy to English supremacy.

There is this radical difference between the character of the French and English. The former will sacrifice the future for the gratification of a present desire. The latter weigh carefully all the facts and, before acting, determine what course will be in the end most to their advantage. They can wait and wait, until the opportune moment arrives.

The acquisition of Cyprus, after the Berlin Congress, and the evident "*entente amicale*" between England and the Sultan undoubtedly gave to the English, in the mind of the Khedive, a position of power much more to be feared than that of the French. The English were also more practical and knew better how to adapt themselves to the conditions of the country. This, with the more effective aid of their Government, enabled them to secure a large portion of the most lucrative positions in Egypt and to flood the country with English employees.

The workings of the new Ministry were wholly satisfactory and popular with all classes. No one could find any fault with the Khedive for the manner in which he conducted the Government, nor even claim that he was not doing the best that could be done under the circumstances. France, however, under the influence of the bondholders, continued against him, with increased asperity, the newspaper war that she had unjustly waged for three years. When England hesitated, and seemed ready to abandon her, she sounded the Cabinets of all the leading Powers of Europe, asking their moral support.

At the time of the Berlin Congress of 1878, organized to settle the questions growing out of the Turco-Russian war, England had need of the influence of France. This she obtained by procuring the assent of the Powers to the proposition that Egyptian matters should not be discussed and by such promises as led France to believe that her policy in regard to Egypt was to be adopted. It was under the pressure of the questions pending in Berlin that England, against the advice of her Consul-General and other representative Englishmen in Egypt, aided in enforcing the full payment of the May coupons of that year.

But conditions had changed. England no longer had need of France. The preponderance of her influence in Egypt seemed assured. Notwithstanding all that had taken place, the Khedive showed a decided preference for the English. The party of English in Egypt, which was against the Anglo-French Ministry and which included the Consul-General, was stronger than that Ministry's partisans. Moreover, England disliked to embark in this new enterprise in partnership with France. Their alleged cordiality was only an outside appearance. High English officials often stated to me that their Government had unwisely allowed itself to be drawn into a disagreeable and complicated alliance. Their ideas of what ought to be done were wholly different from those of the French. They could agree neither upon a general policy, nor upon its details. Their jealousies were strong, each thinking that the other had some covert political designs in every movement made. That each did in most cases have such designs was undoubtedly true.

The financial question became one of secondary importance. This fact made their working together in harmony still more difficult. France thought that she, by virtue of the conquests of the first Napoleon, had in Egypt prior acquired rights of the fruits of which she had been deprived by the English. England was there, if not at that time with the intention of remaining, at least with the design of preventing France from obtaining any permanent foothold. The motive of the present movement on the part of the French was also to a large degree hatred of the Khedive. England, who really had no cause of complaint, remained undecided. She was considering the final results. France was acting from impulse. England knew from experience that the dethroning of a strong, capable prince, and the setting up in his place of a young, inexperienced man, meant the assumption of the Government. Such a responsibility she would not hesitate to take upon herself; but how could this dual government, this partnership with France in the governing business, be managed?

By reason of these considerations and the satisfactory· working of the Government in Egypt, the balance seemed turning in favor of the Khedive, when, suddenly, a new element entered into the contest from a wholly unexpected source. It was nothing less than an apparent alliance on the pending Egyptian question between Prince Bismarck and France. Although nothing at the time could be more surprising, it was not difficult for one who had watched and been acquainted with diplomatic affairs at Cairo for the preceding two years to comprehend some of the causes that had led to this unexpected event.

Germany had heretofore played a very modest rôle in the affairs of the Orient, having, in comparison with England and France, very little influence. She was, however, interested in the floating debt of Egypt to the amount of $750,000. Austria was in a similar situation.

The Consuls-General of these countries complained that while the Khedive heeded the demands of the Consuls-General of England and France, he paid no attention to theirs. They frequently said that there were only two Consuls-General in Egypt, those of England and France, and that the others might as well go home. Bismarck was offended at this secondary position of Germany and saw his opportunity to make his influence felt and to obtain a position in Egypt more in accordance with the dignity of the new empire he had lately founded. The facts were that all the resources of the country, including the estates of the Khedivial family, were in the hands of the European comptrollers, and were applied by them to the payment of the interest on the bonded indebtedness. The European

Ministry had not kept the promise it made to the Khedive, at the time he turned over his private estates, to pay the floating debt. This debt was constantly increasing, and the Khedive could do nothing to relieve this embarrassing situation so long as the bondholders were permitted to absorb all the revenues.

Whether the attitude of Germany had any influence upon England we do not know. However that may be, as soon as she was informed of the policy of the Kaiser's Government, she consented to the French scheme of deposing the Khedive.

Thus, from her avowed and most dreaded enemy, France obtained what was then considered valuable aid in an undertaking to which she attached the greatest importance, and for the accomplishment of which she had persistently labored with all her force. Deservedly, this success was not only the cause of her loss of power in Egypt, but it led to an estrangement between her and England which lasted through two decades. Once England decided to act, the dethronement of the Khedive was easy to accomplish. The only important question was the manner in which it should be done.

About the middle of June, the English representative, Mr. Vivian, orally, and as was then claimed, unofficially, advised the Khedive to abdicate and immediately afterwards left Egypt not to return. Soon afterwards, Monsieur Tricou, a newly arrived French Consul-General, who seemed to have been sent for the special work in hand, gave in his discourteous manner the same advice.

Monsieur Tricou had previously represented France in Egypt and had been recalled at the instance of the Khedive. His return at this time was a direct insult to his Highness and plainly showed the animus of those having control of the French Government.

The day following the verbal communication, Monsieur Tricou and Mr. Lascelles, the English *chargé d'affaires*, read to his Highness a joint official note of the same import. During the day and previous to the presentation of the note, I had an interview with the Khedive at his palace. He appeared dejected, and there was an absence of the vivacity that generally characterized his interviews, even at the time of his most serious troubles. He talked freely of the situation, but expressed no opinion as to its probable outcome. He was already advised of the official note that was to be presented asking him to abdicate, but he did not then expect its presentation till the next day. In a conversation the same day with Cherîf Pasha I found him full of hope as to the final result.

The Khedive was given forty-eight hours in which to answer the demands of the Powers. When the Consuls-General called, at the expiration of this time, he informed them that he had telegraphed to Constantinople for instructions from the Sultan, that he had not yet received a reply and that, when it came, he would have to trouble them to come to receive his answer. He said he had received his authority from the Sultan and could not relieve himself of the responsibilities of the Government without his Majesty's orders. The French Consul-General was much irritated at the unexpected response, and, in his usual manner, said, "How long has your Highness been the humble servant of the Porte?" "Since my birth, Monsieur," was the quick reply of the Khedive.

The Powers were very anxious to have the Khedive abdicate voluntarily in order to avoid contracting any obligations to the Sultan. The French Consul-General continued to urge the abdication, and, the conversation becoming animated, he accused the Khedive of frequently disobeying the Sultan. "I defy you to name an instance" retorted the Khedive. Monsieur Tricou being unable to answer, Mr. Lascelles came to his rescue by politely asking the Khedive if it would not be better in this instance, to act on his own responsibility? To this, the Khedive replied in the most courteous manner, "My dear sir, as the first use you desire me to make of my independence of the Sultan is to relinquish the authority he has given me, I do not see what I am to gain."

All possible pressure was employed to obtain the abdication of the Khedive without waiting for the decision of the Sultan. Promises were made of a civil list, certain private property and the accession of his son Mehemet Tewfik, in case of his acquiescence, and threats of being succeeded by Halim Pasha and sent away without anything, in case he did not acquiesce.

Afterwards, the French and German Consuls-General went to the palace and had the Khedive called at three o'clock in the morning, thereby causing great terror of assassination in the harem. They informed him that they had come to give him the last opportunity of abdicating in favor of his son; that, in a few hours, Halim would be appointed Khedive, and it would then be too late. The Khedive coolly said: "There will be plenty of time to abdicate, I will see you to-morrow. Good night, Gentlemen," and went back to his rooms.

Prince Halim was the red flag that was for years flaunted by the French in the face of the Khedive whenever he refused to accede to their demands. When Napoleon III was the all-powerful monarch in Europe, the Khedive trembled at the simple announcement of a visit from the French Consul-General. "What does he want now?" the Khedive would say, or "He has come to insist on the demand he made yesterday."

Halim was the uncle of the Khedive and, on the latter's death or abdication, would have been, according to Mohammedan law, entitled to the succession, being the oldest male descendant of Mohammed Ali. In 1866, the Khedive had procured a firman from the Sultan, Abdul Aziz, changing the order of succession, so that the Viceroyalty should descend from father to son instead of going to the oldest male member of the reigning family.

A large party of influential Moslems, composed mostly of people living in Constantinople, were opposed to this change. Halim resided in that city and, on the accession of the new Sultan, Abdul Hamid, there were constant intrigues against the Khedive and attempts to restore the old order of succession. To counteract this influence, he was obliged to send large sums of money to Constantinople, in addition to the annual tribute, which had been increased to three million four hundred thousand dollars on account of various concessions, among which was the title of Khedive, a dignity not enjoyed by his predecessors.

These conditions account for his dread of having the influence of any powerful European Government thrown into the balance against him. They also account for the anxiety of the representatives of the Powers to have the Khedive abdicate in favor of his son. They feared that Halim might be too independent or too much under the influence of the Sultan, and that the Sultan might attempt, if they relied upon his action, to profit by the occasion to regain prerogatives that had been bartered away by his predecessor. This last was precisely what did happen. It was only the positive and firm refusal of England and France to yield that prevented the success of the Sultan's attempt and secured to Tewfik Pasha the continuance of the privileges that had been granted to his father, so far as they were thought essential. This was only securing privileges for themselves, however, as Tewfik, whom they were setting on the throne, had no voice in the negotiations, and was afterwards compelled to do their bidding.

At an early stage in the negotiations, before the question of abdication had been broached to Ismaîl, the Sultan had been consulted. His Majesty had expressed a willingness to make

Halim Khedive, but he consented to the appointment of Tewfik only under the strong pressure of England.

The day following the midnight visit of the French and German Consuls-General to the Khedive, attempts to procure his voluntary abdication were continued, based on information claimed to have been received from Constantinople, that the Sultan was about to designate Halim as his successor. Offers were made of written guarantees of what had been promised, but the Khedive said firmly that he would only resign his power into the hands of the Sultan, or by his order.

During these scenes at Cairo the Ambassadors of England and France were busy at Constantinople.

In 1831, Mohammed Ali commenced a war against the Porte to secure his independence. In the following year, his armies, under the command of his adopted son, Ibrahim, the father of Ismaîl, conquered Syria. The intervention of the Powers prevented him from besieging Constantinople, but, under the treaty which followed, he retained the government of Syria. In 1839, England induced the Sultan to renew hostilities. The Sultan suffered a decisive defeat, but England, assisted by Austria, came to his support and arrested the victorious march of the forces of Mohammed Ali. They also compelled him to give up Syria, which had welcomed his coming and been satisfied with his reign and they restored this unhappy country, against its will, to the rule of the Turk. They also compelled him to acknowledge the suzerainty of the Sultan and pay to him an annual tribute amounting to one and a half million dollars. This action of England in replacing Egypt under the suzerainty of the Sultan has cost that country two hundred million dollars.

It has always been the policy of England to sustain Turkey as a bulwark against Russia. However cruel the Turk, he could always count on England's support whenever the integrity of his empire was endangered. Under the treaties, the Sultan could not remove the Khedive without the consent of the Powers that joined in the treaty compelling Mohammed Ali to accept for himself and his successors the sovereignty of Turkey.

When information came from Cairo that there were no hopes of the Khedive's voluntary abdication, the Sultan was much gratified to be able, on the invitation of the Powers, to exercise his prerogative of sovereignty in changing the ruler of Egypt. This privilege had been denied to him and his predecessors since the time that Mohammed Ali proclaimed his independence. He was the more willing and even pleased to do this, as he had never been friendly to the Khedive. This was for the reason, probably, that since the accession of his Sublime Majesty to the throne of the Khalifs in 1876, the exchequer of Egypt had not been such as to enable the Khedive to send to Constantinople such large sums as the Sultan, Abdul Aziz, and the members of his court were accustomed to receive.

In the forenoon of the twenty-sixth of June, a telegram came to the palace at Cairo addressed to "His Highness, Ismaîl Pasha, ex-Khedive of Egypt." In the excitement of the crisis, an unusual number of persons were in the rooms of the Master of Ceremonies, many of whom were waiting in the hope of obtaining an interview with the Khedive.

In olden times, the bearer of bad news to an Eastern potentate often forfeited his life. According to Herodotus, Xerxes said to Pythius, the Lydian, "Learn this well, that the spirit of man dwells in his ears which, when he hears pleasing things, fills the whole body with delight, but when he hears the contrary swells with indignation." [1]

Prejudice against communicating unpleasant information is still strong in the East. The Master of Ceremonies, Zekieh Pasha, read the address upon the despatch and quickly dropped

[1] Her. VII, 39.

it upon the table. Neither he nor his assistant, Tonino Bey, nor any other of the palace officials would venture to take the fatal message upstairs to his Highness. Fortunately, at this moment, Cherif Pasha entered. He was too much of a man to be influenced by any narrow prejudice or superstitious ideas and immediately took the message to the Khedive. His Highness is said to have opened and read it without any visible change of countenance. It was as follows: [1]

"The Grand Vizier of Turkey to Ismail Pasha, ex-Khedive of Egypt:

"The difficulties of Egypt both internal and external have assumed great importance, and the prolongation of the present state of affairs would be dangerous both to Egypt and the Ottoman Empire.

"It is one of the most important duties of the Imperial Government to find means of maintaining the tranquillity and assuring the well-being of the people, and the stipulations of the Imperial Firmans have been drawn with that object. It is evident that your remaining in the position of Khedive can have no other result than to increase and aggravate the present difficulties.

"Consequently, his Imperial Majesty, the Sultan, following a decision of his Council of Ministers, has decided to appoint, to the position of Khedive, his Excellency, Mehemet Tewfik Pasha, and an Imperial decree to this effect has been made.

"This important decision is communicated to his Excellency by another despatch, and I ask you to withdraw from the affairs of the Government in conformity to the order of his Imperial Majesty, the Sultan.

"The 6 Redjeb, 1296 (26 June, 1879)."

His Highness had till this moment relied upon the support of the Sultan and, when he had finished reading the despatch, he is said to have exclaimed, "That is what I receive for having sent during my reign £20,000,000 ($100,000,000) to Constantinople." He then quietly folded the despatch, saying, "Send for Tewfik immediately." Cherif quickly descended the stairs to a side door and, instead of sending for Tewfik, entered his carriage and went for him himself.

Tewfik was then residing at the palace Isma'ilfyeh, near the

[1] Translation from the Turkish.

Nile Bridge, half a mile distant from Abdîn. Here was hope, perhaps expectation, on the part of a young man of twenty-six years, who was as yet living with his family, quietly, without ostentation, and who bore himself with a modesty bordering on diffidence.

At the time of sending the despatch from Constantinople to Ismaîl Pasha, another was sent to Tewfik informing him of his appointment to the position of Khedive and ordering him to assume the direction of the Government. There was neither hesitation nor delay in the delivery of this despatch. The hope of reward stimulated the fortunate bearer of such welcome tidings.

It is said that the native telegraph operator who at night awaited the expected telegram announcing the death of Saîd Pasha, in 1863, and took it to Ismaîl his successor, was rewarded by immediate promotion, which was followed by others, until be became a Pasha.

On Cherîf's arrival at the palace of Tewfik, he found him ready to enter his waiting carriage and about to drive to Abdîn. Cherîf took a seat by his side and, as they drove out of the palace gate, Tewfik handed him the despatch, which he read as the carriage rolled hurriedly toward Abdîn. It was as follows: [1]

"Grand Vizier of Turkey to Mehemet Tewfik Pasha:
"The firm desire of his Majesty, the Sultan, is to secure the means of progress and tranquillity in Egypt which is an integrant part of the Empire, and the privileges which have been granted to the Government of this province sufficiently prove this supremely good intention. But, for some time, interior and exterior difficulties have arisen in this province which necessitate the removal of your august father Ismaîl Pasha.
"Your capacity and intelligence, tried and recognized by his Majesty, the Sultan, gives promise that you will be able to properly govern this province and to re-establish peace and tranquillity in conformity to the high and august desire of his Majesty, the Sultan. Consequently his Imperial Majesty has, by

[1] Translation.

Tewfik Pasha.

an Imperial decree, appointed you Khedive of Egypt, and the Imperial firman will be delivered to you with the usual ceremony.

"Ismaîl Pasha is invited by another despatch to retire from the affairs of the Government. Consequently, on receiving this despatch, you will assemble all the Ulemas, the functionaries, the notables of the country, and the employees of the Government, communicate to them the stipulations of the Imperial decree concerning your appointment and commence the direction of the affairs of the Government.

"This high and just appointment is a recompense for your capacities, and your accession will be the commencement of order and progress which will reign in the country, whose Government you are called to administer.

"I wish you great success, and I felicitate you on your accession."

"The 6 Redjeb, 1296."

In returning the despatch, Cherîf said, "Your Highness will take measures to be proclaimed Khedive at the Citadel this afternoon?" Tewfik assented.

The carriage quickly arrived at the grand entrance of Abdîn. They mounted in a moment the palatial stairway and were met by Ismaîl at the entrance of the reception room. His Highness took the hand of his son, raised it to his lips, according to the Oriental custom of familiar homage and said, "I salute you as my Effendina" (Lord), as the Khedive is usually styled among the natives. He then kissed him on both cheeks and added, "I hope you will not forget that I am your father," after which he retired immediately to his private apartments.

Thus, suddenly, all the responsibilities of the Government of Egypt and the Sudân from the Mediterranean to the lakes of Albert and Victoria Nyanza fell upon this young prince, and he became the absolute ruler of over ten million people, to whom his word was law. The Mahdi was soon to relieve him of the responsibility of the Sudân and Central Africa, and England and France were to assume the principal share of the Government of Egypt, but his cares and burdens were to be increased rather than lessened thereby.

CHAPTER XXII

THE INSTALLATION OF TEWFIK PASHA AND THE DEPARTURE OF
ISMAÎL

THE members of the Ministry were soon afterwards assembled
at the palace. Ismaîl Pasha appeared before them and formally
consented to the accession of his son to the throne of Egypt.
Official notices of the change of ruler were immediately sent to
the diplomatic representatives, accompanied with an invitation
to meet his Highness, Tewfik Pasha, that afternoon at his palace,
Isma'îlîyeh, and accompany him to the Citadel for the ceremony of his proclamation as Khedive.

At the appointed hour, we were at the palace and were received by his Highness. All were in dress uniforms, except the
representative of the United States. He was compelled to appear on this, as on other official occasions, in a plain dress-suit.
The lack of knowledge on the part of the members of Congress
of the customs of other countries and their desire to force their
Brother Jonathan ideas upon the whole world induced them, a
few years ago, to deny to their foreign representatives the
privilege of wearing uniforms according to the universal diplomatic custom.

We were joined at the palace by such judges of the New
Tribunal, or International Court, as were in Cairo. They were
in their official dress, which consisted of the red tarboosh; the
stamboul (a single breasted black coat with standing collar);
a broad scarlet scarf, with gold tassels at its ends, which passed

over the left shoulder and was attached at the waist on the right side; and a large chest plaque, upon which was engraved in relief the rising sun and in Arabic, in black enamel, the words "Justice is the foundation of all good government." The new Khedive, his brothers (Princes Hussein and Hassan), the members of the Ministry and the other court officials and high officers, all wore brilliant uniforms. The Ulemas (Doctors of Law), native judges and other notables were in their flowing native costumes.

The Khedive left the palace in a calash with his two brothers and Cherif Pasha. Then followed the carriages of the Consuls-General, the Judges and a long procession of Europeans and a few natives. The Citadel was over two miles distant, on a high point at the southeastern extremity of the city, which is a spur of the Mokattam Hills. Companies of cavalry were stationed on either side of the street leading from the palace, and, for a considerable distance before arriving at the Citadel, there were soldiers arranged in the same manner.

Information of the change of Government was not given to the public until two o'clock that afternoon. The news spread rapidly, and the crowd became so great near the end of our route that it was with difficulty that the soldiers could keep the passage clear. As we slowly mounted the high hill by a narrow passage with massive walls on either side, one hundred and one guns were fired from the overlooking parapets, announcing to the people the entry upon his reign of a new Khedive, and the sad termination of the reign of Ismaîl Pasha which had had such a brilliant beginning a little over sixteen years before.

As we reached the summit, turning back we saw the city spread out before us with its numerous gardens, its flat roofs, its extensive cemeteries, its historic, domed tombs of Mamelukes, Sultans, Khalîfs, Pashas and Beys, its numerous mosques with their domes and minarets. It was a unique and most delightful picture, covering a space very much more extensive than a city of half a million inhabitants would be expected to cover. On the west was the thread of the Nile and beyond the green fields, and, at the other side of the valley, the pyramids and the mountains of the Lybian desert. In front of us were the mosques and palaces of the Citadel for which the yellow deserts of the Mokattam Hills served as a background.

The Citadel was built by Saladin (Melik Yûsuf Salâheddîn), the founder of a dynasty of Kurds in Egypt, in 1166, of stone taken from the small pyramids of Gizeh. It is of little importance at the present day, in a military point of view, except as a temporary defense against any sudden revolt of the people of the city. An old, narrow passage with high walls on either side leads up to it. This passage was the scene of the horrid tragedies on the first day of March, 1811, in which over four hundred Mamelukes were slaughtered by the soldiers of Mohammed Ali, leaving him the sole ruler of Egypt.

The Mamelukes were originally slaves, as the name implies, trained as soldiers and forming the bodyguards of the Sultans. In 1250, they usurped the throne of Egypt, established a dynasty, and, with various changes, ruled the country for two hundred and fifty years. Those who had previously been slaves frequently became Sultans. In 1517, the Turks conquered the country and reduced the Mameluke Beys to the condition of petty princes. The Beys were made governors of the provinces, but Pashas to whom the Beys promised allegiance were sent to govern the country at large. The Pashas' authority, however, soon became little more than nominal, since the Beys, although paying them tribute, had absolute control of the provinces. The Beys sometimes rebelled and became almost independent of the Ottoman Government.

This was the condition of the country when Mohammed Ali became its governor, or the ruling Pasha. The Mameluke Beys

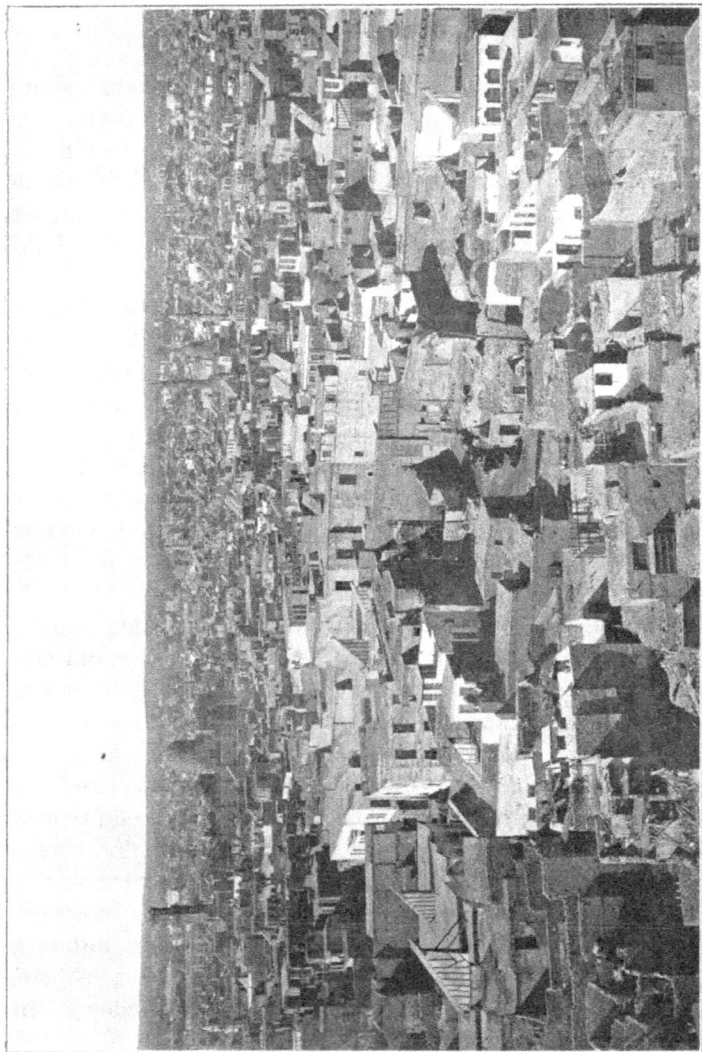

Cairo.

formed an aristocracy that in reality controlled the Government, the Turkish authority being only nominal. Mohammed Ali found that he could do nothing without their consent. Tired of this restraint, he conceived the idea of their utter extermination, and, having made preliminary arrangements to this end, he invited all the Mamelukes in Egypt to a grand reception at his palace in the Citadel.

The invitation of a ruler is always considered a command, and the Mamelukes, having no suspicion of his designs, willingly obeyed. When the reception was finished, he invited them to join in a procession and march through the city. To this they readily assented. Mounted on their richly caparisoned Arab steeds they would make an imposing spectacle, not only delighting the people, but inspiring in them an awe of the power of the combined force of the Mameluke princes.

When they had all entered the narrow passage, with files of the Pasha's soldiers arranged as a guard of honor on either side, the Pasha caused the great gates behind them as well as those at the foot of the hill to be closed, thus shutting them in between high walls. The order was given, the troops fell upon them, and the whole number, variously stated at from four to nearly five hundred, were slain. Only one escaped, and he, because he arrived at the Citadel too late to enter before the lower gate was closed. He heard the noise within and on his fleet horse made his escape into Syria. By a single stroke, the most successful *coup d'état* in history, a numerous aristocracy that had governed the country for over five centuries were exterminated. Thus was founded the power of Mohammed Ali, the son of a Turkish tobacconist of Kavala Roumelia, who was then forty-three years old. He is often called the great-grandfather of Tewfik, whom we were about to see proclaimed as Khedive. In fact, neither Ismaîl nor his son were descendants of Mohammed Ali. Ismaîl's father, Ibrâhîm Pasha, a great general,

who succeeded Mohammed Ali as ruler of Egypt, was only his
adopted son. He was the real son of one of the wives of
Mohammed Ali by a previous husband and was born in
Turkey.

The Citadel is sufficiently large to contain a small town, and
there are in it several very old mosques and a very large palace,
used when I was first in Egypt for offices of the Department of
War. The palace built by Mohammed Ali was of modest size
and used principally for ceremonial receptions, and it was to
this that our procession was directed.

There was to be a more formal ceremony on the arrival of
the firman. This one, therefore, was short, consisting merely
of the reading of the Imperial message before the Ministers, the
Ulemas, high functionaries, notables and employees of the Government, and a reception of the principal personages in the
country, foreign and native.

The Diplomatic and Consular Corps were received first. The
young Khedive, his brothers and the Ministers were seated in a
large reception room. As we entered, his Highness arose and
came forward to meet us.

The Doyen of the Diplomatic Corps made a short complimentary speech in French, in behalf of himself and his colleagues,
and the Khedive replied in the same language. We were seated,
smoked the chibûk, drank coffee, had a short conversation and
took our leave. The Judges were next presented, and then
various civil, religious and military bodies offered their homage
to their new sovereign, many humbly prostrating themselves in
his presence. None were seated nor served with coffee and pipes
except the diplomatic representatives.

During this time Ismaîl was at his palace, Abdîn. I went
directly from the Citadel to visit him, being probably the only
Consul-General who did so. My position of friendliness during
his Highness's troubles permitted me to do what could not con-

sistently be done by other Consuls-General representing Great Powers, except the representative of Russia.

His Highness talked freely of the situation, and said he should embark on the next Sunday or Monday and go directly to Constantinople, where he expected to pass the rest of his days. Knowing of his education in France and his love of European civilization, I ventured the suggestion that some European country other than Turkey might be more agreeable. "Yes," he replied, "perhaps for me personally, but for my family, with our customs, this would be disagreeable, impossible." On taking leave of his Highness, on previous visits, he had accompanied me only to the door of the reception room. On this occasion he accompanied me, while constantly talking, along the hall to the head of the stairs, and started to descend with me before I perceived his object. I did not permit him to go farther, and, as a response to my dissent, he said as we shook hands and separated, "I am no longer Khedive." He had a delicate appreciation of the forms of etiquette, and by accompanying me he wished to renounce all claims arising from his former sovereignty.

Two days later, Saturday, I again visited his Highness, and he informed me that the Sultan had refused him permission to come to Constantinople. He was much disappointed, but stated that he should leave Cairo on Monday morning and Alexandria the evening of the same day. Within twenty-four hours after the abdication, the French Consul-General called on him to inquire when he was to leave, making as an excuse that he wished to give orders to the French war-vessels at Alexandria to render him, on his departure, such honors as were due to a sovereign.

On Saturday afternoon, fearing that there might be some delay, he called again with the acting English Consul-General, both on the young Khedive and his father and insisted on the atter's leaving immediately. The two Powers also required the

Princes, Hussein and Hassan, to leave the country, as they both informed me. Thus the Khedive was required by his Christian guardians to exile, by nearly his first official act, not only his father, but two brothers about his own age against whom no complaints had ever been made. Four days after the abdication, the exiles sailed from Alexandria with their families for an unknown destination.

There was no exultation in Egypt over the change of Government, but only marks of sympathy and respect for the fallen sovereign. Notwithstanding the Oriental custom of abandoning the fallen to their disgrace, his palace was thronged, from the day of the abdication, with visitors who came to express their sympathy, and immense crowds of people accompanied him to the station. There, the separation of the family was a sad scene. The young Khedive embraced his father and brothers, and there were tears in the eyes of all beholders. Only the father was able to control his feelings. It was to be his last meeting with the son, to secure whose accession to the throne he had sacrificed large sums in gifts to the Sultan and his court.

All along the route to Alexandria, there were large numbers of people at the stations, all manifesting feelings of sympathy and respect. At Alexandria, the crowd was so great that it was necessary for the Khedive to go to the ship by an unexpected route. The war-vessels in the harbor manned the yardarms and fired the usual royal salute. Large numbers of people went on board the steamer to take leave and were received by his Highness with the utmost cordiality and calmness. He took leave of one after another by the shaking of the hand, saying a kind word to the more intimate and friendly, and occasionally, according to the habit of Orientals, warmly embracing an old and true friend. I stood some time on the deck talking with the two Princes, and saw some kissing the ex-Khedive's hand and others his garments, while many bowed to him with the greatest reverence. Thus one after another during over two hours took a final farewell of the late Effendina. The hour for sailing arrived and the *Mahroussa*, which had been his Highness's fast and favorite steamer in the height of his power, and was now consigned to take him and his family into exile, moved out of the harbor amid the renewed roar of cannon.

We soon learned of the exultation in Paris over the diplomatic victory, and the *"revanche éclatante;"* but in Egypt the feeling was only that of a conquered people parting with their sovereign at the dictation of hated foreigners. The French thought to strengthen their waning power in the Orient by this achievement, but they were only preparing the way to lose that which had survived their deplorably bad policy. Through this policy, the bondholders had added to their wealth, but the nation was to suffer not only in prestige, but commercially, in a degree wholly disproportional to what had been gained.

The Khedive went first to Naples. Stopping in that city a month later, I found his Highness and his family still on the steamer in the harbor, not yet knowing their final destination. Two years afterwards I visited him at the Favorita. This is a royal palace on the Bay of Naples at the foot of Vesuvius, which had been assigned him as a residence by the King of Italy. If public rumor was correct, this favor was only a partial payment of considerable sums of money that had been loaned by the Khedive personally to the King's father, Victor Emmanuel, and which had not been repaid. On this occasion, the Khedive was apparently very much affected by my visit. He embraced me in true Oriental style, kissing me on both cheeks, and, as he stood, still having his hand upon my shoulder, tears started from his eyes. All his warmth of welcome and the cordiality with which he frequently charmed the visitor when he was Khedive has been characterized by his detractors as theatrical, designed to please, mere "stage play," without any foundation of sincerity or real cordiality. That he possessed in a high degree a talent for pleasing is certain, and that he may have used it at times simply for the results produced is not improbable; but from my personal knowledge of his character I believe that he also formed strong friendships, to which he was generally true, until there was at least an apparent reason for a change of sentiment.

I remained at the palace one or two hours talking of Egyptian affairs, and on my return to Naples, the carriage of the Princes, Hussein and Hassan, followed close after mine to return the visit.

In the fall of 1881, I breakfasted with the Khedive at Milan and again, in the winter of 1882–83, in Paris. On the latter occasion General Stone, on his return from Egypt after a service of about ten years, was present. The English had then taken possession of the country and insisted on the General's retirement, though the young Khedive preferred to have him remain.

When I last saw Ismaîl, at Paris, he had changed his tarboosh for a tall, silk hat and had the appearance of a European. He resided at the Favorita until 1888, when he was permitted to make Constantinople his home. In so doing, he became virtually a prisoner of the Sultan, Abdul Hamid, his old enemy. He could thereafter leave that city only by his Majesty's special permission and was even a part of the time confined in his palace. A short while before his death, having long been in poor health and knowing he had but a short time to live, he made an effort to obtain permission to return to Egypt, desiring to spend his last days in its genial climate and die in his own country. This boon was refused by those who ruled its destinies. After his death, which occurred in March, 1895, they did permit his body to be taken to Cairo and placed in the mausoleum of the Khedivial family. Thus, the principal actor in the Egyptian drama of 1875 to 1879 disappeared. His two sons, Tewfik and Hassan, Cherîf Pasha, Lord Vivian and others had preceded him. The leading Americans who were in the service of the Khedive (Generals Stone and Loring, Colonels Colston, Field and many others) have also disappeared. The same may be said of the prominent Americans who visited the land of the Nile in that period, and who were kindly received by Ismaïl: Grant, Sherman, Washburn, Maynard and Noyes.

CHAPTER XXIII

ISMAÎL PASHA AND HIS REIGN

THERE are different opinions as to the merits and demerits of the reign of Ismaîl Pasha, according to the sources of information and the standard by which he is judged. Few persons were ever so excessively extolled at first and afterwards so shamefully traduced. Until he became financially embarrassed, not only the persons with whom he was immediately surrounded, but European journals of all classes and persons in high positions indulged in the most extravagant praises of the marvelous development of Egypt and its rapid advancement under its enlightened and progressive ruler, the "Napoleon of the Orient."

On his visit to Europe he was received as a royal guest and lodged in royal palaces at Florence, Vienna, Berlin, Paris and London. Emperors, kings, queens and princes vied with each other in bestowing upon him royal honors. In 1867, Queen Victoria conferred upon him the Grand Cross of the Bath and, in 1868, the Grand Cross of the Star of India, and Lord Napier was sent to Cairo to invest his Highness with this latter high decoration. When the financial conditions changed, his newspaper adulators, without any consideration of the causes, turned upon him their batteries of slander and vituperation.

The things he had done for the advancement of education, for modern civilization and for the material improvement of his country, which had before elicited such unstinted eulogies, were then attributed to selfish motives. He had done them either to enrich himself, or, to use the language of his detractors, "to throw dust in the eyes of Europeans." All that had previously been worthy of the highest praise was then only evidence of selfishness, deceit, low cunning, or other base sentiments.

Most of the writers of the history of the period are English. Many of these have written with a semblance of fairness. They are, however, constantly searching for an excuse for being in Egypt, and find no other than that of the claim of the bad administration of Ismaîl Pasha. It is not my purpose to undertake a defense of his Government. It would be difficult, with our ideas of what constitutes good government, to justify the acts of any Oriental prince.

If England and France had desired to depose the Emir of Afghanistan, the Shah of Persia, or the Sultan, they would have had no difficulty in finding a pretext of bad government and establishing the fact to the entire satisfaction of the whole civilized world. What I do wish to say is, that of all these governments, that of the Khedive was decidedly the best. The people were governed arbitrarily, and what we should term harshly, as in all Oriental countries. There are few prisons and, in the larger number of cases, the *koorbash* and the *bastinado* took the place of confinement.

But there were no riots, no periodic slaughtering of Christians, as throughout the whole of the rest of the Ottoman Empire. These slaughtered Christians are numbered by the thousands, and the massacres are nearly as numerous as the passing years. Still, the so-called Christian Powers are constantly combining to give their support to the maintenance of the integrity of the Sultan's dominions.

During all the reign of Ismaîl Pasha, the Christian was as secure in his rights of property, liberty and life as the Mussulman. The stranger, of any nationality or religion, could travel throughout all his dominions, from the sea to Central Africa, as safely as in any country in the world. Had he remained Khedive, with his authority as a ruler untrammeled, the same conditions would have continued. There would have been no revolts in 1881–82, no rule of Arabi Pasha, no bombardment, pillage and burning of Alexandria, with all their attendant horrors, and no $20,000,000 indemnity to be paid by the Egyptian Government and added to the national debt.

There would have been no Tell el-Kebîr with its slaughter of unarmed natives, no successful Mahdi, no defeat and massacre in Kordofân of Hicks Pasha and his ten thousand Egyptian soldiers, no terrible defeats and slaughters at Suakin, no disastrous expedition up the Nile in a vain effort to rescue Gordon Pasha, no loss to Egypt of the Sudân and the other provinces of Central Africa, and no expedition of Egyptian and English soldiers, at great expense to the Egyptian treasury, to recover the lost territories.

All of these events, with their attendant losses of tens of thousands of lives and scores of millions of dollars, were the direct result of the removal of a strong and competent ruler and the placing of the Government in the hands of irresponsible agents of the Paris and London bankers. And this removal was a sequence of Lord Beaconsfield's consent to join with France in an attempt to extort excessive interest on loans of which only fifty to sixty per cent had actually been received by the Egyptian Government.

An English writer, anent this subject, says, "This forcible intervention on the part of both of these Powers was brute force overriding public law for the meanest motive that ever influenced Christian Governments." "Such a departure" he adds "from every previous principle of English policy could not fail to be serious."

Ismaîl Pasha was in many respects a most remarkable man. In energy, administrative ability and intelligence, he far surpassed all other Oriental rulers. Under his guiding hand, Egypt advanced more in all that pertains to modern civilization during the sixteen years of his reign than it had in the previous five hundred years. In the promotion of education, in the preservation of the monuments of antiquity, in vast explorations—scientific and geographic—in the construction of railways and telegraphic lines, in the matter of steam navigation and in reclaiming land from the desert, it accomplished more than had been accomplished by the whole Ottoman Empire since the days of Osman, its founder.

When Ismaîl commenced his reign, Egypt had 246 miles of railway, to which he added 960 miles, at a cost of about $60,000,000; it had 350 miles of telegraph, to which he added over 5,600 miles; it had 4,052,000 acres of tillable land, to which there was added during his reign, mostly by him, 1,370,000 acres, an increase of 33 per cent; it had 44,000 miles of irrigating canals, to which he added 8,400. The cost of the great canal from Cairo to Ismailiya as already stated was not less than 50,000,000 francs. He constructed the harbors of Alexandria and Suez at a cost of $20,000,000.

He built docks, bridges and immense sugar factories. He erected lighthouses and instituted an excellent lighthouse service on all the coasts of Egypt. He purchased steamers and established regular steamship lines on the Mediterranean and the Red Sea. He had constructed in France and removed to Alexandria a large dry dock. The annual exports were increased during his reign more than three-fold, from £4,454,000 to £13,810,000. He added to his dominions large extents of territory in Central Africa and on the Red Sea, including Suakin, Massowah and Zeila. He caused these countries to be surveyed and mapped and established in them his Government, the authority of which was everywhere respected. This vast territory with the old Sudân now constitute what the English with great pride term the "New British Empire of the Sudân." It was all under the full, peaceable control of the Khedive at the time he was dethroned.

At the commencement of his reign, Cairo was wholly an Oriental city. The streets were narrow, many of them only wide enough for a single camel or horse. They were not lighted. Each person who went out at night carried his lantern or was preceded by a torch bearer. There was no available water-supply except the canal running through the town, from which the water was carried in skins. When the canal was dry, which was the case for some months each year, the water was taken from cisterns where it had been stored at the time of the high Nile. Ismaîl established good systems of gas and water both in Cairo and Alexandria. To the former city, he made large additions of streets, boulevards and public gardens, thus creating a beautiful European town, with modern comforts and conveniences, alongside the old town.

Egypt has the benefit to-day of these numerous internal improvements, as well as of the increased amount of tillable land, the railroads, telegraph lines, harbors, docks and lighthouses.

Ismaîl Pasha also abolished the slave trade in his dominions and the horrid practice of the mutilation of colored boys for service in the harems, making such mutilation a crime punishable with death. He stopped the importation of slaves, expended very large sums of money in an attempt to end completely the slave trade in the Sudân and the provinces of Central Africa, and to prevent the transportation of slaves across the Red Sea, whence the slave dealers took them to Turkey and Persia.

He also made a law, according to the provisions of which the sale of slaves, both white and black, from family to family was to cease in August, 1884. As there were rarely any slaves born in Egypt, this would soon have ended slavery in that country. He permitted his sons to have only one wife each, in order to set an example for the discontinuance of polygamy and the consequent importation of white slaves.

Previous to his reign, there was an open slave market at Cairo where both white and black slaves were sold; and negroes were being constantly captured in Central Africa and brought down the Nile or taken across the Red Sea and sold as slaves.

A short time before his dethronement, I negotiated with Cherîf Pasha, with the approbation of his Highness, a treaty in which were embodied, in the form of an agreement on the part of the Khedive, provisions for the abolition of traffic in slaves. This was done in accordance with a verbal understanding on the subject with the Government at Washington. I sent Mr. Evarts a draft of the treaty in English and French, but, in consequence of the change of Khedive and the English and French control, it was never executed.

This treaty contained also a provision giving to cruisers of the United States a right to "visit, search and detain, in order to hand over to the most convenient Egyptian authority for trial, any Egyptian vessel found engaged in the traffic in slaves, or which might be fairly suspected of being intended for that traffic."

It would require a volume to give a history of the improvement in educational facilities during Ismaîl's administration. At the close of the reign of his immediate predecessor, Saîd Pasha, the whole number of public schools was only 185. During the reign of Ismaîl the number was increased to 4,817. These schools provided for between eighty and one hundred thousand pupils—a percentage of the whole number of boys in the country eight times greater than the percentage of public school pupils in the Russian Empire, and three-fourths as great as the percentage in Italy.

In the last year of the reign of Saîd Pasha, the whole sum appropriated by the Government for schools was only $30,000. Ismaîl had increased this amount in 1872 to $400,000. Under the bondholders' reign, this sum was reduced in 1880 to $200,000, precisely the amount of the salaries of twelve European comptrollers imposed upon the country.[1] The Arabs have a great desire for learning. Their aptitude in acquiring knowledge is universally admitted and their advancement under the reign of Ismaîl was without parallel. They are also capable of the highest degree of culture. In his attempts to raise the standard of education, the Khedive had to encounter the almost universal illiteracy among the masses, but he had no prejudices to combat.

In all other departments than that of education he had tremendous obstacles to overcome. We of the Occident cannot comprehend the full significance of his innovations. The ruler who attempts to graft modern civilization upon the old Oriental stock, with all its ignorance, its prejudices and conservatism, has no aid. He must not only originate and direct every change, but must actually impose it by the force of his authority.[2]

---

[1] "Influenced by his third wife, a woman of considerable learning, the Khedive Ismaîl caused to be constructed most extensive school buildings to be devoted to the higher education of Mohammedan girls ; but this promising institution was suppressed, as a measure of economy, in 1876, through the English and French intervention in Egyptian financial affairs, and these beautiful buildings are now occupied by the administration of public works. A similar " economical " measure was employed in the suppression of the extensive schools for soldiers' children established by General Stone Pasha, the American chief of Ismaîl's military household."—GEN. GEORGE S. BATCHELLER in North American Review of Aug. 2, 1907, p. 776.

[2] An experience of my own while traveling in Syria will show the difficulties of improvements in these countries.

I was returning southward from a trip to the Great Cedars, along the highest mountain path. Near sunset on the second day, I suddenly came to the brow

The Khedive was personally of amiable disposition. No other testimony would be given by any of his numerous palace employees, either foreign or native. He discontinued the severe punishments, which had previously prevailed in Egypt. There

of a mountain declivity whence could be seen, a thousand feet below, a picturesque village in a plateau on the side of the mountain.

My company consisted of an interpreter, a fifteen year old son of Dr. Bliss, president of the American College at Beirut, a cook and two muleteers. We had three riding horses and mules to carry tents, provisions and camp equipage. The descent appeared difficult and, for the horses impossible, but others had descended by the same path and why not we. Our animals were so accustomed to mountain travel that they could even mount and descend ordinary stairs. The baggage having been fastened so that it could not slip forward, the horses and mules slowly crept down the mountain, sliding, at times, for considerable distances.

That night, by permission, we pitched our tents on a lawn in front of the dwelling of a former Emir of the Lebanon. Previous to 1860, he was a petty prince governing by hereditary right, subject to the Sultan. In consequence of the massacres of that year, the Lebanon was placed under a special government, the Governor being appointed by the Sultan, but subject to the approval of the Great Powers. The Emir lost his hereditary authority, but retained great influence among the people.

In the evening, I called upon the Emir. He was very old and deaf, and only his wife could make him understand. Our conversation was, therefore, through the interpreter and the wife. Rustoum Pasha was then the Governor of the Lebanon, and an exceptionally good ruler. We had lately had our tents pitched close by each other for two weeks, and he had told me of some of his plans for improving the country.

Among them, was a wagon road from Beirut to Damascus by the way of the Dog River (Lycus of the Romans), which was a little east of the village of the Emir but much lower. The only wagon road in Syria at that time in a condition to be used was one between these two cities constructed over the mountains by a French company under a fifty-year concession. The tolls were designedly fixed at a figure sufficiently high to exclude all travel, except by the company's conveyances. This gave it the monopoly of the passenger and freight traffic, which was so large that the business required sixteen hundred horses and mules and four hundred men.

Stages left each end of the route morning and evening and large trains of wagons loaded with merchandise each day. I naturally thought that a new road that would end this oppressive monopoly, and give an outlet to the inhabitants of this and many other secluded villages, would very much please

were no confiscations, scarcely any banishments and very few
capital punishments. I heard of only one of the last named
during the three years that he reigned, after my arrival. There
is the one exceptional case, it is true, that of the Minister of
Finance, Ismaîl Sadik Pasha. In the absolute Oriental government, the sovereign must in many cases necessarily take the
place of the judge, and there may have been injustice in some
cases. But Ismaîl's record is white, in this respect, in comparison with that of any other Oriental potentate. Even the English in the Government of non-Christian countries cannot show
a better record. They never hesitate to try, shoot, or hang
people summarily, whenever they believe it necessary to assure
or strengthen their supremacy. On their landing at Alexandria
after the bombardment of that city, they adopted some of these
summary methods.

While Egypt was so rapidly advancing in all that pertains to
modern civilization (even including the luxury of creating a
large national debt, in which most European countries indulge
to the extent of their credit), what was being done in the rest

the Emir. During the conversation I mentioned the subject. The wife had
not the patience to do more than announce the subject to her deaf consort.
She commenced at once to express her own decided opinions, which were,
undoubtedly, also those of her husband.

"Yes," she said, "the Governor wanted their people to help build this road"
but he would get "no aid from them." "What do we want of a road?"
"What purpose can we put it to? How can we use it?" and other exclama-
tions of the same character were repeated in quick succession with nervousness
and emphasis. "No, he will get no aid from us. We want nothing to do with
his road."

The poor woman had probably never seen a cart, wagon or carriage, certainly not in her own town, and such innovations were not to be tolerated.
The next morning, we descended one thousand feet to the river by an incline
nearly as sharp as that by which we had reached the village. We then mounted
two thousand feet on the other side, a part of the distance by broad steps.
We passed on the way people with pack mules loaded with wood going to
Beirut, twenty miles distant. And yet what did they want of a road?

of the Ottoman Empire? Although his Sublime Majesty's Government was upheld and kept from disintegration by the European Powers, was there any printers' ink used, during this period, in praise of the material improvements of his country, or of the amelioration of the condition of the inhabitants of the dominions over which he ruled? No; there was only a record of a constant cry of agonizing humanity, of massacres of Armenians, Bulgarians and other Christians, and of congresses to impose reforms and keep the Turk on his feet. The Ottoman debt did not fail to be increased, not only to the extent of the borrowing capacity of the Government, but even beyond any expectation of its ability to pay. And, for this, there was nothing to show but annals of murders.

In all Syria, there was not a harbor, a railroad, nor even a wagon road except the one from Beirut to Damascus. The internal commerce of the country was carried on by means of pack mules and camels over rough, rugged paths which had not been improved in the least for centuries. Steamers coming along the coasts were obliged to anchor out in the sea, to transfer their cargoes and passengers to the shore in small boats, if the weather permitted, or, if the sea was too rough for this, to steam on without landing either.

In Asia Minor, there was only one railroad. That had been built by an English company from Smyrna a short distance into the interior. Turkey in Europe could not show much more advancement. Everywhere, there were misery, oppression and the cruelty of the Turk. But the Sultan was upheld as a superior moral being and was asked, in the interests of good government and of the happiness of his beloved subjects, to remove the Khedive, who was in the way of the giving of a free hand to those who were pocketing the resources of Egypt. He could not do otherwise than obey, even if he had been so disposed.

The results were tersely expressed in 1887 by the now vener-

able member of the English Parliament, Sir Wilfrid Lawson, in
seconding a motion to amend the address in reply to the Queen's
speech and demand an immediate recall of the English forces
in Egypt. He said:

"We have raised the funded debt of Egypt from £90,000,000
to £100,000,000, slaughtered many thousands of the natives,
crippled the National Chamber, bombarded the principal city
of the country under circumstances of the greatest horror,
increased taxation, promoted horrible debauchery in the capital,
sown dissensions between the Khedive and the people, and
crushed out the first little sparks of independence that had been
seen in Eastern nations for ages past."

The causes of the financial embarrassments of Ismaîl Pasha
are attributed, by those who attempt to justify his forced
abdication, to his extreme prodigality, and on this theme they
have embroidered the most extravagant romance. Any little
summer house on the desert has been classed as one of his
Highness's "magnificent and costly palaces."

There were only two residences built by Ismaîl that were
worthy of the name of palaces, and the cost of these was in-
significant in comparison with royal European residences. Like
other buildings in Cairo, they were of common rough stone, laid
in mortar and plastered inside and out. They had plain, flat,
cemented roofs and their cost was in no way disproportionate
to his Highness's private wealth before he became Viceroy.
The receptions and dinners given by him after my arrival in
Egypt were few in number, and in no way extravagant; and yet
an English writer, who claimed great candor and conservatism
in the statements of his book, called them "revels" and "Bel-
shazzar's feasts."

According to the newspaper accounts, the balls and other
entertainments given by his immediate successors, under their

European advisers, have been greater in number and far more sumptuous; but there is no claim of extravagance.

When Mr. Goschen came to Egypt, with all the prestige of an ex-member of the English Cabinet, to continue the work of "spoiling the Egyptians," which he had commenced years before as a member of the firm of Fruhling-Goschen, one of the great crimes he charged against the Khedive was that of aiding in the maintenance of the theater at Cairo.

This theatre was largely patronized by European and American visitors, who came in the winter to Egypt for health, or pleasure. The operas and principal theaters of Paris, Berlin and other European cities are maintained, or largely aided, by their respective Governments. The theater at Cairo still exists; but there are now no criticisms.

All of these pretended extravagances, which for years furnished themes for the newspaper correspondence carried on in the interest of the bondholders, counted but little in the sum of the national debt. The most serious unnecessary expenditures were those arising from the Khedivial hospitality in entertaining the imperial, royal and princely guests with their numerous retinues, the Ambassadors, Ministers and newspaper correspondents, who visited Egypt at the time of the opening of the Suez Canal.

Among these guests were Francis Joseph, Emperor of Austria, the Empress Eugénie, the Crown Prince of Prussia and numerous scions of royalty and nobility. From these, down through a long list to correspondents of obscure newspapers and nobodies, there were in all, it is claimed, over three thousand who through some official influence managed to be classed among the invited. All these visitors were sumptuously entertained in palaces and hotels, and many were furnished with steamers for the voyage up the Nile. This was a foolish expenditure, an excessive manifestation of Oriental hospitality, the cost of which might properly have been placed to the charge of the private estate of the Khedive.

His Highness then thought that the canal, to the construction of which he had so largely contributed, was to be his crowning glory. It did not occur to him that it was to lead to his own and Egypt's ruin, nor that the nation which had given it no aid and had as far as possible obstructed the work would ultimately reap its vast commercial benefits, and, through it, augment its possessions and its political power to an inestimable extent. Probably, the suavity of the ever captivating Monsieur de Lesseps, as well as his own Oriental largeness of hospitality, led him to this unjustifiable expenditure. Whatever may be said of the great accomplishment of Monsieur de Lesseps, he was certainly the evil genius of Egypt, and the Suez Canal the primary cause of its ruin.

The Prince of Wales and many other royal or celebrated personages were also entertained by Ismaîl with a lavishness similar to that which he had practiced at the time of the opening of the canal. Outlays of this character added to the total of the indebtedness, but they were not the causes of the financial embarrassments. These causes were the same that have frequently produced great numbers of failures among business men,—the attempt to do too much at a flood-tide of prosperity which is soon to be followed by a low ebb.

Ismaîl came to the throne in 1863 at the time of the high price of cotton. Egypt had been producing considerable quantities of this commodity for some years. The high prices then prevailing, and a belief in the continuance of the war in the United States, caused a great extension in this department of Egyptian agriculture. In 1864, the exports of Egypt amounted to the unprecedented sum of $72,000,000. This prosperity excited all classes and produced the wildest ideas as to the mines of wealth in the soil of the Delta of the Nile. Egypt was henceforth to be the great cotton-producing country of the world. Even the common fellah could indulge in a second wife. The best business men lost their conservatism and were carried away in the current of financial speculation. The Khedive, who had previously been very successful in all his business enterprises, imbibed the spirit of the day and thought there was no end to Egypt's wealth.

Orientals are proverbially improvident. With prosperity comes ostentation and love of pompous show. The Khedive, unfortunately, knew Europe too well. He loved its splendor, and, with his grand and noble ideas of enlarging the boundaries of Egypt, creating an African Empire on the model of European civilization, with numerous railroads, telegraphic facilities, harbors, docks, steamboat lines and general education, came also the desire for fine cities, beautiful gardens and parks and all the attendant luxuries of modern civilization. He was surrounded by a legion of European flatterers, who extolled him and exaggerated the wealth of the country, and he was soon launched into a multitude of costly schemes of territorial enlargement and internal improvement.

In the fall of 1864, on the requisition of the Sultan, a small army was sent by Egypt, at its own expense, to put down a rebellion in the Hedjaz; and, in the spring of the following year, another was sent to Crete to aid the Turk in suppressing the Christian revolt.

With the addition of expenses came a reduction in revenues. In 1866, in consequence of the decline in cotton, the exports had decreased thirty-three per cent, about $23,000,000. Great projects were under way, contracts were made, and, because there was everywhere hope of better times and of an increased revenue from uncompleted improvements, there was no curtailment of expenses. They were rather constantly increasing, each new work requiring additional outlay. The harbors required docks and the railroads rolling stock. There were also great wastages, enormous leakages. All the works were new to the natives, and were carried on by contracts with Europeans, who formed a body of cormorants ever seeking lucrative "jobs."

The Khedive had few competent and trustworthy agents. He was obliged to supervise every department of his Government, and, in order to do so, had to familiarize and occupy himself with the railroads, the telegraphs, the steamer lines, the harbors, the docks, the lighthouse system, the municipal improvements, the armies, the vast explorations and conquests in Central Africa, and the establishment of his authority in the equatorial provinces and at Suakin and Massowah.

All these departments were under his immediate control, and not a contract could be made, nor a car purchased, nor a new switch put in, nor a rod of track laid without his direction. In addition to this and to the personal government of his millions of subjects, his vast personal estates and those of his family, the cleaning and constructing of irrigating canals, and the reclaiming of desert lands, all required his attention.

The management of his lands with their hundreds of thousands of laborers, their great sugar factories, their railroads, boats, camels, cattle and utensils, would have been sufficient to have prostrated the most able administrator. Yet, with all his other cares, he did not neglect his personal estates. His knowledge of the details of every applicance and utensil, from the shaduf and mattock to the steam pump, the locomotive and steamship, was always an occasion of the greatest surprise to those who conversed with him for the first time, and the constant wonder of those Europeans who were the most familiar with him and the country.

He made all contracts of importance, and even the smaller ones were under his supervision. It was far too much for one brain; and it is doubtful if any one person ever undertook to direct so many, and such varied and extended enterprises,— to say nothing of the endless cares of his Government. The results were necessarily great wastes through incapable and dishonest agents.

Notwithstanding these losses, his administration would have met all its liabilities except for the usurious interest paid on its loans. As already stated, Egypt had, as early as 1882, repaid the full amount of all moneys it had actually received on the sale of bonds with six per cent annual interest, and had left to its credit in over-payments eighteen million dollars. The loans so repaid included those made to pay the fifty million dollar debt legacy of Saîd Pasha and the many millions taken by the Suez Canal Company through the award of Napoleon III. The four hundred and fifty million dollar debt now placed to Egypt's account, and the interest paid thereon since 1882, amounting to as much as the nominal principal, are all usury, and without any equitable consideration.

The annual interest on the sum still remaining is, in round numbers, eighteen million dollars. This is a naked tribute which must be paid annually to Europe for an indefinite period, probably for generations, like the tribute paid to Turkey imposed by the Powers, at the instigation of England, in the time of Mohammed Ali. Ismaîl Pasha's real crime consisted in putting himself into the hands of the Shylocks of London and Paris. These Shylocks, who were mostly Jewish bankers, had sufficient power to control the Governments of England and France and to induce them to establish a new precedent relative to official aid in the collection of contractual debts, even those not resting upon any moral obligation.

It was for the collection of claims of this character, which would enable the Rothschilds, Oppenheims, Goschen and others of the financial groups to reap the full harvest of their financial ventures, that the two Great Powers first gave their official aid and England, later, its military support.

Very few English people have ever received correct information relative to the causes of the financial failure in Egypt. Having had no information to the contrary, they believe that the money was honestly loaned, that the indebtedness remaining is the balance unpaid, and that these hundreds of millions were squandered by Ismaîl Pasha in riotous living. They are justly proud of what Lord Cromer has done toward giving the people a good Government, but they know nothing of the facts relative to the burdens imposed, which Lord Cromer could do little to alleviate. He could do nothing to relieve this little country, one-fifth as large as the state of New York, from the annual payment of eighteen million dollars unjustly exacted and forced from this oppressed people by military power; nor from the payment of the three and a half millions of tribute to Turkey, which, I am informed, has long been hypothecated and goes direct to England.

When we speak of the extent of Egypt, we do not include the surrounding deserts nor the Sudân and other southern provinces. These are not yet any more than self-supporting, neither are they any longer a part of Egyptian territory. Egypt paid the expense of the reconquest and is permitted, as compensation, the empty honor of having her flag raised, for the time being, beside that of the English.

The new departure of certain aggressive European Powers from well-established principles, in their attempts to collect claims based on contracts and other claims the equity of which is doubtful by the use of ironclads, opens a wide door for the perpetration of gross wrongs against small and weak countries. Any encouragement of, or even acquiescence in, acts of this character against weak American Powers would be likely to lead us into serious international complications. Aiding, or in any manner participating in the forced collection of claims of the character of the larger part of those against Egypt would be a crime which it is hoped there will be no occasion to charge to the Government of the United States. If we strictly adhere to the course we have thus far pursued, we shall avoid not only the danger but the injustice of such a policy. Secretary of State Elihu Root, in his late speech at Buenos Aires, Argentina, said: "The United States has never employed and never will employ her army or navy for the collection of debts contracted by governments or private individuals." "Such measures," he added, "lend themselves to speculation and are based on sordid objects."

CHAPTER XXIV

INTERNATIONAL TRIBUNALS

THE Mixed Tribunals or International Courts of Egypt constitute a unique institution. They are composed of foreign and native judges. To constitute a court for the trial of a cause requires five judges, three foreign and two native. There are no juries, the court finding the facts and deciding the questions of law. The court in which the trial takes place is known as the Court of First Instance and has two branches, the civil and the commercial. The former has jurisdiction in what would be termed equity actions in an English or American court and the latter in actions at law. There are, however, important exceptions to this line of division.

In the commercial court, there are two assessors, one native and one foreigner, chosen from the prominent business men of the city in which the court is held. They serve for a stated time, at the end of which others are selected to take their place, in a manner similar to that of selecting jurors in the United States. They sit with the judges on the trial and have a vote in the decision of the case. The Europeans are residents of Egypt, and the natives are chosen from among the prominent local merchants. Being acquainted with the commercial customs of the people, they are valuable aids to the court. Actions in which the sum in controversy is below a fixed amount are tried before a single European judge in a court known as the Court of Justice Sommaire.

There is also a Court of Appeal, a forum of last resort, to which cases may be appealed from the trial courts. It has seven foreign judges, one from each of the seven Great Powers, and five natives. General George S. Batcheller has lately been designated by President Roosevelt to represent the United States in this Court. He was, under President Harrison, Assistant Secretary of the Treasury at Washington and Minister to Portugal. Having served in the Court of First Instance at Cairo for over ten years, he is eminently fitted for his new position.

There are in all these International Courts thirty-four foreign and twenty-one native judges. Of the former, there are three from each of the seven Great Powers, including the United States, and one and sometimes two from the Christian Powers of the second class, such as Belgium, Holland, Greece and Spain. The courts have jurisdiction in civil actions in all mixed cases, that is, actions in which there are parties of different nationalities,—as a native and an Englishman or an Englishman and a German. They also have jurisdiction in cases of crimes committed in opposing the execution of their judgments. They were instituted under the Khedive, Ismaïl Pasha, to take the place of a large number of consular courts which had been established under the extraterritorial jurisdiction granted to the Christian Powers.

Christian governments have never acknowledged the jurisdiction over their citizens of the courts of non-Christian countries. Whenever these countries have been opened to commerce and the residence, temporary or permanent, of foreigners, treaties have been made or concessions granted allowing extraterritorial jurisdiction. This is the right of the Christian country to govern, through its Consuls, its own citizens who may, either temporarily or as permanent residents, be in the non-Christian country. Japan has lately been made an exception to this rule, whether wisely or not the future action of her courts will determine. Already serious complaints have been made by European merchants.

In the case of the Turkish Empire, the Khalîfs and Sultans could not formerly treat with infidels. To have entered into agreements with them would have been to acknowledge that they had rights which even a Khalîf was bound to respect. Instead of entering into agreements or making treaties, the Khalîfs issued letters containing grants of privileges. These letters, known to Orientals as Imperial Diplomas and to Europeans as Capitulations, granted to the foreign sailors and merchants who came to trade in the Khalîf's dominions immunity from arrest or molestation by the local authorities. They were first issued as early as the twelfth century. Christian nations were never over modest in making claims under a very elastic construction of these grants of privileges. As favorable opportunities occurred, they also obtained additional grants, until in the principal cities of Egypt, more especially in Alexandria, it became a question whether the foreign governments or the local authority was the ruling power. The extraterritorial rights, claimed and enjoyed, resulted in the establishment of numerous sovereignties in Egypt.

Christian foreigners were, as to their government and all judicial proceedings, considered as residing in their own country. There were fourteen Christian Powers, at one time eighteen, represented by Consuls, each of whom was a *de facto* governor of the members of his colony and a judge to try and decide all complaints or actions brought against them, from whose decisions there was no appeal except to his own Government. There was, however, no means of executing judgments rendered against a native except through the local authorities, nor against a foreigner except through the courtesy of the Consul of the party against whom the judgment had been rendered.

Foreigners were not only exempt from arrest and trial by the local authorities, but their children, born in Egypt, took the nationality of their parents, and this might continue, as it actually did in some cases, for generations. To secure this right of the nationality of both the parent and child, it was only necessary that the family records should be properly entered and preserved at the Consulate.

There were residing in Egypt in 1878 thirty thousand Greeks, ten thousand Italians and many of other nationalities. The bankers, a large portion of the principal merchants and other business men of the country were foreigners. Commercial enterprises were largely in their hands. With fourteen independent judicial systems, often rendering opposing decisions, since each Consul acted under the laws of his own country, there could only be endless confusion resulting in most serious difficulties.

Different plans to avoid this confusion were tried, but the first efficacious solution was the International Courts. It was only through long and difficult negotiations and, it is said, by a free use of money at Constantinople and with the press of London and Paris, that the Khedive succeeded in establishing them. Several of the Powers clung tenaciously to the privileges granted, or acquired by long usage and by forced construction of the Capitulations. Jurisdiction in criminal cases is still retained by the Consular Courts.

The position of a foreign judge is no sinecure, though he has each year three and a half months' leave of absence, usually taken in the hot months from June to October. Three foreign judges, however, must remain during the vacation to hold a court in case of urgency. These take their vacation at a later date. From October to June, the court is always overloaded with work.

The judgments are prepared by the judges and are in the

nature of the report of a referee, containing the findings of fact, the legal opinion, and the order of execution. By the French system, a party against whom a judgment is rendered must be informed by the judgment itself of the facts and reasons of its being rendered; otherwise, the judgment is void on its face and cannot be executed.

The legal languages of the courts have been, until a very recent date, French, Italian and Arabic. English has now been added. In practice, French is the principal language, all the judges, except the Italian, and most of the lawyers employ no other in their court proceedings. The papers used in evidence are in many languages besides those mentioned,—Greek, German, Spanish, Turkish, and even Hebrew. This necessitates a large number of clerks and interpreters.

The court is an independent body, employing and discharging at its pleasure its clerks, sheriffs and interpreters, paying their salaries and those of its members. Large fees are received from suitors and for the services of clerks, sheriffs and interpreters and also a percentage on the judgments rendered. The revenues from these sources and for the registration of deeds, bonds, mortgages and for notarial acts are more than sufficient to pay all the expenses of the courts. The surplus is paid to the Egyptian Government. During the first twenty-eight years of the sitting of these courts, ending October 31, 1903, the number of cases adjudged was 229,807 and the receipts therefrom and from the other sources I have mentioned were 7,184,722 Egyptian pounds, equalling $35,923,610. The expenses of the courts during this period were $18,843,715, leaving a surplus of $17,079,895 which was paid to the Egyptian Government. During the last decade, the business of the courts has increased very rapidly. The receipts for the year 1904 were $3,910,000; those for 1905, $5,048,000. The surplus paid to the Government in the latter year was $3,978,000. Thus these courts, instead of being an expense to the Government, as our courts are, are a fruitful source of revenue. This is a species of taxation to which we, happily, have not yet had recourse.

The judges hold their positions for life, or as long as these courts are maintained. They can neither be removed by their own Governments nor by that of Egypt. They may, however, be removed by the Court of Appeal for misconduct or incompetency.

Oral testimony is rarely permitted in the trial of a cause, and then only by an interlocutory judgment allowing certain prescribed questions to be asked or some isolated fact to be proved. If such evidence were permitted as is permitted in an American or English court, it would be of little advantage to litigants, as no employee, employer, servant, master, business associate, or person within the fourth degree of relationship to a party is a competent witness. The system is the same in principle as that in France and other Continental countries. It is based on the supposition that no one interested, however remotely, is to be believed.

If contracts are not in writing, there is generally no legal remedy. The honor of the party must be relied upon. Even the payment of money upon a contract cannot be proven orally, but the party claimed to have received it may be ordered by the court to appear and answer the simple question as to whether it is true that payment was made as claimed. If he does not appear as ordered, he loses his case. If he does and denies the payment, that settles the question. His denial cannot be disproved by oral testimony. In criminal cases, oral testimony is taken as under the English or common-law system.

The value of property or the amount of loss sustained by damage to it is determined by experts appointed by the court. Application for such appraisal must be made immediately after the event causing the damage claimed, and the expert must promptly make and deliver to the court his report to be used whenever the case is heard.

Books of account, when kept in a prescribed manner, and letter-press copies are admissible as evidence in actions between merchants only; but the condition of the accounts and the balances are determined by the written reports of expert accountants, also appointed by the court.

Documents, promissory notes, letters and other writings are admitted in evidence without proof of authenticity. The party against whom they are introduced, however, can enter a plea of forgery or any other, which, if proved, would invalidate the document. In that case, the action is suspended and a special issue formed and tried before a single judge under the limitations of a judgment of the court as to the oral evidence to be admitted. In the event of failure of a party to sustain his allegations, he is not only condemned to pay the costs of the special proceeding, but in case of bad faith or of an accusation of forgery he may be fined.

The court is generally in session every forenoon, except on the Moslem Sunday (which is our Friday) and the Christian Sunday. The trial of a cause consists of short arguments by the attorneys on the papers produced, including reports of experts, if there are any, and generally does not occupy more than an hour, often not half that time.

The papers with the briefs of the attorneys are taken by the court and the cases divided among the judges, generally only among the foreign judges, for examination. A decision is agreed upon at a council held each week, in accordance with which a judgment is drawn by the judge who first took the papers for examination and is read in open court by the presiding justice. The proceeding is very summary and the judgment is generally rendered within a very short time after the commencement of the action.

All decisions are *per curiam* in accordance with the votes of a majority of the judges or the judges and assessors sitting on the trial. No dissenting opinions are permitted, nor can the differences in opinion of the judges, if any, be divulged. The judgment stands as that of the court, and is, so far as the public is informed, the unanimous opinion of the judges. It is thought that dissenting opinions or a knowledge that there is any disagreement among the judges weakens the effect of the judgment and lessens the confidence in and the respect for the court. There are advocates of the adoption of the same system in the courts of our country.

The want of more explicit and more detailed evidence is often very perplexing to the judge, and the uneducated native undoubtedly frequently suffers great wrong; but I am not prepared to say that the truth is not quite as often arrived at as by our system of voluminous, conflicting and often directly contradictory evidence. Certainly, the ascertaining of damages to property by experts, acting immediately, is more satisfactory than that of oral testimony as taken in our courts, often after the lapse of years. The European judges in these courts are strongly opposed to oral testimony, claiming that its introduction would only be opening the doors to perjury and gross frauds.

The Mixed Tribunals were organized in 1875, and a code, which was a modification of the Code Napoleon, adopted for their use. The modifications were such as were thought necessary to adapt it to the customs and conditions of the country. Its application by the courts proved the desirability of other changes. In 1880, an International Commission was organized for the purpose of making additional modifications. President Hayes appointed Hon. George S. Batcheller, then judge in these courts at Cairo, and the writer, to represent the United States on this commission. The commission met in Cairo from time to time during the winter of 1880–81, but did not finish its work on account of disagreement regarding several important questions.

While in the United States on a leave of absence in the summer of 1881, I received a telegram from the chief clerk in the Department of State, requesting my presence in Washington. On arriving in that city on the morning of the first day of July, I was informed that the President, Mr. Garfield, wished to see me. By an arrangement of Mr. Blaine, then Secretary of State, an interview was had at the close of the Cabinet meeting held that day. It was the last Cabinet meeting at which this lamented President presided. As I entered the room by invitation of Mr. Blaine, the other members of the Cabinet were conversing and arranging their papers preparatory to leaving. After a few words of greeting, I was seated near the President who commenced a conversation relative to the judgeship in the courts of Egypt, which had become vacated by the appointment of Judge Morgan to the position of Envoy Extraordinary and Minister Plenipotentiary in Mexico. He asked me if I would like the place, stating that Mr. Blaine had recommended me as a suitable person for the position and that he would be pleased to offer it to me if it would be acceptable.

The President had planned an excursion to New England and was to leave Washington the following morning. As the members of the Cabinet were about to leave the room, he turned toward them and raising his voice asked, "Who is to accompany me to-morrow?" I believe Mr. Blaine said he intended going. Others said they would join him later.

The offer of the President was accepted and a telegram sent that evening to Egypt by the Department of State announcing my designation for the position. I was in New York the next morning, when the report came that the President had been assassinated. On my arrival in Egypt in October, I was assigned to the court at Alexandria.

CHAPTER XXV

RIOTS OF ALEXANDRIA

WHILE busily engaged during the winter of 1881–82 with my new duties in the courts, the foreign financial pressure that had been continued since the dethronement of the Khedive, Ismaîl Pasha, was fast hastening the country to its final crisis. The discontent of the people was constantly increasing. There was no feeling of opposition to the Khedive, but hatred against the foreign financial domination.

It cannot be admitted that the ruling spirits at London, who dictated the English policy relating to Egypt, did not foresee the result of their action. The English Ministry had been changed, but the foreign representatives and the bureaucratic departments remained in the control of that Jingo element of the Conservative Party which believes in advancing English interests in every part of the world without regard to the rights of those not of their own nationality. They were actuated by the same motives that were afterwards typified by the Jameson raid and the policy of Cecil Rhodes in South Africa.

After various changes in the Egyptian Ministry, effected sometimes by means indicating incipient rebellion, Arabi Pasha became its ruling power. He did not interfere with the revenues that had been devoted to the payment of the interest on the public debt. No real fault could be found with his policy, except that it diminished the prestige of the foreign Powers, and might in the end, if allowed to continue, give again to Egypt self-control.

He was the idol of the people. No patriot was ever more popular. His appearance in Alexandria was the occasion of an ovation seldom surpassed among these phlegmatic people. The streets were thronged and the demonstrations showed that the natives were practically unanimous in his support. This made him the more unacceptable to those who dictated the policy of the Government. Patriotic movements are always in a degree stimulated and aided by private ambitions, but from what afterwards transpired, it was evident that no patriot was ever less actuated by motives of personal ambition than Arabi. In fact, after the most searching inquiry, no evidence could be found which indicated anything other than a passionate desire to be freed from an oppressive foreign domination.

That the Khedive was in sympathy with the movement to free the country from the bondholders' rule, there is no doubt. He would gladly have aided it, could he have been assured success. To have aided it and failed would have lost him even his shadow of authority. For him, there was no other safe course than that of obeying the rulers that "had been set over him."

Opposition to the European Powers at that late day was ill-advised. The people were already "bound hand and foot." There was no army worth mentioning, and no means of creating one. Egypt had not had control of its own finances for five years and much more than its net revenues had been taken to Paris and London in the interests of their great banking institutions. There was little left for the people. Even their previous accumulations and those of their ancestors were exhausted. Only the land remained and much of that was mortgaged to, or already in the hands of, those who had loaned them money to pay their taxes. Whatever the results might be, the foreign Governments had no intention of relinquishing the foothold they had obtained, without bloodshed, but through a long series of negotiations and through diplomatic pressure at Cairo and Constantinople so strenuous that it could not be resisted.

England and France sent their fleets of war vessels to Alexandria and anchored them in its harbor. Other nations, with the object of watching their movements, followed their example. Among the war vessels arriving were several of the Greek navy. Between the lower classes of Greeks in Alexandria and the Arabs there was little friendship. The presence of the vessels stimulated the pride and increased the arrogance of the former and correspondingly aroused the hatred of the latter. The tension of public feeling was strong and all classes were in a state of excitement that would not have existed, except for the many war vessels in the harbor. Perfect quiet would have reigned had they not arrived.

Some weeks after the arrival of the French and English fleets, an incident occurred, due to the state of excitement that had been created, which led to a serious riot. By a gross misrepresentation of the facts, this gave some color of justification to the subsequent action of England.

The eastern part of Alexandria is occupied largely by Europeans and the better class of natives; the western, by natives and the lowest class of foreigners. Among the latter were at that time many Greeks noted then as now for their quarrelsome and, in other respects, bad character. A riot occurred on a Sunday in this part of the city. The exact details, as in the case of most riots, will never be fully known. We do know that the rioting was instigated by an English subject, a Maltese Greek. A large part of the laboring class of both the native and foreign population, being that day unemployed, were either in the native cafés, or taking their siestas. An Arab had a dispute with the Greek concerning a small claim for money. The Greek, who was said to have been intoxicated, became enraged, drew a knife and fatally stabbed the Arab in the abdomen. The sight of the helpless and bleeding victim, as he was carried away, and the account of the affair which spread quickly, excited the natives who soon commenced gathering in large numbers.

The Arabs of Egypt have been for many generations subjects of an arbitrary and generally an oppressive government. If they were originally of a different disposition, they have become the most peaceable, submissive and easily governed people in the world. As the news spread, the crowd increased and became turbulent, but it was not until the Greeks and Maltese had commenced firing from their windows and flat housetops upon the unarmed natives, and some of their number had been killed and others wounded, that they were aroused to violent acts of vengeance.

The natives, excepting the Beduins, were not allowed the luxury of firearms. They could only provide themselves with clubs. These, for the most part, were large canes, such as the fellâhîn generally carry when walking in the fields. They are rough, round saplings, one and a half to two inches in diameter and about five feet long. They are heavy and resemble clubs rather than canes. There are no timber lands in Egypt and these are brought across the Mediterranean and sold in the Arab quarters. The Greeks had been imprudently provided with firearms by the permission of their Consul, under the claim that it was necessary for their protection. As a result of the firing, the Arabs became thoroughly aroused and maddened and came swarming into this part of the city, clubbing to death every European they found in the streets.

The Hôtel de l'Europe, where I was then taking my meals, was at the lower end of the Place Mohammed-Ali, and near the Arab quarter. My rooms were three-fourths of a mile distant. I left the hotel about two o'clock. Little more than an hour afterwards, it became necessary to barricade the *porte-cochère* of the hotel to protect the inmates from the mob. Thieves took advantage of the situation and many stores were pillaged in the native quarter. Some American naval officers who were on the shore in civilian dress had a narrow escape. The police were wholly unable to cope with so formidable a riot.

During the hot summer, it is customary in Egypt to take a short nap after the noon-day meal. The stores, banks and other business places are closed from twelve till three o'clock. No one is to be disturbed in his repose during this time. The principal persons charged with the government of Alexandria were, at the time of the commencement of the difficulties, indulging in their usual siestas. It was nearly an hour after the stabbing of the Arab before the Governor was aroused and fully informed of the seriousness of the situation. There was at the time no Minister of the Interior and the Governor received his instructions direct from the Cabinet of the Khedive. Much time was spent by him in communicating with Cairo and with the commanders of the English and French fleets. Finally, he summoned the soldiers. They came promptly and on their arrival order was quickly restored.

It was between four and five o'clock when I was first informed that there was "fighting in the streets down town." Though advised that it was dangerous, I immediately started for the Place Mohammed-Ali. I met only a few persons in the streets, and these were running from the disturbed quarters. As I entered the upper end of the square, the soldiers, having come from the forts on what was formerly the Island of Pharos, entered at the other end. Standing upon the high steps of the Palace of Justice, I saw only a few persons and these were fleeing as fast as possible. As soon as it was known that the soldiers were approaching, the mob disappeared with magical celerity.

About sixty foreigners lost their lives in this riot. These

were of the lower classes and most of them resided in the Arab quarters. It was claimed during the following two days, without contradiction, that several times that number of Arabs were killed. One Greek, the next morning, boasted of having shot five.

This is as correct a statement as can be given of what has been characterized by historians as the Alexandrian massacre of the Christians by the Moslems. For three days no one termed it anything other than a lamentable and serious riot, commenced by a foreigner.

The French Consul in the report made to his Government dated the following day, called it a riot (*émeute*). Among other things, he said: "About three o'clock a Maltese and a native quarreled and the latter received a stab of a knife in the stomach. At his cries, the Arabs gathered. The quarter is inhabited by Maltese and Greeks. The latter had been imprudently armed. Revolvers having been fired from the windows, the strife became general. Troops of Arabs came from all quarters armed with clubs and beat to death the Europeans." Commander Batcheller, of the American man-of-war, *Galena*, was one of the American officers who were on shore at the time. In his report, he called it a "serious riot, in which many Europeans and natives were killed." Similar accounts were published the next day in the London papers. In the *Daily News* was the following paragraph: "The Europeans fired from the windows, killing many Arabs, who in their turn dealt terrible havoc among the Europeans in the streets." Other papers contained statements to the same effect.

When the European correspondents, who had come to Egypt on the arrival of the fleets, arrived from Cairo, the riot was quickly changed to a massacre, chargeable to Moslem fanaticism. They even went so far as to charge upon Arabi Pasha, without a shadow-reason, the inciting and organization of the mob.

The European dead and wounded were taken to the European hospitals. The natives immediately buried their dead and the exact number was never given.

Accounts, a large part of which were due to the creative imagination of the different correspondents, were published and republished in England, on the Continent, and in the Egyptian journals owned by Europeans until not only the people of England and the Continent, but the mass of the European residents of Egypt believed them to be true. The more intelligent Europeans, who knew the facts, thought their interest would be subserved by a foreign occupation and allowed the reports to go without public contradiction. Thus is history made.

A week after the riots, in a copy of one of the leading newspapers of London, the writer read an entirely incorrect statement of what was known to have taken place. Having become somewhat acquainted with the correspondent of that paper, he took the liberty of criticising his statements. He asked him why he had suppressed a part of the facts and characterized the riots as a premeditated massacre of Christians by Mohammedans, when he knew that they were commenced by an English subject and that many more natives were killed than foreigners. The correspondent was not in the least disturbed by the question and coolly answered that he was in Egypt for a purpose and was fulfilling the object of his mission. Then smiling and raising his hands in the attitude of one holding and reading a newspaper he jocosely added; "I send a despatch to London every day. The next morning the subscribers all over England read it over their coffee with all the seriousness and confidence that they read their Bible." [1]

[1] A few weeks later, the English army was in possession of Alexandria. Arabi Pasha had erected earthworks at Kafr ed-Dawar, twelve miles inland from Ramleh in the direction of Cairo. The English commander, probably for the sake of getting information as to the character of these works, or, perhaps, to keep up the idea that the invasion was to be made from this point,

The published accounts and the information given by the Consuls to their citizens that war was imminent, created general alarm. Every train from the interior was crowded with Europeans who took the first steamer for their country, or, in their fright, sought refuge aboard some ship in the harbor. The courts continued their work as long as suitors or their attorneys appeared. Ships of war continued to arrive, until the harbor presented an array of war engines such as is seldom witnessed. Even the United States with its then very limited navy was represented by four vessels.

Steamers of various nations were constantly coming and going, generally sailing away loaded with refugees. French, Italian, and Greek vessels, crowded with people of their own

---

sent one of his popular regiments on a reconnoissance. It crossed the grassy marsh, then nearly dry, on the east of Lake Mareotis to the vicinity of the new earthworks. Before its arrival within gunshot, the Egyptians commenced firing. According to statements of persons who claimed to have witnessed the movement, the soldiers suddenly broke their ranks and fled, returning to camp without "formality in the order of their going." The correspondent mentioned in the text immediately telegraphed to his paper in London an account of this reported military exploit.

The next day a member of the English Parliament rose and asked if it were true that the regiment mentioned had behaved badly. The representative of the War Office replied that he had received no information of that character, and would ascertain the facts. Inquiry was made by telegram and an answer received denying the truth of what had been published. The English Admiral immediately ordered the correspondent to leave the British lines within twenty-four hours. As there was no other means of departure he was obliged to take passage for England on a freight boat. The next week appeared in *Punch* a cartoon, of which the harbor of Alexandria and the British ships supplied the background, and which represented the British Admiral, a colossal figure, as holding this correspondent by the back of the neck preparatory to hurling him over the British lines. Thus one correspondent, who was "in Egypt for a purpose," learned the difference, in results, between misrepresenting facts relative to those who have no one to protect them, and misrepresenting facts relative to those who have protectors. If he had reported what he believed to be true, as is possible, his disillusion must have been just so much the more bitter.

nationalities, most of whom could not pay their transportation, were lying at anchor in the harbor. There were then no docks approached by steamers at which passengers could be landed and embarked. Hence, the waters were covered with small native boats going to and from the vessels, some of them rowed, but most of them provided with sails of the Oriental type. The boatmen who wore their native costumes, with the red tarboosh, fez or turban, were all active and noisy.

Uniformed officers in their gigs, manned with sailors in costumes representing their nationality, were going to or coming from the shore, or paying friendly visits to the officers of the other vessels. The beautiful weather, the bunting displayed by the numerous ships, the activity of the native boatmen, made joyous by their increased business and indifferent to the future, gave the whole scene the appearance of a gala-day without a suggestion of impending disaster. It was the peaceful calm before the awful storm of war. The city and the whole country were as peaceful and quiet as the harbor.

There was a serious attempt made at the time to obtain evidence showing that Arabi Pasha was responsible for the riots and that they were the result of plans prepared by him and his associates. The English Government had political reasons for wishing to establish some criminal acts against these parties. It employed an attorney at Alexandria and obtained a mass of unreliable and contradictory statements, principally from Maltese and Greeks, without finding anything to prove that which was desired. The attention of the British agents was particularly directed, by a despatch from Lord Granville, to the obtaining of evidence implicating Arabi and those acting under him. The task became hopeless and was abandoned.

The Egyptian Government desired a full and complete examination and formed a Commission of Inquiry. The English attorney whom I have mentioned was designated by the English Consul as a member of this commission to represent his Government. As soon as this was known in London, Lord Granville sent instructions to have the English representatives "hold themselves aloof from it." The French representative also withdrew. Without the co-operation of these two Governments, nothing could be accomplished. Under the extraterritorial privileges enjoyed by foreigners in Egypt, they could not be brought before the commission to testify nor could their houses be searched for the property stolen during the riots without the consent and co-operation of their Consuls. This consent was refused. Thus all further inquiry was prevented by Lord Granville.

There have never been any proofs that the riots were the result of any previously prepared plans. The fact, however, that such claims were made, the sudden discontinuance of all investigation when it was found that no blame could be charged to Arabi, and the refusal of the English Government to co-operate with those who wished and had a moral right to have the most searching inquiry made, left a suspicion in the minds of many Englishmen that there were facts which their Government desired to conceal. Lord Randolph Churchill prepared papers which were presented to the English Parliament asking further investigation. His Lordship's statements cast suspicion upon an entirely different class of people than those desired to be inculpated.

In a despatch of May seventh, 1882, Sir Edward Malet, the English Diplomatic Representative in Cairo, wrote Lord Granville, the British Minister of Foreign Affairs, as follows: "I believe that some complication of an acute character must supervene before any satisfactory solution of the Egyptian question can be attained, and that it would be wiser to hasten it than retard it." This means, of course, "satisfactory" from an English point of view.

At this time, the National Party was in power. The governmental proceedings were satisfactory to all, except the foreigners, who wished to govern the country wholly in their own interest, and those who were in the employ of the foreigners or who dared not do otherwise than obey their orders. There was profound peace among the people in every part of Egypt. Yet the English Consul at Alexandria was secretly arming the Maltese Greeks and, through his advice, the Greek Consul was pursuing the same course with his people. Thus the worst, the most disorderly and dangerous class in Egypt were provided with the means that gave to the riots their sanguinary character.

The British Admiral lent his aid and detailed an officer of his squadron to assist in making plans and effecting an organization. It does not appear that the French took any part in these preparations, and the Austrian and Italian Consuls did not become aware of the secret till the ninth of June, two days before the riots. The matter was then brought to the knowledge of the Consuls-General at Cairo. Sir Edward had been kept informed of the action of the English Consul, but had up to this time remained silent. A meeting of the Consuls-General was held on the morning of the Sunday of the riots. They were of the opinion that the arming was a "most dangerous course and likely at any moment in itself to cause a collision." This decision was communicated to the English Consul at Alexandria and two hours after its receipt the riots were at their fullest intensity.

There is another peculiar fact. It is known that during the riots the telegraph wires were busy with despatches between the Governor of Alexandria, the squadron and consular authorities and the Government at Cairo. None of these have been published. Arabi was in council with Dervish Pasha, the special Turkish Commissioner, and had no information of what was taking place at Alexandria until the riots were ended.

I was well acquainted for a number of years with Mr. Cookson, the English Consul at Alexandria. He was an honorable man and I am certain did nothing except what he considered his official duty. He could not do otherwise than view everything from an English standpoint, that is, with an eye to English interests. Whatever his intentions or those of other English representatives may have been, there are certain conclusions that are unavoidable to anyone personally familiar with the facts, or who has carefully studied the official documents.

1. The riots were a great grief to Arabi and his friends. It was for their interest that the most perfect order should be maintained. This they well knew.

2. The riots were welcomed by those who desired foreign military occupation. They were the "complications of an acute character" which in their opinion "must intervene before any satisfactory solution of the Egyptian question could be attained" and which "it was wiser to hasten than retard."

3. Whatever the object of arming the Maltese and Greeks might have been, it is certain that if this did not actually cause the riots it was the cause of their extremely bloody character.

The English and French fleets came to Egypt, as it was claimed, to assure the maintenance of peace. Their presence had created a condition wholly unexpected by France. She had relied on securing her ends by diplomatic pressure and a simple show of force. Thus far, her part had been played to satisfy the bondholders of Paris, to maintain her prestige and prevent England from obtaining a preponderance of influence in Egypt. She had not intended to engage in any actual hostilities nor could her Parliament be induced to authorize such action. Her irreparable mistake had been made in instigating the dethronement of a strong, able ruler, and the putting in his place of one who was only to obey the orders of comptrollers sent from Paris and London. The sending of her fleet to Alexandria, though she had no intention of having it engage in operations, was an unfortunate declaration on her part that coercion by force was necessary. Her discomfiture was England's opportunity, and it was hastily embraced.

When a nation is ready for war, and has in view a rich conquest, reasons for commencing hostilities are easily found. Under a claim, denied by Arabi and the Khedive, that Arabi was mounting additional guns in the forts, thus strengthening his position and placing in jeopardy the British fleet in the harbor, Admiral Seymour commenced hostile operations.

A month had passed since the riots, and during this time the foreigners, wholly unmolested, had been leaving the country. A demand was made for the surrender of the forts which was not granted, and immediate preparations were made for the bombardment. I had been frequently invited to go aboard one of our vessels in the harbor, but had answered that when notice of the expected commencement of hostilities was given I would do so. Until then, I saw no reason for leaving the city.

CHAPTER XXVI

BOMBARDMENT OF ALEXANDRIA

SUNDAY forenoon, July ninth, I received information from a private and confidential source that notices of the bombardment, to take place twenty-four hours later, would be printed that night in different languages aboard the English Admiral's ship and sent out early the next morning.

Just at dusk, I was taken to the *Lancaster*, the flagship of the United States Rear-Admiral, Nicholson. He was much surprised at the information I gave him and doubted its correctness. He said he was in daily communication with the British Admiral, and would certainly have been informed had the time been set for the bombardment. He added: "You have lived in the Orient long enough not to believe unauthorized rumors." I answered that I was not at liberty to give him the source of my information, but that he might rely on its being correct. The commanders of the other American vessels were summoned and came aboard the Admiral's ship. A consultation was held, but the Admiral remained unconvinced. I went for the night on board the *Galena* and was afterwards transferred to the *Quinnebaug*. The *Galena* had been ordered away and sailed on the morning of the bombardment.

At early dawn, orders came from Admiral Nicholson to "fire up," and a few minutes later to "fire up quickly!" He had received at midnight official information of the intended bombardment. Going on deck I was greeted with an impressive and beautiful scene. We were lying in the capacious roadstead opposite the Khedivial palace, Râs-et-Tîn, a mile or more from the ordinary landing. There was a very large number of vessels in the harbor. Besides the ships of war, there were steamers, sailing vessels from the different parts of the Mediterranean, ships, schooners, sloops, fishing smacks and other small craft in great numbers. Some were square rigged, others had long lateen-sails.

Already, there was a line of sailing boats moving past us toward the sea, each flying its national ensign. This continued for several hours. The American vessels, though under steam, remained till the arrival in the afternoon of the train bringing from Cairo the American Vice-Consul General and his suite. We then moved out of the harbor and anchored just behind the English fleet as near as the Admiral thought it prudent.

Here we awaited the events of the morrow. Behind us were the merchant vessels and warships of nearly all the neutral European Powers. The French fleet had withdrawn and sailed to Port Said. The light sea-breeze of the day had died away, and as the sun disappeared its last rays were reflected by placid waters. Sixty or seventy vessels were anchored a short distance from the low, sandy beach that lies along the margin of the sea and separates it from the city. The city itself was then in full view, quiet and peaceful.

Who could tell what was to happen there, what scenes of horror would be witnessed, when once its people should be wrought to madness by the shrieking shells of a hostile fleet and the slaughter of the innocent inhabitants? The submarine cable was controlled by an English company, and the Egyptian shore end had been removed to a vessel lying several miles out at sea. During the night, the English fleet was throwing its calcium lights along the shore defenses.

The sun rose the next day in a clear sky. It was one of

Egypt's beautiful summer mornings. The shore was lined with old fortifications, some of them dating from the time of Mohammed-Ali. None of them were at all adapted to resist modern engines of war, nor to protect properly the men serving the guns. Some of them were built of stone in such a manner that it would be difficult to find a more dangerous place for a soldier within reach of the shells of a well-equipped, modern man-of-war. They proved veritable slaughter-houses.

Looking southward, we had, on our left, Forts Pharos and Ada, the former on the site of the old Phare, once one of the seven wonders of the world. On our right was the entrance to the modern harbor, the new lighthouse and other fortifications. Far behind them, on a slight elevation, appeared the tall, granite column, known as Pompey's Pillar. Further eastward, in the background, was the doomed city.

The ancient Phare was at the east end of what was an island when Alexander ordered the building of the city. This was the place of entry to the Greek and Roman harbor. The new lighthouse is at the west and close to the entrance of the modern harbor. Near this were fortifications. There were still others along the coast west of the entrance for a distance of six miles.

Directly in front of us, cleared for action, was a modern fleet, the most powerful ever assembled for hostile purposes up to that time. There were eight ironclads and five wooden vessels. They were placed in position at an early hour in the morning. The *Inflexible* had a sandwiched armor of wood and iron, the entire thickness of the plates of iron being from sixteen to twenty-six inches, and the sandwiched wood from seventeen to twenty-five inches. This ship was the largest man-of-war that had then been built. It was armed with eighty-ton guns, capable of throwing shells weighing seventeen hundred pounds five miles.

At precisely seven o'clock in the morning, a signal gun announced the commencement of the bombardment. The fire was immediately returned from the forts. It had been expected by military experts that the guns of the Egyptians would be silenced within an hour. It was thought that it would not be possible for any troops, in such fortifications, to withstand, even for a short time, such a rain of bursting shells as would be thrown upon them by the fleet. In a conversation with General Stone, a few days previous, I asked him what time would be required for the fleet to silence the guns of the forts. After a few moments' reflection, he answered: "About thirty minutes." All were disappointed.

During the whole day we heard only the deafening roar of cannon, saw the bursting shells and the smoke of battle which was driven inland by the sea-breeze and enveloped the city as with a cloud. The thirteen vessels of war showered upon the brave men at their guns in the forts exploding shells to the number of over three thousand. The explosions could be distinctly seen and were eagerly watched from our ships. Occasionally they burst prematurely high in the air; sometimes, just above the heads of the Arabs in the forts, scattering their missiles of death in every direction. Some entered deep into the earth or the masonry and there exploded, sending up clouds of dust and *débris* and leaving large craters. Some of these craters were as deep as eight feet and sixteen feet and more broad. Occasionally a shell passed over a fort and entered the city.

The bravery of the Arabs at their guns greatly astonished military men. Immediately after the clearing away of the dust and smoke of a bursting shell that must have left all in its vicinity torn in pieces, a little cloud of smoke from a gun close by would show that the living were still at their post.

During the day there were three explosions in the forts,

which we thought, at the time, were the powder magazines or arsenals, throwing high in the air clouds of smoke and *débris*. One of these explosions, at Fort Ada, silenced its guns and killed nearly everyone in the fort, showing the utter inadequacy of these old fortifications to withstand the force of great, modern guns. All the guns of the fortifications were not silenced till five o'clock in the afternoon, and the English did not cease firing until six o'clock. The ships received a large number of shots and were considerably, but not seriously, damaged. Their number of killed and wounded was small, six killed and twenty-seven wounded. The Admiral said in his report that it was "impossible to account for the very small loss considering the amount of shell and shot which struck them." There were about fifteen hundred men in the forts, a large part of whom died at their posts.

After the battle commenced, an occasional shell from the forts passed the English ships and fell near us. About ten o'clock we moved a little further out, but remained nearer to the scene of action than any other of the unengaged ships.

The next morning, all was quiet and the English buried their dead at sea. Two or three shells were fired into the forts, but no reply was made. In the afternoon we saw a dense smoke rising from the upper part of the town. This increased, and, as the night came, we could see the flames gradually extending over the European quarter, threatening the destruction of that part of the city. All the next day and the following night the burning district grew larger and larger. This part of the town was owned principally by Europeans, but there were no soldiers to land and save the property from destruction. During the evening of the thirteenth a party of English were landed. They did not enter the interior of the town, but took positions along its southern side.

Friday forenoon (the fourteenth) the American Admiral tired

of waiting and, without having received any communication from the English, moved into the harbor in advance of any other neutral ships. He soon afterwards sent one hundred and seventy-five marines into the town to re-establish the American Consulate, and do what they could to arrest the destruction of the fire. This was done at the request of the English Admiral and with the consent of the Khedive, who had then returned to his palace, Râs-et-Tîn. In the morning, some English marines had taken possession of the inner forts and some of the gates of the walled city. Though the town had been abandoned by the Egyptian soldiers since Wednesday forenoon, the English did not enter its interior until Saturday, the day after our little band had established its quarters and raised the American flag at the upper end of the Place Mohammed-Ali.

I also entered the town on Saturday. A large part of the European quarter was a mass of burning ruins. The streets which the fire had not reached were like those of Pompeii in their solitude. The shops had been pillaged and there was scarcely a person to be seen. For two days after the local authorities had been driven away by the shells of the fleet, the city had been wholly in the hands of thieves. The result was what might have been expected, but no worse than it would have been in London or New York. Drive the local authorities from either of these cities, and a swarm of pillaging thieves and robbers would fill the streets in an hour.

The heart of the town could only be approached by circuitous routes. The walls of the buildings were generally high and three feet thick, made of rough stone and mortar, bound together with wood and plastered inside and out. The mass of ruins was therefore so great that it covered the ground ten and fifteen feet deep and filled even wide streets. Miles of great blocks had been destroyed, and the fire was still spreading. Fortunately, from the amount of stone, cement and mortar used in every part of the buildings, and the small amount of wood, they were what were termed "slow burners."

The Palace of Justice, the American Consulate and a considerable number of other buildings were saved by our marines, who were commanded by Lieutenant-Commander, now Rear-Admiral, Casper F. Goodrich, from the flagship, *Lancaster*. There were a few unexploded shells lying in the streets, and marks of others in the remaining buildings. According to the official reports, about two hundred of the unarmed inhabitants were killed by these stray shells and the fragments of others. It was afterwards shown that fires were set by the evacuating troops. It is probable that others were caused by the shells. It is known that an adjoining dependence of the palace Râs-et-Tîn was thus set on fire.

A visit to the forts after the bombardment showed the terrible ordeal to which the Egyptian soldiers had been subjected in these open, unprotected fortifications. No words can paint the scenes. The dismounted guns and shattered walls, with the *débris* of bursted shells and broken stones scattered over the entire inner surface of the forts, were such as to render it apparently impossible for anyone to have escaped this holocaust of death. The appearance of Fort Ada, where the explosion of the magazine "caused the retreat of the remaining garrison," as the English Admiral laconically puts it, was the most appalling. Apparently, there could have been no one left living to have retreated. Shells and their fragments and *débris* of all kinds were thrown broadcast in such quantities, in every direction, as to have rendered it almost impossible for anyone to have escaped.

Notwithstanding this condition, I find in the account of a military writer the following: "The English, while surprised by the tenacity of their opponents, were the first to confess that men of a stamp at all similar to their own would have

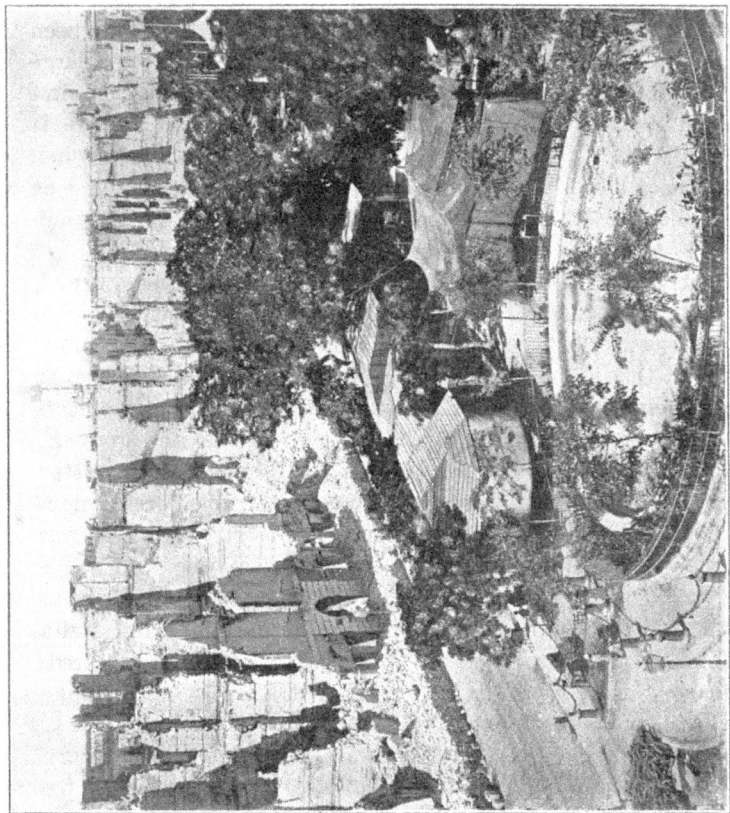

Place Mohammed Ali, Alexandria, after the Bombardment
and Burning of the City.

accepted the gage thrown down the next day, and have renewed the fight." The men for the most part were either dead, or *hors de combat*. If there had been fifteen hundred more Egyptian artillerymen that could have been used, and they had been placed on the morrow in these open slaughter pens, to a large extent dismantled, they would have been sacrificed as the first fifteen hundred had been. And to what purpose? There is no doubt as to the bravery of the English troops, but when and where have they stood at their guns to be slaughtered as these men were? If there had been the least hope of final success, even greater sacrifice might have been justified.

Nearly all the business part of the city had been burned, and the part that had escaped the flames had been pillaged. There was much discussion at the time as to who was accountable for this appalling disaster. Admitting, as claimed, that the principal part of the damages were caused by the officers of the defeated Egyptians and native thieves and robbers, who was responsible for creating the conditions that permitted these acts? In other words, who was responsible for the non-landing of men to take possession of the city when it was evacuated? If it was for want of men, who was responsible for the commencement of hostilities without a force ready to land? There were English troops both at Cyprus and at Malta and only a very small body of men would have been required. Four days' delay would have been ample time in which to make all necessary preparations.

Even admitting that England was justified in the military occupation of Egypt, admitting that she would have been for this purpose justified in taking forcible possession of Alexandria, even then, there was no justification for the bombardment at the time, and in the manner it was executed. I never heard an Englishman attempt its justification. Even those who attempted an apology admitted it was a mistake. I have heard

English officers, both of the navy and army, speak of it as a lamentable military error to have commenced the bombardment without an adequate landing force. Some of the army officers attributed it to the ambition of the Admiral and his desire to connect his name with an historical event, and give his arm of the service a part of the glory of a conquest that he knew was about to be made. There is only one other possible explanation, and that is that the English authorities hastened the event in order to have a *fait accompli*, fearing political complications.

A few words will explain the situation. The eyes of the world were, from the first, designedly kept fixed upon Alexandria, as the official reports afterwards published show, although England had no intention of entering Egypt by that city. How long the plan for the invasion of Egypt had been under consideration we do not know. That it had been perfected in all its details eight days before the bombardment appears from published official papers. Egypt was to be seized by an invasion by the way of the Suez Canal.

A force of about twenty thousand men was to enter at Port Said. Another division was to be brought from India and enter at Suez. These were to meet at Isma'ilīya near the center of the canal. After an expected easy victory in the vicinity of Tell el-Kebîr, on the eastern edge of the cultivated lands, a hasty cavalry expedition was to be made to Cairo before the defeated Egyptians had time to re-form. This was precisely what happened two months later, as soon as the troops could be forwarded. When there is only a shadow of armed resistance it is easy to form military plans and carry them out to the letter, as in a sham battle.

At the date mentioned, plans had been made even as to the means of transport across the desert from the canal to Tell el-Kebîr and, along the desert, to Cairo. Proposals were made

Interior of Fort Ada, Alexandria, after the Bombardment.

for the purchase of one thousand mules in America for immediate shipment.   Secret orders were given to officers and a long
list of details arranged.   Sir Archibald Alison left England for
Cyprus to take charge of the troops to be landed there and
organized for sailing to Port Said.

In all these multitudinous military preparations, made previous to the bombardment at Alexandria, no mention is made
of any expected co-operation by the French.   Their fleet remained at Alexandria with that of England, up to the time
notice was given of the bombardment, without any apparent
want of harmony.   The military preparations were secret, and
it was evident that England had for a considerable time known
through secret agents, if not otherwise, that the French Parliament would not authorize any military hostilities.[1]

She seized with avidity the opportunity offered to disem-
barrass herself of an alliance that had long been a source of
annoyance.   The opportunity for which she had long watched
and waited had arrived.   Egypt was to be hers without any
participation in its Government by the French.   It may be that
fear of some new turn or complications in the negotiations with
the French hastened the commencement of an actual occupation.   In that case, the premature bombardment, causing one
of the greatest disasters of the nineteenth century, may have
been the result of direct orders from London.   The reasons
given to the public at the time for the bombardment were:
that the English, by means of their calcium lights, had discovered that the Egyptians were strengthening their positions

---

[1] It would appear from the official despatches afterwards published that
France had no official information of the plans and intentions of the English.
On the day of the bombardment, Lord Lyons, the English Ambassador at
Paris, by order of Lord Granville, stated to M. de Freycinet, the French Minister of Foreign Affairs, that "the bombardment was considered as a legitimate
act of defense and that there was no hidden purpose (arrière pensée) on the
part of the British Government."

in the forts; that they had mounted one or more additional cannon; that the Admiral had informed his Government of the facts claiming that his fleet was endangered; and that, on these representations, he had obtained permission to take the forts if he thought it necessary. The Egyptian Ministry denied this statement, and even offered to permit the dismounting of two cannon for every one claimed to have been mounted. The reasons assigned were too ludicrous to merit a moment's consideration. They evidently had no influence in determining the plan of the Admiral. He well knew that anything that the Egyptians could do in strengthening their position would not have a feather's weight in determining the results of any attack on the fortifications. He also knew that there was no intention or disposition on their part of commencing hostilities.

CHAPTER XXVII

AFTER THE BOMBARDMENT

THE return of the refugees who had been driven inland by the bombardment was a melancholy drama. It was understood, even by the well informed, that only the forts were to be attacked, and that the only danger in remaining in any part of the city not in their immediate vicinity would be from the aroused frenzy of the natives.

Of the two hundred and fifty thousand inhabitants, it is probable that not more than sixty thousand had left when the explosion of the first great shell awakened those remaining from their phlegmatic indifference. A large majority had believed that nothing serious would happen. Had not the impregnable stone forts and the old cannon with which they were manned protected them from hostilities since the childhood of the oldest inhabitant? Why should they fear now? Would not the soldiers in the fort sink the English fleet or drive it from their shores?

It was not till the stray shells commenced falling in their midst that the great mass of the lower class realized their danger. Then their flight commenced and soon became general. Many, even in this hour of terror, clung to and carried away with them their scanty possessions. Lake Mareotis bounds Alexandria on the south. On the west, a long, narrow beach separates the lake from the sea. The most practical route of scape for the fleeing multitude—men, women and children—

was eastward toward, or south of, Ramleh, a small suburb, built on the desert, near the sea. In this direction many thousands sought a place of safety.

Troops began to arrive from Cyprus on Monday, six days after the bombardment. When outposts had been established and a force received sufficient to police the city, messengers informed the refugees, who were encamped on the sands, that they could safely return. They eagerly sought their homes, miserable though they were. Entering the city by the Rosetta or Ramleh gate, they passed down a broad street filling it from side to side for hours. It was a constant stream of impoverished humanity. All were poorly and scantily clad and begrimed with dirt and dust. The natives were barefooted and barelimbed; the women bore their infants in their arms, while their half-naked children trudged at their sides; men and women, old and young carried such effects as they still possessed. Occasionally one of the more well-to-do had a donkey, a poor horse, or a buffalo cow on whose back the burdens were packed. There were also a few creaking vehicles loaded with personal effects. Such was the motley mass passing down the streets, still smoking with burning ruins, to their own quarter of the town. Fortunately, the fire had done little damage in that part of the city, but it had been pillaged of whatever was of sufficient value to tempt thieves.

The Khedive remained at his palace in Ramleh, outside but near the southeastern part of the city, during the bombardment, and returned to Râs-et-Tîn early in the morning of the day of the landing of the American marines. General Stone, keeping his solemn promise made to the ex-Khedive, Ismaîl Pasha, that he would remain with and be true to his son, did not leave him during these trying days.

In an interview that I had with his Highness soon afterwards, he stated that he had ordered Arabi not to permit the English to land and he seemed, by his conversation, to censure him because he had been unable to execute his orders. He added: "As the representative of the Sultan, it is my duty to defend the country and I cannot voluntarily surrender the least particle of territory."

All the talk afterwards heard charging Arabi with the intention of injuring him was pure fiction. If anything of this kind could have been proved, he would have been hung instead of being banished. His Highness gave me a detailed account of what actually took place. Arabi wished the Khedive to retire inland and remain there and sent officers to accompany him. This would have increased largely the prestige of the National Party. The same reasons made his possession by the English desirable. They tried to have him go, as he stated to me, on board of one of their vessels before the bombardment. This he declined to do, preferring to remain with his people.

Whether his Highness really expected Arabi to be successful in the defense of the country may never be known. That he wished it is certain. He could easily have managed Arabi, but he well knew, being advised by good counsellors, that England's hand once closed upon Egypt would never be opened. When he saw that further resistance was hopeless, he gave himself up as the only means of saving his viceroyalty with its semblance of power. From that time until his death he had no alternative but to execute the will of his captors. The alleged treason of Arabi consisted solely in disobeying the Khedive's orders when the latter was virtually a prisoner.

After the arrival of the English fleet in the month of May, Arabi and his Ministry, on the demand of the English, resigned. At the request of the Austrian, German and Italian Diplomatic Representatives, Arabi was reappointed by the Khedive and retained in power till after the bombardment. The English then made strenuous efforts, both at Constantinople and in

Egypt, to have him officially declared a traitor. This, in their opinion, was necessary in order to keep up the fiction that they were the friends of the Khedive and had come to his support. There were important political reasons of an international character why the Government should be continued in the name of his Highness. If Arabi could be thus disgraced, it would also tend to aid in the execution of the military plans that had been formed. Up to this time he had acted, in opposing the English, in obedience to the orders of both the Sultan and the Khedive. The facts were so well known that the Khedive hesitated to comply with the anomalous demands made upon him.

The mission of the fleet, as claimed, was to restore the full authority of the Khedive and assure the peace of the country which, up to the time of its arrival, had not been disturbed. To be more explicit, the English came ostensibly as friends of his Highness to aid him against the influence of Arabi and the National Party. The Khedive ordered Arabi to fire upon these friends and their ships, in case of their aggression, and not to allow them to land upon the soil of Egypt. Arabi tried to the best of his ability to execute these orders. He did as well as any General could have done with the means he possessed, and much better than any military judge thought possible. The forts were destroyed, the artillerymen were killed and, as an incident of the war, the city was burned, in the defense of the country against the friends of the Khedive! The ironclads and the eighty-ton guns were the stronger and Arabi was obliged to yield to the inevitable.

Whatever the facts, the Khedive could not long resist the demands of those into whose hands he had fallen, and retain even a semblance of his sovereignty. Finally, some ingenious person prepared for him the following most remarkable proclamation and he had only to issue it and send it out to his people:

"Let those who read this Order know the cause of the dismissal of Ahmed Pasha Arabi, and for the edification of all, this is truth.

"After ten hours of bombardment our fortifications were annihilated, 400 of our cannons destroyed, and the greater part of our artillerymen killed or disabled, while the English fleet had only lost five men, and its vessels had undergone no serious damage.

"Ahmed Pasha Arabi then came to us at the Palace of Ramleh to announce the painful news of the destruction of our forts.

"On his side the Admiral of the English fleet had demanded of us the 'evacuation of the forts of El-Adjemi, of Dekhile, and of Mex, for them to be occupied by his troops.' The Council of Ministers assisted by his Excellency Dervish Pasha, having also assembled, it was decided that the forts could not be surrendered without the express order of his Imperial Majesty the Sultan, and that on the contrary it was necessary to provide for their defense by reinforcing the garrisons to oppose a disembarkation of foreign troops. At the same time a telegraphic despatch was addressed to the Sublime Porte.

"But Arabi Pasha then repaired to the Rosetta Gate at Alexandria, without taking any military measure. I had him followed by one of my Aides-de-camp to remind him that he should send reinforcements to the positions agreed upon.

"Arabi Pasha answered that he could not send a single soldier; he ordered the troops to retire with him, and repair to Kafr ed-Dawâr, thus leaving the town deprived of defenders.

"The next day the English troops disembarked at Alexandria, the most important point of our country, and took possession of the town without a single shot having been fired, a fact which would dishonor the Egyptian Army if the ineffaceable shame did not wholly fall on him who had the command—on Arabi Pasha." [1]

[1] Translated from the Arabic.

This proclamation, to those acquainted with the facts, was a most extraordinary and even ludicrous document. But it was drawn for the class of people among whom it was to be circulated and was thought by those then in control to be a clever means of discrediting Arabi among the mass of ignorant Egyptians. This class had believed in the invincibility of the old guns of the fortifications. They also believed in the infallible authority of the Khedive. To have him charge upon Arabi the responsibility of the failure of sinking the English vessels or driving them from their shores was regarded as a crushing blow to his prestige. It was also a justification of the Khedive and would render him a more useful instrument in governing the country.

The incoming steamers gradually brought back the foreign residents, and the city again showed some signs of life. Many of the streets were wholly obstructed by the *débris* of the burned buildings, and others were rendered dangerous by the falling walls. The Hôtel de l'Europe, to which I had removed before the bombardment, had been burned with my books and other effects. The building where I had previously resided in the upper part of the city had been taken as quarters for English officers. Fortunately, I found for occupation poor rooms in a native building near the edge of the water of the old eastern harbor, that of the Ptolemies and Romans.

Many clerks and other employees of the courts remained or soon returned. All the judges except myself were absent during the summer. While charged with all the responsibilities, my duties were only administrative. No one attempted any judicial proceedings. Arabi had withdrawn to Kafr ed-Dawâr, a point on the railroad to Cairo just beyond Lake Mareotis, seventeen miles distant.

Outposts were established about the city and the war vessels remained in the harbor, but all offensive military movements were temporarily suspended. It was the opinion of military experts at that time, that a very small army of well disciplined soldiers could easily march to Cairo or any other place in Lower Egypt. The English, however, were not ready to execute the plans that had been matured in London by Sir Garnet Wolseley. These plans were to give England an opportunity of showing Europe that in an emergency it had other sources than the British Islands from which to draw troops.

It was known that there would be no serious fighting and thought to be perfectly safe and a fine stroke of policy to exhibit the native Indian forces commanded by English officers. The English have ever since congratulated themselves on the clever manner in which they were enabled to show their vast military resources. On the arrival of these troops and others from England, the Suez Canal was used as a military base. Although M. de Lesseps then had full authority over the canal, his protests and strenuous opposition were of no avail. It was simply a question of military power, of an army and a navy. It will be the same with the Panama Canal in time of war. Its possession and use will depend upon our ability to hold it against all adversaries.

Arabi sent one of his officers to Tell el-Kebîr to erect fortifications, that being considered the most available point of entry from the canal. He could easily have blocked the canal, but, relying upon the promises of M. de Lesseps, he left it open for the entry of the hostile forces until it was too late. After the surrender of the Khedive, many of the native officers began to provide for their future. The officer in charge at Tell el-Kebîr communicated with the authorities at Alexandria through the family of General Stone and arranged to desert his post instead of pushing the work assigned him. He escaped by the way of the Suez Canal, giving the English full knowledge of the condition of the fortifications.

There were only about eight thousand drilled native troops
in Arabi's army. These were mostly stationed at Kafr ed-
Dawâr and at Rosetta and Damietta, the present mouths of
the Nile. The other Egyptian soldiers were either old men,
or undrilled fellâhîn, ten thousand of whom could be put to
flight by a thousand well drilled troops. The so-called battle
of Tell el-Kebîr gave Sir Garnet Wolseley a peerage. Yet compared with the great battles that have been fought in Europe,
Asia and America during the last fifty years, it was, on the part
of the English, a mere skirmish. There were great gaps in the
fortifications through which the cavalry could ride, and, though
there were two lines of earthworks, cannons had been mounted
only in one.

A march was made for a considerable distance across the
desert in a very "dark night," and the attack made in a mist at
early dawn. No outposts were found, and the march was wholly
unobstructed. So still and successful was this movement, and
so utterly surprised were the Egyptians, that some of the
English troops commenced mounting the parapets before a gun
was fired. Then, for a few minutes, there was a desultory fire
by the suddenly awakened Arabs in the darkness, still so great
that it was difficult to distinguish friend from foe. Arabi was
awakened by the noise of the guns, but, before he was dressed,
his soldiers were in full retreat. "They threw away their arms
and begged for mercy," according to the English official report.

In this battle, lasting but a few minutes, the English lost in
killed, including officers that afterwards died of wounds, fifty-
eight. The Egyptians, according to the best information at-
tainable, lost twenty-two hundred killed and a great number
died afterwards from wounds. The English approached and
entered the works, according to the commander's orders, without firing a gun. Considering these circumstances and the
short time of any resistance, it is not surprising that the English

official published reports are ominously silent as to the native losses. It was a slaughter, rather than a battle.

Most of the natives then at Tell el-Kebîr were unarmed fellâhîn. They were brought there in great numbers to construct earthworks in the same manner that they were accustomed to be summoned to dig and clean the irrigating canals under the system known as the *corvée*. In such cases, they slept at night on the ground at the place of their work, having at most a blanket for protection. At the time of the English attack, thousands of these unarmed natives were lying asleep on the ground where they had been at work the previous day. These were indiscriminately slaughtered, along with the fleeing soldiers, by the Indian troops.

An English officer who was in the action of Tell el-Kebîr stated to me, in explanation of this affair, that some of the Indians having been wounded, these troops became maddened, and that before the officers could get them under control the lamentable work had been done. This was undoubtedly true. No English officer of the present day would have willingly permitted such a slaughter. It was simply a case of "letting loose the dogs of war." It was an unexpected object lesson for Christian Europe of the result of using soldiers of this class.

After Tell el-Kebîr, all open opposition to the English occupation ceased, and the seat of Government was again transferred to Cairo. As a guard of honor, a body of Indian cavalry was brought to Alexandria and used in escorting the Khedive to the station. Well mounted and attired in their gay, native uniforms, they made a pleasing picture. This display was designed to further impress Europeans, as well as natives, with an idea of the Empire's great reserve force in the heart of India. As the Khedive rode, thus escorted, beside Sir Edward Malet, the English Diplomatic Agent and Consul-General, along the principal street lined with people, there was no applause, no manifestation of joy.

During the summer and fall, the permanent military occupation of the country was well established and, from that time, there has been abject submission. The Khedive is required, as a condition of retaining his position, to sign such papers as are prepared for him. This he is expected to do without criticism or comment, as a military subaltern executes the orders of his superiors. A mild attempt, some years ago, of the present young Khedive to exercise some of the prerogatives of a sovereign was summarily suppressed by the English authorities.[1]

Immediately after the taking of Alexandria, there were serious complaints by its European residents on account of their losses, caused by the bombardment and subsequent burning and pillage of the city.

The Khedive issued a decree making these losses a charge upon Egypt. What else could he do? It has become almost a principle of international law that the conquered shall be charged with the cost of the conquest. The losses incurred at Alexandria were only an incident in the war. In actions between litigants in our courts, the party failing is generally charged with the cost of the proceeding on the ground that he was wrong

[1] A story was lately current in Egypt of another instance of a little insubordination. It shows the precise situation. According to the account, Lord Cromer went to the palace, Abdîn, with some document that required the official signature of the Khedive. The contents of the paper were not agreeable to his Highness and he indulged in some criticisms. Finally, he asked, "What if I do not affix my signature?" "Ceylon, your Highness" replied the real ruler of Egypt. This was the island to which Arabi and his associates were banished and where they were held in captivity many years. Still hesitating, the Khedive added "What if I still disregard what you say and refuse to sign?" There was a body of English soldiers then drilling on the large square in front of the palace. A military force is always near by and ready at a moment's call. Lord Cromer invited the Khedive to accompany him to the window and silently pointed to the soldiers. The document was signed and the incident closed.

in his pretensions. Among nations, might practically makes right. Consequently, the weaker must pay the cost of failure.

Negotiations between the Powers were instituted, which resulted in an agreement for an International Commission of Indemnities. Its members were appointed by the different Governments, and their labors commenced the following winter. There were in all eleven commissioners, two from Egypt, one from each of the seven Great Powers, one from Greece, on account of the number of its claims, and one representing the other Powers of the second class. The writer was designated by President Arthur as the commissioner from the United States.

The claims were so numerous that their examination was necessarily summary. They numbered over ten thousand. To have examined them minutely and taken evidence, as in an American court of claims, would have required many years. The proceedings were, however, very similar to those of the French courts in the trial of a civil action, except that the attorneys did not appear in person, but submitted their observations in writing. No oral testimony was taken and the sessions of the Commission were secret. Full justice could not be expected as a result of work of such summary character. The claimants, however, demanded speedy adjudications; saying that one-half of the amounts of their losses paid without a long delay and used in rebuilding or re-establishing their business would be preferable to the whole paid many years later.

The parties submitted detailed, verified claims, accompanied by affidavits and certificates of persons claiming to have knowledge of the facts. Their attorneys added brief statements summarizing the proofs and giving their conclusions as to the amounts to which their clients were entitled. In the cases of buildings destroyed, the opinions of experts, builders, contractors and architects were added. The writings thus produced formed what the French call a *dossier*. This was submitted to the attorneys of the Government, who examined the papers and added their opinions and conclusions. In this form, each claim was brought before the Commission, which appointed committees among which the work was divided.

The *dossiers* were divided among the members of the committees for examination, and, after such examination, reports were made to the whole committee, by which they were adopted, modified or rejected. On one day of each week, the whole Commission met and received the reports of the committees. These reports were generally adopted without dissent, but, in the more important cases, there was often a divergence of opinion and sometimes long and animated discussions.

The Commission finished its work in eleven months, having examined and made final decisions on the ten thousand claims presented, allowing on them over twenty millions of dollars. It was the intention to render as small awards as the facts would permit. Few claims were wholly rejected, but nearly all were very much reduced, and, in some cases, but a small part was allowed. In the uncertainty surrounding a large part of the claims, the Egyptian Government was given the benefit of all doubts, and it is probable that the total amount awarded was not very much more than half the aggregate of the actual losses.

CHAPTER XXVIII

THE FUTURE OF EGYPT

WHAT is to be the future of Egypt? is a question often asked. Politically, the countries bordering upon the Nile, from the Mediterranean to the great lakes of Central Africa, will remain practically English provinces as long as England holds India and her other colonial acquisitions, and is able, as at present, to maintain naval supremacy.

In a conversation with Sir Edward Malet, just before leaving the hotel to board an American vessel, on the eve of the bombardment, he stated to me that, were it not for the Suez Canal, they would be out of Egypt within twenty-four hours. That was probably, at the time, the sentiment of the English Cabinet with Gladstone at its head. It would be different to-day, even if there were no canal. A valuable territorial acquisition once made is never abandoned by England. As long as she holds Gibraltar, she will hold Egypt.

The control of the Suez Canal is to her of the most vital importance. In case of an international war, it would be one of her most effective aids. She secured its control for less than $20,000,000. The Panama Canal, though of less national importance to us, will cost $200,000,000. Each is of very great value, both commercially and for strategic purposes. Neither Government will yield these acquired rights so long as they hold their present advanced position among the great world Powers.

Why does not England abandon all disguise and make Egypt

an English province instead of governing the country by an illusory, advisory system?

Primarily, because it is easier to govern the people through the Khedive, one of their own language and religion. They regard him as their legitimate and rightful sovereign and respect his authority, even more than we do that of the President. They know that a foreign Power occupies the country and that the Khedive must conform to its wishes. They believe that he does many things that are not in accordance with his desires, but they are ever hopeful of an end of the foreign domination.

The English are careful to make the Khedive and his family adequate pecuniary allowances and to have him surrounded with the pomp that gives him the appearance of a real sovereign. By thus maintaining his Highness's prestige, the country can be governed principally by natives, necessitating only a small force of English soldiers. The real governing power, claiming to act only as advisory, in this way escapes the responsibility of its own acts and policies, which it would not always wish to assume. The Khedive, in theory, is the absolute ruler, making and enforcing all the laws. All decrees are issued and orders given in his name. Under his supposed authority, the natives quietly submit to burdens that would otherwise be endured only by the application of military force. When in Upper Egypt, some years since, I had a conversation relative to the land-tax with a native living between Luxor and the First Cataract. He was the owner of what was considered a large tract of land in that very narrow and thickly settled valley. He informed me that the tax had been so high that it left very little or nothing for him; but that the Khedive had been up the river, and, after a personal investigation, had reduced the tax in that section, having found it too high. This man was only a fellah, but one of the most prominent where he resided. He had a son who had been well educated, and yet both were under the delusion that the Khedive, of his own will, as former Egyptian rulers had done, could change the amount of the land-tax. This manner of maintaining the Khedive's prestige with his own people is certainly very adroit and only persons who had had long experience in the government of the Indian provinces would be able to produce and maintain such a delusion through a series of years.

If England should make Egypt one of her provinces, it would still be subject to the debts which she has sanctioned and which are due largely to English people. It would also be subject to the tribute to Turkey which virtually belongs to English bankers.

There are also reasons of an international character for continuing this advisory system of government. England has twice promised to withdraw its military forces, one promise having been made by the Liberals, when in power, and the other by the Conservatives. Though the question of the permanent occupation may be considered as settled by the long, silent acquiescence of the Powers, they have never given their formal consent. France still has her claims, though recent negotiations indicate that they have to a large extent been abandoned, in exchange for a "free hand" and English support in Morocco.

All of the Christian Powers have extraterritorial rights which led to the formation of the International Courts. Some of the Powers would yield these only under great pressure.

The rights of the Sultan must also be considered. His Majesty is, by the admission of all the Powers of Europe, the real sovereign of Egypt. His authority is at present only nominal, but the assumption of sovereignty by England would be an infringement upon his prerogatives likely to produce lasting feelings of hostility.

In her policy of shutting Russia up among the icefields of the north, England will always have need of the Sultan's aid in keeping the Dardanelles closed. In case of the serious war with that Power, which, for two generations, has been the continuous nightmare of the English statesman, his Sublime Majesty, if so disposed, might make a religious appeal. He could thus easily arouse the millions of Mussulmans in India, who acknowledge him as their Khalíf, the successor of Mohammed, the head of Islam. Unless some satisfactory agreement can be made with the Porte for the transfer of the sovereignty of Egypt, its present form of government will probably continue indefinitely, even if all other political difficulties should be removed.

What will be the future condition of the people of Egypt? That of the working classes, who constitute the great mass of the population, will remain substantially what it now is, what it has been as far back as our knowledge extends. In this condition there has been little change for centuries, and there will be little for centuries to come. The land is being rapidly acquired by foreigners. English companies and individuals are already the owners of large tracts. But, whoever owns the soil, European, Turk or native, the condition of those who till it, dig and clean the canals, maintain the Nile levees, and perform the immense amount of labor required by the necessity of irrigation, will not be materially changed.

The rough and, sometimes, cruel modes of government of ancient rulers have been and are being ameliorated, as in other countries. But the people receive such a pittance for their labor that substantial improvement either in mental culture, or in the conditions of living is impossible. They earn from ten to fifteen cents a day, and are employed only a part of the year. This is more than they formerly received, but the cost of living is proportionally still higher. They provide their own food and that of their families. Under these conditions, there is nothing in reserve for them but ignorance, the mud hut or pen, and the scantiest possible quantity, that will maintain their physical being, of the coarsest food.

The abolition of the *corvée* under the late Khedive, Tewfik

Pasha, was a step in the right direction, much to be commended. The system had outlived the time of its necessity. The labor of cleaning the canals and repairing the Nile levees is so great that up to a very recent period it is doubtful whether it could have been accomplished otherwise than by the *corvée*, which was a form of taxation upon the masses. Neglect or delay of this work would have been disastrous. The water controlled in the river and distributed by the canals is the life of Egypt.

Under the *corvée* system, the people of the fellah-villages along the lines of the numerous canals were compelled to perform the work, necessary in their vicinity, without pay, as road work is done in some parts of the United States. The manner of living during the continuance of this labor was not materially different from that to which they were accustomed. According to our ideas of living, it was a great hardship. As compared with theirs, the difference was not as great as that between the life of our soldiers in time of peace and that of civilians.

The debt of Egypt is practically what it was twenty-five years ago and there are political reasons why it will not be the policy of the English Government to have it materially lessened. The debt was the alleged cause of their coming and it will be a continuous alleged reason for remaining. Some of the lands and other properties, gifts to the state made by the Khedive, Ismaîl Pasha, have been sold and the proceeds applied to the debt. Other liabilities have been incurred, through the losses at Alexandria, the war in the Sudân and various public improvements. The dam at Assuân and the barrage at Assuît have added $800,000 to the amount of annual taxation for thirty years. The high rate of interest has been very materially lessened, but this interest, the tribute to Turkey and the expensive English occupation and administration foot up so great a total that the working class will remain in a state of poverty. The landholders, in consequence of the reduction of the interest to a more reasonable rate, are in a better condition than formerly and, by obtaining the labor of the people at the small sum now paid, they are able to realize fair revenues on the capital invested.

The common laboring fellah will continue in the future, as in the past, what he is often called by the higher classes, both European and native, "the beast of burden." The useful donkey, which he overloads and goads to his work, lives in a condition but little lower. In saying this, it is not intended to censure the present rulers, nor to charge these conditions to them. They certainly cannot be rightfully accused of being in Egypt on any benevolent, humanizing, civilizing or Christianizing mission. Their Government is there because it believes the commercial and political welfare of the Empire demands it; its citizens, official and unofficial, are there, for their individual interests.

Lord Cromer's administration has been the best it could be, considering the conditions under which it was commenced. To him, too much praise cannot be accorded. But he and his official sucessors must continue to exact from the people the annual payment of the tribute to the bondholders and to Turkey. His administration has been in reality a personal government. Its success depended upon his good intentions and personal ability. Will England find a second Lord Cromer? The question of the sovereignty of Egypt is still open and the eyes of Europe are fixed upon the administration of its Government. It is certainly in the interest of England that this administration should be the best that can be attained, not only for political but also for commercial reasons. That the latter are not neglected, was tersely expressed to me by an Egyptian Pasha holding an official position when I was last in Egypt. He said: "The English govern well, but they govern for themselves." It is England who is to reap the harvest. Unless the land is well tilled, the sheaves all collected and the grain carefully garnered, the large amount required to satisfy the claims cannot be realized. But however good the intentions, the attempt to make any very material change in the condition of the fellâhîn with the debt that has been imposed upon them unpaid, would be hopeless. Their condition might be ameliorated if the country could be relieved of its unjust burdens, but the improvement of the mass of the laboring people would not be very marked. It is only by long and continued observation that the real situation can be understood.

In the United States, with its sparse population, its vast extent of fertile lands, its rich and exhaustless mines, life is, or should be, easy. Certainly material and mental advancement are within the grasp of all, and have become the ruling passions of the people. Egypt, not including the Sudân and the Central African provinces and including only its productive lands, is a very small country surrounded by sea and desert. Its resources are in the soil. It contains a little less than 6,000,000 acres of productive land. Its debt is $450,000,000 or $75 on each acre. If we capitalize the tribute of $3,500,000 paid to Turkey at the rate of three and a half per cent, another $100,000,000 will be added to the interest-bearing debt, making in all $90 on each acre. This is virtually a mortgage of $9,000 on each hundred acres of land, the interest on which must be paid semi-annually. The population of Egypt proper is now said to be 10,000,000. Thus, each 100 acres must sustain 166 persons, pay the interest on $9,000 and the expenses of the Government, including those of the cities, schools and the foreign occupation and administration. How much can remain for those who till the soil?

The fine new hotels, the increase of facilities for luxurious living and the passing of a pleasant winter in the capital, or up the river, in the society of educated, agreeable people and polite English officers, charm the traveler. He is informed by

an abundant English literature and verbal statements that there
is a wonderful transformation in Egypt. He repeats it to his
friends and makes it the basis for articles in newspapers, magazines and books. Rarely do any of these travelers enter a
fellah-hut or make any examination as to the real condition of
this class.

The same effect was produced on the traveler by the won
derful transformation due to Ismaîl Pasha, which caused his
praises to be proclaimed throughout Europe. But neither the
marvelous improvements he made, nor anything that has been
accomplished by his successors, has materially changed the condition of the fellâhîn. You will find them, if you wish to make
the examination, living in the same mud huts, in the same
miserable condition as of yore. The conditions were even more
favorable for the people under the reign of Ismaîl Pasha, up to
the time of the financial crisis, than they have been at any time
since. Money was then flowing into the country in abundance
both from the sale of produce and the proceeds of loans. This
money was expended among the people in the extensive improvements that have been mentioned. Since that time, there
has been a constant stream flowing outward, going to Europe,
which has required all the resources of the country.

Whether living in better or worse conditions, the Egyptians
would be happier under native rulers of their own religion than
under any foreign power. European Governments are more
regular than any native Government would be. But their
system of taxation, as applied to all non-Christian colonies, is a
mill cleverly adjusted to the producing capacities of the country.
Its motion never ceases. It grinds closely and takes all the
flour. For those who, by their toil, produce the wealth of the
country, there remains only a scanty part of the products of
the soil. There is for them no opportunity for accumulation
and, with a failure of crops, comes starvation.

There is no better government for English people than that of England, whether in England or in colonies occupied by her own people. But that of her colonies, in which the people are non-Christian natives who can never be Anglicized, is purely arbitrary and military. The native, except to a very limited extent in certain cities, has no voice in it, nor is he allowed to hold any commanding position, civil or military. His treatment depends upon the character of those placed over him. If it happens to be a Lord Cromer, he has a good master; but it is always a master, and he is kept in abject submission by military force, whenever there is need of it, and is always governed as an inferior being.

On the first establishment of the Anglo-French control, a number of Englishmen of long experience in India were brought to Egypt to occupy the principal governmental positions. After the military occupation was effected, a native army was organized with English officers, as in India, but without carrying out the complete system that has been adopted in that country. England has created in India what may be termed a military aristocracy and, by it, governs the country. The common English soldier in India becomes a person of importance. He has more servants than a major-general in our army. He has a cook, a man to wash and keep his clothes in order, men to black his shoes, to keep him fanned, while he sleeps, with the punkah, and to wait upon and serve him in every menial capacity. If he is a cavalryman, his horse is fed and groomed by a servant. In this manner, the idea of the superiority of the white man is maintained.

The same system is adopted among the native soldiers which form the bulk of the army. Natives are permitted to hold subaltern positions, but they cannot command an Englishman. The Englishman, however low his official position, outranks any native. Subaltern natives also have their retinues of servants,

but their number is not as great as those of the English. Even
the common native soldier has his servants, and his pay is so
much higher than the ordinary wages of the country, that it
gives him a position far above any class of laborers. He is a
privileged person. Once in the service, he does not wish to
abandon his position. Thus, the soldiers become an aristocratic
caste, domineering over the mass of the people and ruling the
country in the most arbitrary manner. They are his Majesty's
soldiers and, anything that they or their superiors need, they
believe they have the right to take without waiting for any
formality in the manner of taking.

Many years ago I was dining at his residence with a retired
English army officer, who had been long in the military service
in India and bore the title of "General." There were a number
of invited guests, all English but myself. The conversation
turned upon India and the Sepoy War, and the General related
some of his experiences. He was present on one of the occasions
when Sepoy prisoners were bound to the mouths of cannon and
blown into fragments. He said: "I was then a lieutenant. The
commanding officer stated to me in the morning that I might
see blood during the day. I did not know what he meant. We
were ordered out and my place was beside a cannon, and the
blood flew over me, staining my clothing." After relating various details connected with this execution he remarked em-
phatically, "Well, we have got their claws cut and intend to
keep them cut." On inquiry being made as to what he meant
by this expression, he answered, "We have got them so poor,
and we intend to keep them so poor that they cannot rebel."

It must not be inferred that this officer was in any sense a
brutal man or devoid of feelings of humanity. I knew him well
and he was a kind, humane, gentleman, and I am sure would
not have knowingly wronged anyone. He was simply a typical
Englishman and saw everything through English eyes, with a

view to English interest. From his standpoint, and in accordance with his education, wherever the English flag had been raised, rightfully or wrongfully, there the authority of the Queen's Government was supreme. Anyone who opposed it was a traitor, an outlaw, who had forfeited his right to life. It was right, and a proper regard for English interests required, that his punishment should be made an example to deter others from acts of rebellion.

The success in keeping the Indians poor is shown by the poverty famines that have lately become so frequent and extensive. In the productive years, the produce is taken away to pay the taxes. Whenever there is a short crop, there is no money with which to buy food. The vigorous, young and middle aged men wander away and generally find means of subsistence. The old, the weak, the decrepit and many women and children perish. In a cold, economical point of view there is no loss. It is the nonproducing class that disappears by thousands. The Hon. Wm. J. Bryan in an article on the "British Rule in India," published in the *Commoner*, July 6, 1906, says: "The poverty of the people of India is distressing in the extreme; millions live on the verge of starvation all the time, and one would think that their very appearance would plead successfully in their behalf." Yet these starving millions pay annually, for the privilege of being governed by Christians, a hundred million dollars for the army and fifteen million dollars for the civil service employed in keeping them from rebellion. England has taken from this country, in the last one hundred and fifty years, thousands of millions of pounds. She is still, according to the best English authorities, taking from these poor people, over and above all expenses, thirty million pounds sterling annually to be added to the enormous wealth she has already accumulated from this country.

Mr. Bryan says that several times while in India he "heard

the plague referred to as a providential remedy for over-popu-
lation." He does not mention the famines as being thus regarded.

The English, not being in Egypt for the benefit of the Egyptians, cannot be expected to govern otherwise than for English
interests. The population, however, as compared with that of
India is small and there are several English military stations
not far distant. Considering the peaceable character of the
people and the other conditions, it will never be necessary to
resort to the extraordinary means of government adopted in
India. It is probable that the best possible government will be
given them under the conditions that have been imposed. This
is for England's interest. Otherwise, such large sums could not
be annually taken from the country. Certainly it will not be
necessary to take any extraordinary methods to keep the masses
in poverty. The fixed charges by which the country's resources
are taken to Europe will inevitably lead to that result. Fortunately, droughts and years of failure of food supplies are rare.
It has been over a quarter of a century since the last famine in
Egypt.

Whatever the conditions, Egypt will always have men of
wealth. There will be prosperous and rich merchants and bankers in Alexandria, and a very limited number in other cities.
Among these, there will be a few natives, but much the larger
number will be Europeans and Syrians. There will also be a
few rich, native landowners whose property has been kept intact
through all the financial vicissitudes which the country has
experienced.

The very richness of the soil of Egypt seems to be its greatest
misfortune. It is said that when the Persians became a powerful people they proposed to their King, Cyrus, to leave their
small rugged country, and occupy some of the fertile neighboring regions. The King consented, but "warned them to prepare

henceforth, not to rule, but to be ruled over," adding "that delicate men spring from delicate countries, that it is not given to the same land to produce excellent fruits and men valiant in war." The Persians, acting on the advice of the King, remained in their ancestral homes, "preferring to live in a barren country, and to command, rather than to cultivate fertile plains and be the slaves of others." [1] We have a marked exemplification of the wisdom of the ancient ruler in the government to-day of three hundred and fifty-six millions of alien races by thirty-five millions of people inhabiting England and Scotland.

The people of Egypt, during a large portion of their history since the Persian invasion, have been slaves to foreign domination. They are peaceful and love a quiet life. Their rich fields, in the future as in the past, will attract the cupidity of the foreigner. Besides the many political advantages accruing from its occupation, twenty-five million dollars can be annually abstracted from this country. It is now the ruling principle of the Great Powers of Europe by the allotment of "spheres of influence" or by direct partition, according to interests acquired or claimed, to divide among themselves the territory of such non-Christian countries as are unable to defend their rights successfully. Under these conditions, it cannot be expected that Egypt will not remain in the control of or be allotted to one of the greater of these Powers. Whoever shall be their masters, English, French or Turk, the great mass of the people, the laboring classes of Egypt will continue to be bondmen, occupying the richest and most productive land in the world, but living in poverty, destitution and squalor.

---

[1] Her. IX, 122.